"Equal parts shocking and poignant, this captivating book outlines the bold reforms so urgently needed in healthcare services and shines a light on women's real-life stories and experiences of traumatic birth. Vividly written and packed with deeply moving accounts of the impact of birth trauma, *Breaking the Taboo* is a vital insight into the scandal that is the postcode lottery of this country's maternity provision. Put a copy on the desk of every MP."
HARRIET HARMAN, DEPUTY LEADER
OF THE LABOUR PARTY 2007–2015

"*Breaking the Taboo* is a gripping, courageous and urgent account of the extraordinary experience of becoming a mother while serving as an MP and a damning indictment of how we treat new mothers. Theo has started the much-needed #MeToo movement for inadequate maternity care. Essential reading for all about how life can begin in a maternity system that we as a society should be ashamed of."
LUCY JONES, AUTHOR OF *MATRESCENCE:
ON THE METAMORPHOSIS OF PREGNANCY,
CHILDBIRTH AND MOTHERHOOD*

"A painfully honest, important testimony to traumatic birth – vital reading for both parents and policy makers."
RORY STEWART, FORMER GOVERNMENT MINISTER
AND CO-HOST OF *THE REST IS POLITICS*

"*Breaking the Taboo* is a book that truly touched my heart. Theo Clarke brings a much-needed voice to the experience of birth trauma and, in doing so, offers a sense of comfort and understanding that many of us are missing. If you've carried the weight of a difficult birth, this book will help you feel seen and heard."
LOUISE THOMPSON, BROADCASTER AND AUTHOR OF *LUCKY:
LEARNING TO LIVE AGAIN*

"*Breaking the Taboo* is a jaw-dropping insight into the postcode lottery of maternity care in the UK. Theo's account of what it is like to be a new mother and an MP at the same time left me reeling – as did the descriptions of the birth trauma suffered by her and the other mothers who have so bravely shared their stories. Inspiring and powerful, this is a must-read."
DAME ANDREA LEADSOM, FORMER BUSINESS SECRETARY

"As a clinician committed to supporting women who have been affected by birth trauma, I pay tribute to Theo and all the women who have shared their stories for this powerful new book. It's essential that we break the silence around birth trauma so we can learn from these experiences and do everything possible to ensure that every woman receives the high-quality care she deserves."

RANEE THAKAR, PRESIDENT OF THE ROYAL COLLEGE OF OBSTETRICIANS AND GYNAECOLOGISTS

"*Breaking the Taboo* is a brave, personal and at times brutal account of how Theo's own experience of birth trauma led to her groundbreaking campaign to protect new mums. It also offers a fascinating glimpse into the reality of pregnancy and early motherhood as a politician during one of the most turbulent periods in recent British history."

JUSTINE ROBERTS, CEO AND FOUNDER OF MUMSNET

"I wish Theo hadn't had to write this book, but I'm so glad she did. We need to move the needle on maternity and post-partum care, and it starts with vital stories like this one."

STACEY HALLS, NOVELIST AND BESTSELLING AUTHOR OF *THE FAMILIARS*

"*Breaking the Taboo* is a powerful personal account of being a new mother experiencing birth trauma. Theo charts our work together in Parliament to break the silence surrounding the subject and correctly identifies the serious need for a #MeToo movement around birth trauma. Her moving and candid book will help to spark much-needed change."

ROSIE DUFFIELD MP, CO-CHAIR OF THE ALL-PARTY PARLIAMENTARY GROUP ON BIRTH TRAUMA

"This book does not stand alone. It is one part of the positive action taken by a courageous campaigner and mother, together with the huge number of women she has created a platform for. They have all been able to tell their stories and telling those stories will lead to change. This book should be widely read, especially by those who can help make that change."

PENNY MORDAUNT, FORMER LEADER OF THE HOUSE OF COMMONS

THEO CLARKE

Breaking

WHY WE NEED TO TALK

the

ABOUT BIRTH TRAUMA

Taboo

Biteback Publishing

First published in Great Britain in 2025 by
Biteback Publishing Ltd, London
Copyright © Theo Clarke 2025

Theo Clarke has asserted her right under the Copyright, Designs and Patents Act 1988 to be identified as the author of this work.

All rights reserved. No part of this publication may be reproduced, stored in a retrieval system or transmitted, in any form or by any means, without the publisher's prior permission in writing.

This book is sold subject to the condition that it shall not, by way of trade or otherwise, be lent, resold, hired out or otherwise circulated without the publisher's prior consent in any form of binding or cover other than that in which it is published and without a similar condition, including this condition, being imposed on the subsequent purchaser.

Every reasonable effort has been made to trace copyright holders of material reproduced in this book, but if any have been inadvertently overlooked the publisher would be glad to hear from them.

This book is based on the author's personal experience and is not intended to be a substitute for taking medical advice on pregnancy and childbirth.

ISBN 978-1-78590-935-1

10 9 8 7 6 5 4 3 2 1

A CIP catalogue record for this book is available from the British Library.

Set in Minion Pro

Printed and bound in Great Britain by
CPI Group (UK) Ltd, Croydon CR0 4YY

For my daughter, Arabella

'Believe you can and you're halfway there.'
THEODORE ROOSEVELT

CONTENTS

Foreword *by* Donna Ockenden — xi
Preface — xv

PART I — BECOMING AN MP AND MOTHER
Chapter One — Pregnant in Parliament — 3
Chapter Two — Fear of childbirth — 13
Chapter Three — Preparing for birth — 19
Chapter Four — Final trimester — 23
Chapter Five — Resigning in hospital — 29
Chapter Six — Leadership election — 37
Chapter Seven — Overdue — 43
Chapter Eight — Induction — 53

PART II — BUILDING A MOVEMENT
Chapter Nine — My birth trauma — 63
Chapter Ten — Home — 73
Chapter Eleven — Recovery — 83
Chapter Twelve — Unexpected news — 93
Chapter Thirteen — Government in crisis — 101

Chapter Fourteen	Chequers	109
Chapter Fifteen	Return to work	121
Chapter Sixteen	Friends and foes	133
Chapter Seventeen	Breaking the taboo	139
Chapter Eighteen	Recruiting unlikely allies	147
Chapter Nineteen	A historic debate	157
Chapter Twenty	Reshuffle	165
Chapter Twenty-One	Defying the Prime Minister	177
Chapter Twenty-Two	The Birth Trauma Inquiry	187
Chapter Twenty-Three	Negotiations with 10 Downing Street	197
Chapter Twenty-Four	General election	207

PART III	PERSONAL STORIES	
Chapter Twenty-Five	Birth injuries	215
Chapter Twenty-Six	Maternal mental health	225
Chapter Twenty-Seven	Medical emergencies	237
Chapter Twenty-Eight	Fathers and partners	249
Chapter Twenty-Nine	Marginalised groups	261
Chapter Thirty	Baby loss	273
Chapter Thirty-One	The wider impact of birth trauma	287
Chapter Thirty-Two	Covid and lockdown babies	301
Chapter Thirty-Three	Global birth trauma	311
Chapter Thirty-Four	Healing	323

Postscript: The maternity manifesto	337
Modernising Parliament	347
Resources	351
Further reading	357
Acknowledgements	359

FOREWORD

For more than ten years, the UK has seen a significant decline in the quality of maternity care provided by the NHS. A significant contribution to this has been the austerity measures imposed by previous governments. This decline has been outlined through a number of independent investigations and reviews, and following on from the publication of these independent reviews, maternity services find themselves the topic of media headlines, which are followed by an outcry from the public, professional organisations and Members of Parliament. Calls for change are echoed by families across the country, and the NHS workforce are motivated to implement urgent actions to improve the quality of the service they provide.

As time passes, the findings of independent reviews fail to be fully implemented due to a lack of oversight from a government that previously endorsed them. This can be witnessed through a series of reports, such as 'Invisible: Maternity Experiences of Muslim Women from Racialised Minority Communities' and the reports on East Kent, Morecambe Bay and Shrewsbury & Telford NHS trusts. The period in which these investigations were published spans the course of a decade, yet they have all produced similar findings. My biggest concern is that over the course of the past ten years or more, maternity service provision has continued to struggle and as a result of this, more women and families have suffered the consequences.

On 13 May 2024, the already known state of the UK's maternity service provision was once again highlighted. Theo Clarke, former MP, published a report titled 'Listen to Mums: Ending the Postcode Lottery on Perinatal Care', which added to the ongoing national conversation about the widespread failings in perinatal services. The media reported the shock felt by politicians, health professionals and families at accounts they heard of women enduring painful, undignified treatment, sometimes without consent.

This book tells the story of how Theo, following her own traumatic birth and birth injury in 2022, realised her own experience could be a potential catalyst for change. Theo set up an all-party parliamentary group into birth trauma. Before launching the cross-party inquiry, she initiated the first House of Commons debate on birth trauma in Parliament's 1,000-year history.

In the last third of the book, Theo gives parents an opportunity that they were not given by the NHS – a chance to be heard. Their first-hand accounts describe the overwhelming psychological and physical toll arising from poor maternity care. As a midwife of thirty-five years and through my various roles in chairing maternity reviews, I am all too aware of how many maternity services are frequently failing mothers, their babies and staff working in maternity services on the ground. But having been exposed to such experiences does not diminish the heartache I felt in reading the accounts of families that have been let down by the NHS. Too often, women are not listened to, procedures are carried out without consent and women are left without the support they need postnatally.

FOREWORD

The perinatal workforce are struggling to keep up with the demands and pressures they are facing, there is not enough staff to provide the service that mothers and babies need and many midwives and obstetricians are leaving their jobs as a result of burnout. Those who remain are often overworked in an underfunded, under-resourced environment. Professionals become traumatised by what they have witnessed and are offered little to no support to help them navigate these difficulties.

Theo Clarke's book is a sobering read, highlighting once again known structural problems that are difficult to resolve but integral to remedying the declining trajectory of maternity services provided by the NHS. My sincere hope is that there remains a will to change perinatal care for the better; now, let us work together to make it happen.

Donna Ockenden
May 2025

PREFACE

I had never heard the term 'birth trauma' before I suffered my own. I had not planned that campaigning to end the postcode lottery in maternity services would be the focus of my time as a Member of Parliament, but that was the journey I unexpectedly found myself on after I gave an emotional speech in the House of Commons. I shared my experience of emergency surgery following the birth of my daughter and how terrified I was that I was going to die. I was amazed by the huge number of women and families who wrote to me sharing their own stories. There remains a real taboo about speaking about birth trauma, and the debate I led in Parliament – the first in British history – started a long-overdue national conversation on this issue.

I would like to dedicate this book to anyone who has suffered from birth trauma. It was harrowing to read the evidence presented to the first birth trauma inquiry in the UK, which I chaired in Parliament in 2024. Afterwards, I continued to receive further testimonies, both from this country and overseas, and the desire to publish many of these new stories was a key driver for writing this book. I want to ensure that their voices continue to be heard by the government so that maternity care is improved in this country, and I also hope to issue a call to action to other countries around the world to do the same. It is worth noting that while the issues surrounding birth trauma are present across the country, the Birth Trauma Inquiry mainly focused on NHS England. To balance this, I have included two stories from the devolved UK nations in the final part of the book.

I want anyone who has suffered from either physical or mental challenges since having a baby to know that they are not alone. I didn't recognise many of the symptoms of my own birth trauma at first. I didn't know where to find help and I felt too ashamed to ask for it, so I know how tough it is to talk about such a difficult and sensitive topic, but therapy for my mental health and specialist care for my birth injury have helped. This is the first time that I have shared in detail my own experience, symptoms, recovery and the physical and mental health challenges I suffered as a new mother. I hope that this book will point others in the direction of where they too can find help to heal and recover from their own birth trauma.

I owe a huge debt to the many individuals and organisations who have campaigned tirelessly on this issue for many years before me. Particular thanks to Rosie Duffield MP, who co-chaired the All-Party Parliamentary Group on Birth Trauma with me and supported me in leading a genuinely cross-party national campaign to effect policy change. Also thanks to the Birth Trauma Association, who first introduced me to other mothers who had been affected, helped me to understand the scale of the problem in the UK and acted as secretariat to the Birth Trauma Inquiry. Their chief executive Kim Thomas wrote the official report, provided policy briefs for the parliamentary committee and helped with collating and reading the huge volume of submissions for both the inquiry and this book.

PREFACE

Many other groups and individuals have also advised my campaign, including Mumsnet, MASIC, Maternal Mental Health Alliance, Make Birth Better, birth injuries campaigner Gill Castle, midwife Donna Ockenden (who led the independent review of maternity services for the government at several hospital trusts) and Dr Ranee Thakar, president of the Royal College of Obstetricians and Gynaecology. My thanks also to the United Nations Population Fund (UNFPA), who helped me to collect stories in the field of global birth trauma from women from as far afield as Afghanistan, Guinea and Yemen, who rarely have their voices heard.

My final trimester, labour and the period of recovery from my own traumatic birth, in the summer and autumn of 2022, coincided with a turbulent and extraordinary moment in British history, with the UK experiencing three Prime Ministers and two monarchs within just four months. While memories can be incomplete, I have tried to recall as much as I can about this and to be honest about my experiences. I have referred to medical notes, diaries and the news where it was possible to do so. I also wanted to share the experience of what it was like to give birth, be a new mother and recover from a difficult birth while also working in the unique job of being an MP. The House of Commons Library believes that I'm only the fifty-sixth female MP to give birth while elected. I have seen how the lack of female representation in Parliament contributes to women's health often being ignored in government policy. We need to achieve gender parity for this to change. It is also essential to make Parliament more family friendly, in order to better support new mothers.

Finally, I hope that this book helps to lift the curtain on what it was like to be a backbench MP running a campaign to effect change. It was a huge collective effort to improve government policy on maternal health. I pay tribute to former Prime Minister Rishi Sunak for responding to my call for a new comprehensive national maternity strategy and to former Health Secretary Vicky Atkins for adding birth trauma to the Women's Health Strategy. I hope that current and future British governments will implement in full the recommendations outlined in the Birth Trauma Inquiry so that no mother endures what I or others in this book did. Despite losing my seat in the recent general election, I continue to campaign to ensure that all mothers in this country and around the world get the care that they need and deserve. This book is a testament to them for bravely sharing their stories with me.

PART I

BECOMING AN MP AND MOTHER

CHAPTER ONE

PREGNANT IN PARLIAMENT

My political journey began when I was first elected in the Boris Johnson landslide in December 2019 to the Stafford constituency, a West Midlands seat in Staffordshire. I had stepped into the shoes of my Conservative predecessor Jeremy Lefroy, who I knew well from our time together volunteering in Africa.

The election campaign was dominated by my party's pledge to 'Get Brexit Done', but within 100 days of becoming an MP, the first cases of Covid-19 had been diagnosed in the UK and the country went into lockdown. It was a fraught, tense period, and I felt the weight of the responsibility of representing my constituents during a global pandemic. I spent much of my time attending daily briefings with the Department for Health and Social Care as they worked out how to save lives. I lobbied for my hospital to have more ventilators, dealt with patients being discharged from hospitals to care homes, grappled to understand the endless new emergency legislation that Covid generated, advocated for funding through the furlough scheme to prevent businesses from going bankrupt during restrictions, resolved individual pieces of casework from weddings being cancelled to schools being closed, and worked with the local council on operational logistics for the new vaccine rollout across Stafford.

It was a huge challenge to be a new MP during such an unexpected crisis. There was no job description for what I was expected to do, and I never knew what the next day was going to entail. I was also always expected to vote with the government and if I failed to do so and broke what was called a 'three-line whip', it could result in expulsion from the party. The only way around this was for me to attend a local event in my constituency or be overseas so that I couldn't be in Parliament on the day of the vote. Very rarely and only if there was a specific local issue that I had raised with the whips – who acted like prefects in a boarding school, enforcing good behaviour – in advance could they choose to 'slip' me, which meant I had permission to miss a vote for a constituency visit, but this remained unusual.

The government liked to keep us on a short leash, especially our new intake of Conservative MPs, who they found increasingly hard to manage. We were seen by our older, more experienced colleagues as too independent, unruly and ambitious to make our mark. This was mainly a reflection of our intake's demographic, with many of us elected for the first time and a significant proportion having worked outside the Westminster bubble. I had spent the previous few years as chief executive of not-for-profit organisation Coalition for Global Prosperity, which worked to tackle global poverty and was backed by the Gates Foundation. I had experienced first-hand the poverty and suffering in many parts of the developing world, which had shaped my view that Britain should be a force for good in the world. I had slept in refugee camps as far afield as Uganda and Bangladesh, visited water and sanitation projects in India and Sierra Leone and campaigned to improve global policy on everything from girls' education to deforestation, in order to help the world's most vulnerable people.

I had always believed that it was a good thing for legislators to have had real-life experience before politics, so I was pleased that my intake of MPs was so varied and included former teachers, entrepreneurs and lawyers. Unfortunately, due to the pandemic we spent many months separated as we worked from our constituencies and voted remotely, which made networking with colleagues and building relationships difficult. I was very grateful that I had several friends who were already elected to lean on for advice, such as Tobias Ellwood who helped me prep for my first speeches in the Chamber and Tom Tugendhat who let me hot desk in his office until I could open my own.

I also set up the '109' WhatsApp group for my intake to communicate with each other privately, which clearly put hackles up in the Whips' Office and labelled me as a future troublemaker – something that was only compounded when I ran the slate to get our intake elected on to select committees by block voting, much to the annoyance of older MPs. I joined the International Development Select Committee, continuing my interest in foreign affairs, and got involved on issues that affected my constituency, including HS2, farming and defence.

I gave my maiden speech within a few weeks, as I was chomping at the bit to be allowed to speak and I was unable to ask a question to ministers on behalf of constituents until I had delivered it. I remember vividly jumping up and down for the first time on the historic green benches as I tried to catch the Speaker's eye and how nervous I felt as I delivered my first speech live on television during the Queen's Speech debate on global Britain. I have always been a big supporter of women's rights, so my first question in the

Chamber was about period poverty in schools, and I enjoyed watching the older male MPs squirm with embarrassment, which made me chuckle. It was an important moment in my career and I was proud of myself for being the first ever female MP to be elected in my constituency. My feminist credentials obviously struck a chord with some of my younger residents – I remember visiting a local primary school in Ranton for World Book Day, where one of the young girls, aged around nine or ten, had dressed as a suffragette with a coloured sash with 'Votes for women' written on it. I beamed when she told me that I had broken the glass ceiling in Stafford and that she planned to be our next MP.

In Parliament, I was kept busy on bill committees scrutinising legislation line by line, which I must admit was not always my favourite activity. I spent hours listening to oral evidence sessions on technical aspects of trade, agriculture or building regulations, with hundreds of pages of briefs. It became impossible to plan my diary too much, as things constantly changed due to urgent meetings with ministers being rescheduled or votes being called. The division bell would ring at the most inconvenient times – I could be in the middle of a select committee hearing, speaking on a panel with my local chamber of commerce, giving a tour to constituents or speaking to my partner Henry when I'd have to apologise and leave immediately to go and join the stampede to vote. One minute I'd be talking potholes and the next I'd be in the queue standing next to the Prime Minister. Occasionally I'd get held up on a call and would have to run to make it to the Chamber, so I decided to ditch my high heels and took to wearing flats or even trainers. When we were on a three-line whip to defend the government's legislative programme, I didn't dare even go for a short walk in St James's Park, which was just in front of my office, in case I didn't make it back to vote within the allotted minutes before the doors were locked.

One of the highlights of my first year was being appointed by Boris Johnson as the Prime Minister's trade envoy to Kenya, which meant I would also visit Nairobi to undertake trade deal negotiations on behalf of the British government to help deliver the Economic Partnership Agreement. My appointment came after I had several challenging encounters with the then Chief Whip Mark Spencer about upcoming contentious votes. Mark asked me outright what I wanted in order to support the government and six months later I was appointed to what I had asked for. Clearly there were some advantages to being seen as a troublemaker so early on.

It was a constant struggle to balance personal commitments with being an elected representative. During Monday to Thursday, I would spend time in the House of Commons and on Fridays I would be in my constituency office for my regular surgery and local meetings. The weekend would be dominated by constituency events, where I enjoyed village fetes, 'families day' at the army base or civic services with the mayor or borough council. However, one of my greatest challenges was attempting to work my way through the never-ending list of invites and trying not to let down any businesses, charities, schools or voluntary groups in Stafford. The only way to do this was to rotate around the constituency, trying to offend as few people as possible.

It also became increasingly difficult to get away to see my partner Henry, who lived several hours' drive away in the Cotswolds and was still getting used to being in a relationship with a politician. My job had changed significantly since we had first met and he found the long hours and hectic environment tough. It felt like my job was always present and often in the way of our relationship and it was impossible to escape it, as even when we stayed with friends and family they commented on that week's drama in Westminster. Politics was a lifestyle, not just a career. It was intense, demanding and frustrating at times, but I also found it hugely fulfilling, especially when I could genuinely make a difference to people's lives – mainly when I picked up a local issue to resolve through my constituency surgeries.

It was halfway through my Parliamentary term, in 2021, that Henry and I got married. Early on we decided to try for a baby, as Henry had turned forty and I was only a few years behind him. I will admit that I had never been obsessed about having a baby. If I hadn't met my husband then I might never have had a child, as my career had always been of paramount importance to me.

I hadn't studied politics at A-level and my university degree was in English literature with history of art. My first interest in politics was in foreign affairs, which was kindled by debating at school and being sent to the United Nations aged sixteen as youth ambassador for the UK at a Global Young Leaders Conference in New York. I was asked to deliver a speech in the General Assembly in front of UN Secretary-General Kofi Annan, which was a huge honour and something I will never forget. I was inspired by the thought of international leaders coming together to tackle global problems, but I also thought that many British politicians were self-serving and completely out of touch with the public, and I was not a member of a political party.

I despaired during the election expenses scandal. However, it was this crisis that galvanised me to door-knock in a general election campaign for the first time and I decided to support Rory Stewart, then a new prospective parliamentary candidate who was running to be an MP for the first time in 2010 up in Penrith & the Border. This gave me my first real insight into political campaigning as, with no prior experience, I found myself helping to organise his street stalls, driving him to debates across his huge rural constituency, doing research prep for his hustings, arranging visits for the press and VIPs and attending visits with him, from farmers affected by foot and mouth disease to local business owners who were struggling. I then went on to support Prime Minister David Cameron in the NOtoAV campaign at the Alternative Vote referendum and delivered my first political speech with future Chancellor Kwasi Kwarteng at Guildford Conservative Association. I had only two hours' notice that I would give the speech; no one on the senior leadership referendum campaign team could attend so I stepped in at the last minute. It was a baptism of fire and accidentally set me on the long road to becoming an MP.

Despite being elected to Parliament in my thirties, I had already campaigned for over a decade in support of the Conservative Party and had fought two exhausting general elections in the safe Labour seat of Bristol East in quick succession during 2015 and 2017 alongside setting up my own arts business. When I finally reached the House of Commons, I worried that having a baby while elected to public office would hold me back in my peer group, as there was a risk that I would never be promoted or become a minister if I took any time out. I had never noticed my age too much before, but the NHS described me as a geriatric mother given that I was over thirty-five. For the first time, I was conscious that I would be an older working parent. If I did manage to have a baby, then it would be much later than my own mother, who had me in her early twenties. Given that I had usually already worked a full five-day week by Wednesday evening, I also knew these hours were not going to be sustainable with a baby.

Most of the politicians on my side of the House either had older children or didn't have any at all. Very few had had a baby while elected and I didn't feel comfortable speaking to the few ministers who had. Some MPs on the Labour benches had had a baby while elected, such as Harriet Harman, Tulip Siddiq and Stella Creasy, and I read what they had to say about the challenges they faced.

I found out that I was pregnant in December 2021 while I was in Parliament, which was unusual for a sitting Friday. I took a test in the toilets outside my office in Derby Gate, impatiently waited for the results and then took two more tests to confirm they were all positive. I was delighted, especially since I had miscarried once early on and I knew I was lucky to get pregnant without needing fertility treatment given my age. That weekend I went to my grandparents' house in Kent, where I told Henry in person. It was tricky to hide the secret from my family over the holidays and to avoid the foods that the NHS advised against eating. I took to hiding cans of Appletiser in cupboards around the house, which I used to secretly replace the expensive Christmas champagne I poured down the toilet. I didn't want to tell anyone until my twelve-week scan as I was worried that I'd lose another baby.

At the end of my first trimester, I began to suffer from bad morning sickness and it became a struggle to face the three-and-a-half hour commute from Stafford to London on a Monday morning and then do a long day in the office followed by evening votes. My new husband and I were separated during the week, which became increasingly stressful while I was pregnant. Henry still worked in Gloucestershire, where he was attempting to sell his house and find a new job, which would enable him to move up to my constituency full time and also be nearer his parents' home in Staffordshire. We told our respective families just before Valentine's Day, after our twelve-week scan, and they were thrilled for us both.

The next few weeks were busy with constituency work and International Women's Day, for which I supported a large number of events including the 50:50 Parliament cross-party campaign to elect more female MPs. My morning sickness soon became all-day-and-night sickness and as my nausea worsened, I asked the Whips' Office to be slipped to go home early. It was a Monday night and we had a vote on the Police and Crime Bill. By midnight, I felt so awful that I went to lie down in the Ladies' Room near Central Lobby, a small room with sofas where female MPs can hang up clothes, read the papers or write correspondence. Next door was a small single bed and a shower.

I was vomiting badly and felt so ill that I didn't feel well enough to get up to walk through the division lobby in support of the government. I requisitioned the bed and put a hastily written note up on the door, which explained that I wasn't feeling well. I felt so embarrassed and I was mortified to have to have to tell my whip that I felt ill and had to sleep, given it was so late and they had refused to let me leave the parliamentary estate. I had always prided myself on being a strong and competent woman and now I was completely vulnerable and reduced to asking for help. The whips came to check on me and nodded me through each vote at 1 a.m. – meaning they vouched for me being in Parliament, so I didn't have to walk through the voting lobby in person – after they had declined my request to go home. The government won the vote by more than forty. I was outraged, but my complaint to the Chief Whip was completely ignored.

It became increasingly difficult to hide that I was pregnant, and in March 2022 we decided that I was going to have the share the news with my local Conservative Association and with my constituents in Stafford. I updated my chairman and drafted a statement for members to be sent first as a courtesy. I deliberately didn't post anything publicly on social media, yet within five minutes of the newsletter going out, I had a call from the political journalist at our local paper asking for a comment. My personal life was suddenly news. It was a shock.

CHAPTER TWO

FEAR OF CHILDBIRTH

Throughout my pregnancy, I began to develop severe anxiety. My maternity appointments took place in London at Chelsea and Westminster Hospital, in order to be near Parliament, but I planned to have my baby up in Staffordshire. I was concerned about the fact that I would be under the care of a completely new team who didn't know my history. I also had several close friends who had shared with me the stories of their traumatic births, which ranged from life-threatening post-partum haemorrhages to suffering through stitches in stirrups with no pain relief. Some had also experienced terrible postnatal depression.

I have never shared this before, but I was referred by the NHS to a maternity trauma and loss care service prior to giving birth due to my fears of blood, needles and having an emergency Caesarean section. I had not previously done any therapy before I was pregnant and I'll be honest that I didn't think I would find it helpful. I was deeply sceptical that it would make any difference. Why pay to speak to somebody when you could talk to your family and friends for free? However, my husband was insistent that I try it as my phobias were extreme and my body would go into complete shutdown in terror.

I used to visit Terri, a specialist midwife, at the adjacent building to the hospital, in a small side room with two white plastic chairs. She was patient, kind, compassionate and never made me feel foolish. Terri talked me through my birth preferences and helped me to design a mental health care plan after she diagnosed me with severe anxiety due to my needle and blood phobias. She listened patiently when I told her about how I had panic attacks and fainted during blood tests and said that she thought I partly had negative associations with hospitals due to death, because the last time I was in the same hospital in London was to see my father when he died back in 2019. When I attended my antenatal appointments, memories would rush back when the lift stopped at the same floor as the ward where he died. Even though on a rational level I knew I was in a hospital and the doctors were there to help me, emotionally I was terrified of the white coats all around me and the beeping machines filled me with fear.

I was clear with Terri that I wanted to have a natural birth and to avoid any medical interventions. I had concerns about complications during birth and my greatest fear was having an emergency C-section. I requested in my birth plan that in this scenario, I would like to be put under a general anaesthetic as I knew I did not have the mental strength to be awake in theatre for an operation. I recalled to Terri the time I had been a volunteer in Sierra Leone and had ended up in a remote rural clinic in West Africa with my best friend who had malaria. When I went into the ward and saw women hooked up to drips, I had passed out on the floor and had to be carried unconscious to a bed by the patients, which was embarrassing.

My family and even my husband did not appreciate at first how extreme my blood and needle phobia could be and how I would actively avoid blood tests, as I would faint or have an anxiety attack. In routine appointments, I would feel dizzy when a blood pressure cuff was put on my arm or if doctors discussed 'having a Venflon [cannula] in situ' – it particularly stressed me out to think about one being put in my hand during labour. I became concerned about passing out during tests in pregnancy or having a panic attack in the hospital, which might affect our baby.

Henry was infinitely patient with me and took the time to come to as many appointments with me as he could. Even he was shocked at how extreme my blood phobia was when he took me to a routine appointment. He described to me that when I had a blood test, it was like I was having my arm amputated.

I spent months having mental health specialist care with the NHS to try to help. However, every time I went into the GP surgery or the hospital, I became hysterical, crying, hyperventilating and shaking uncontrollably. Every time it was the same and I began to ask in appointments if it was necessary to have another blood test. I outright refused to have the one for my gestational diabetes check. That day, it was a different midwife I didn't know at the clinic who had no bedside manner and did not read my notes. I took the required glucose tablets and my daughter whizzed around inside me like a washing machine, but I didn't end up having my sugar levels checked as I was in such distress they abandoned the test. I was so terrified and shaking so much that it was impossible for them to access the vein. My ultimate fear became that I might refuse a blood transfusion in the worst-case scenario of serious birth complications.

Terri taught me various breathing and grounding techniques as coping mechanisms. She told me to breathe in for five seconds and breathe out for five seconds or to look around and think of five things I could see, four things I could touch, three things I could hear, two things I could smell and one thing I could taste. She would ask me to relax different muscles by tensing them for five seconds, relaxing them and notice how different it felt when the muscles relaxed. I found it hard to concentrate doing these exercises and I felt foolish when I was asked to imagine standing on the beach and wiggle my toes in the sand or pretended to hold a mug of hot chocolate in my hands and blew on it to cool it. I was conscious that I was sat in a colourless box room humming with London traffic. I asked to open the window but was told that was not possible – it was kept shut to prevent suicide attempts.

In these appointments, my mind often drifted back to the endless to-do list I had waiting for me back in the office and I would criticise myself for wasting valuable work time by being at the appointment and taking time out for just a phobia. I had discovered that as a politician it was impossible to reach the fabled 'inbox zero', as correspondence would come in at all times of the day or night. I settled instead for 'inbox infinity' and tried to clear email messages and letters in batched times throughout the day. Between these times, I focused on important meetings or specific tasks such as reading a policy brief or writing a speech.

It felt like I was never going to get through all the tasks I had to do in Parliament and my constituency. I didn't have the time to be pregnant for nine long months. I was tired all the time and found it difficult to cope with the late-night hours for divisions. It was not uncommon to get home at midnight on a Monday, after the long commute down from Stafford to London in the morning in order to be in the House of Commons for the Chamber to start sitting for debates and urgent statements.

The toxic culture in Parliament encouraged workaholism. Colleagues used to compete with each other and boast how they often worked an eighty-hour week, which meant they were not able to spend much time with their families. I felt that ministers looked collectively exhausted as they were so stretched for time and their government responsibilities seemed too broad. Even backbench MPs were expected to undertake a colossal amount of work every day and to view the workload as a badge of honour. It was depressing to see, night after night, colleagues calling their young children from the voting lobby to say goodnight as they missed yet another bedtime or parents' evening. I desperately didn't want to become one of them when my own baby arrived. My bump had become huge and uncomfortable and I constantly needed to go to the bathroom. All I wanted to do was lie down on the sofa in my office and go to sleep, especially in the evenings while waiting to vote, rather than tackle the never-ending in-tray.

Many of the relaxing strategies Terri taught me for my phobias didn't seem to work, but one that seemed to help was smell. I'd walk past a barbeque and be transported back to sitting on the beach as a child, eating burgers on a clifftop overlooking a bay in Devon. Smells became acute for me during pregnancy, to the point that I avoided walking down the high street or past anywhere filled with restaurants. The different smells overwhelmed me, especially from Indian curries or Chinese takeaways, which usually I loved but would make me gag. Given that I had a such a good sense of smell, Terri decided we should try a scent that might help me during a stressful situation such as a blood test or labour. I opted for a sea salt perfume, which I would squirt onto a handkerchief, and kept a small bag of dried lavender in my handbag.

I also tried controlled breathing to help me let go of my anxieties. With each breath, I was told to imagine my worries dissolving or floating away. I would put one hand on my chest and one on my stomach, take a deep breath for seven seconds and allow my hands to rise gently, then I would hold the breath for two seconds and release it slowly again for eleven seconds. My worries didn't disappear, but it did calm me down and allowed me to be more present within the room and stop 'to-do' listing in my brain. Touch was also helpful and I decided that I would bring a favourite cuddly toy, a lion, with me during labour.

I felt emotional and scared every time I thought about what would happen during childbirth. I tried all the strategies I was recommended over several months. I experimented with breath meditations on apps, practised grounding techniques. visualised safe places, made playlists of calming music and tried hypnobirthing classes. Very few of these techniques helped and I began to feel very stressed at how I would respond to being in labour. I was not given any medication; instead, the focus was on designing my mental health plan.

I never told any of my colleagues in Parliament. Politics was the worst environment for sharing vulnerabilities. Weaknesses were something to be exploited by opponents and I didn't want any of them to know.

CHAPTER THREE

PREPARING FOR BIRTH

As an organised person who likes to plan, I attempted the same approach with my pregnancy, failing to realise how impossible this was to do. There was no manual that could prepare me for giving birth and looking after a newborn baby; I could only experience it. However, I still tried, reading multiple books that people recommended such as *Expecting Better*, *How to Grow a Baby and Push It Out*, *The Positive Birth Book* and *What to Expect When You're Expecting*, with its month-by-month descriptions. I downloaded the Flo app to track how my baby was progressing in the womb, I read parenting blogs, I listened to podcasts and I rang friends for advice. So it was hardly surprising when I decided to sign my husband and I up for antenatal classes. I wanted to meet other local mums through the classes, to make some friends and to have someone to text for advice in the middle of the night who might also be awake with their baby.

I looked into the Bump Class in central London, but it was too difficult to attend their classes with late-night votes in Parliament. The Conservative whips weren't going to slip me one night a week to miss votes and risk government legislation not passing. So I waited until I moved up to my constituency full time in June, six weeks before my due date. I had done some research online and the best option seemed to be the National Childbirth Trust (NCT). They ran courses across the country on pregnancy, birth and early parenthood, and I signed Henry and me up for Monday evenings, which included a specialist class on breastfeeding.

I paid £210, which was a lot of money, but I couldn't find any free classes offered locally by the NHS either in Stafford or Stoke-on-Trent, where I would have my baby. It remained deeply ironic that despite my public opposition as the local MP, Stafford County Hospital's freestanding birth centre had remained closed since Covid and I was unable to have my baby in my own constituency.

I chose to attend an NCT course in Stone, just outside my constituency, so local families were less likely to know who I was. I had become fed up with the increasing verbal and online abuse and how invasive and pervasive attacks on politicians had become. Along with other female MPs, I received more abuse than my male colleagues. I was tired of being shouted at while getting cash out of the ATM, being harassed while buying a ticket at the railway station or being harangued in the supermarket when I bought tampons or toothpaste. I always carried a panic button with me and the police had installed extra security in our constituency home, with a rapid response patrol car, after they had investigated a local resident for sending me threatening emails and trying to find out where I lived. I didn't tell any of my NCT class what my job was and I hoped I would not be recognised as a local MP. The last thing I wanted on a pregnancy course was to be hassled about casework or controversial government policies.

The first class was in the local church in Stone in their community centre. Our female tutor was friendly and set up a WhatsApp group for us all to communicate. Life had begun to go back to normal after the pandemic and I was grateful to be doing classes in person after they had all moved online during Covid restrictions. Given I was pregnant, I remained vigilant about symptoms and continued to take regular lateral flow tests even though I'd been vaccinated as an expectant mother in a high-risk group. I didn't want to risk becoming unwell.

Henry had finally sold his house in the Cotswolds and had accepted a new job in Staffordshire, which was due to start in a few weeks. When it began, he would move up to the constituency for us to live as a family. I became anxious about going into hospital, knowing that he was several hours' drive away and that I was on my own if anything unexpected happened.

There were six other couples doing our course and it was the first baby for all of us. We were predominately in our thirties or early forties, most of us lived in the Stafford or Stone area and we found it easy to get on after the initial awkward introductions. All of us were unprepared for what to expect during birth and were keen to meet other local parents. Each of the pregnant mothers was very focused on preparing for the birth, but it became apparent that the same was not true of the fathers. The reality of the impending arrival of their babies only seemed to hit them all when our course leader asked them to install our car seats, which shocked them into realising that any of us could go into labour any day.

We had a fun group and we joked that we were on the course to 'learn how to keep baby alive', so we asked about breastfeeding, whether to follow a routine or not and if we should the wake the baby up to feed. We discussed suitable clothing for a newborn, how to set up a safe sleeping environment, how to swaddle, what to wear given the heatwave, what pain relief to ask for in hospital and what vaccinations the baby should be given.

Most of the rest of the course was practical advice, such as how to change a newborn nappy. Our instructor did a hilarious exercise with a doll wearing a nappy. Inside she had hidden bright yellow mustard. It looked completely realistic when Henry was summoned up to the front of the class to deal with his first explosion and we all burst into laughter. The mums were pleased when the dads asked during the course how to recognise the signs of labour, their role as birth partners and how to support us best after they returned to work, given paternity leave was only two weeks in the UK.

I was interested to hear about timings between contractions, when to call the maternity ward and how to wear a baby sling. We asked what to pack in our hospital bag and were told to bring toiletries, spare clothes, a telephone charger, a book to read and fairy lights. We shared our birth plans and I talked about requesting a water birth. However, there was barely any attention given to us as mothers on what might happen post-birth, bar brief references to a C-section, and induction was barely mentioned. None of us gave much thought to our own recovery post-birth or in the event of complications. The course was almost exclusively focused on looking after our future baby.

The class set me up with expectations that everything would be fine during labour, that I could completely trust the NHS staff in the hospital to look after me and that nothing would go wrong. I explicitly asked about what would happen if things went wrong in labour and was told I was unnecessarily worrying myself. Instead, I was sent a video of the newborn breast crawl. The YouTube description said underneath, 'Your amazing newborn can crawl to the breast soon after birth. All mammals know how to find their food source.' This greatly influenced my expectations about what would happen straight after the birth and I imagined my newborn daughter magically crawling up my chest to start breastfeeding.

CHAPTER FOUR

FINAL TRIMESTER

Once I was close to my due date, my doctor advised me to stop driving in case I went into labour alone in my car. I represented a market town surrounded by small villages and farmland in a rural constituency, so it was hard to get around on public transport. My constituency office manager James would drive to my house to collect me so I could attend events such as the opening of the new Shire Hall business centre in Stafford's market square.

That day, the weather was unbearably hot. James was concerned I was overdoing it and made me promise not to stay longer than an hour. This project had been one of my key election pledges, which I had finally delivered after years of lobbying government for the funding. Even though I was heavily pregnant, I knew I had to be there given I had raised the £1.6 million needed to reopen the iconic building in the heart of Stafford. I had committed myself to the project so publicly because I believed it was key to regeneration of the high street and would encourage new businesses to grow. As I stood wilting in the heat, waiting to give my speech alongside the chief executive of Staffordshire County Council and other dignitaries, I realised that being an MP meant there was never a day off.

I had no legitimate substitute like there would be in other professions, such as an acting CEO. Constituents wanted only to see me, in person, and if I sent a representative they felt fobbed off.

Two days later, I was relieved when the Conservatives held our local council by-election in Penkridge North & Acton Trussell, but it was a very close result, with the Liberal Democrats nipping at our heels. I felt guilty that, as his MP, I hadn't been able to campaign more for the excellent local candidate Andy Adams, but I had found door-knocking in rural villages too exhausting.

Towards the end of my third trimester, I no longer felt like attending public events in order to be shouted at by residents and grilled on issues from antisocial behaviour to planning or the contentious proposed asylum seeker centre in Stafford. It didn't feel like I got any time off despite being so close to my baby's arrival, so I decided to skip the neighbourhood watch meeting with residents in Stafford one evening. The councillor was furious and rang me to ask why I hadn't attended, but I was exhausted and my swollen belly felt too cumbersome to leave the house. I also pulled out of attending a fundraising dinner for neighbouring MP Sir Bill Cash, much to the organiser's chagrin.

The expectations of what I could do while heavily pregnant were far too high. I struggled to read several hundred emails a day from constituents with urgent casework or respond to campaigners writing to me about policy, coupled with daily correspondence from the party, the Whips' Office and my select committees. I simply couldn't deal with the volume of work I usually did, which was on average twelve hours a day. My team did a huge amount to help me and I appreciated how much they stepped up, particularly my chief of staff in Parliament, Samantha, and James up in Stafford, but the buck stopped with me as only I was the elected representative.

Everything important still needed my sign-off, and I felt that I was letting everyone down but also potentially causing harm to my baby by not resting more.

I tried to get ready for my daughter's arrival by borrowing items for her nursery such as a baby light and a white noise machine. I sorted her second- and third-hand babygrows by age group into drawers, folded muslins and stocked the nappy changing station with antiseptic cream, nappy bags and wet wipes. I focused solely on items for my baby. It didn't occur to me that I would need much support myself, given I was planning a natural birth. My assumption was that I would be walking within a few days, breastfeeding my baby straightaway and that I'd be able to look after her once Henry's fortnight of paternity leave ended.

My anxiety subsided somewhat once Henry started his new job as an estate agent at James du Pavey in my new constituency. None of my family lived locally so I felt completely dependent on him for support. My father had died the week I got selected as the prospective parliamentary candidate for Stafford, my mother lived several hours' drive away and my siblings were both down in London.

Meanwhile, my blood phobia had not improved, despite attending meetings with specialists for extra psychological support for months, and I would soon be giving birth. I was terrified that nothing had made any difference and I knew that they would want to take my bloods during my hospital stay. I was extremely terrified of ending up in theatre.

I was now so desperate to cure my phobia that I was prepared to try anything, however unusual the intervention. My husband recommended that I speak to an energy healer who specialised in past lives. I had never done anything like this before, but I was determined to get help. Jane offered me a Zoom session to read my chart and asked my higher self and my guides for permission to work with my ancestral energies. She asked me what topic I wanted to ask about and I told her my fear of childbirth and blood. I closed my eyes while she asked questions about whether the emotional blockages were in my past or present lives and whether it was on the maternal or paternal side of my family. Each time her pendulum responded to her with a yes or no, moving over the chart. I sat quietly and tried to concentrate on what she said, but I was sceptical about how useful this approach would be. The only reading I'd ever had was a palm and tarot session in a caravan on Brighton Pier years earlier.

Next, she asked how many years my trauma went back and probed the connected emotions that came up, such as grief, betrayal or low self-worth. She asked specific questions about childbirth and listed a number of emotions that needed healing within my family line. She then cleared my energy using my higher self. Finally, she said that someone had died or nearly died in childbirth several generations back on my father's side. The hair stood up on the back of my neck and I felt cold.

I was spooked by the whole experience and it made me wonder if there was something in my history that had triggered this extreme response in me. Months of specialist healthcare had made no difference and my phobia was so severe that perhaps there was something else going on that I couldn't explain with normal science. Afterwards, I remembered that my father's ancestor Sir Charles Clarke had been royal physician to Queen Adelaide, wife of William IV, and had saved her life in childbirth. I knew the brief facts that he had been a notable surgeon and physician, but I had never properly focused on his history. I looked him up and discovered he had been a fellow at the Royal College of Physicians specialising in midwifery and in women's and children's diseases, which was highly unusual at the time. I didn't know if there was any connection, but it felt like there might be. I slept deeply that night.

The next day I was gutted to miss attending the Queen's Baton Relay in Stafford ahead of the upcoming Commonwealth Games, especially as my constituency would be hosting the mountain biking event. Instead, I attended Royal Stoke University Hospital for another foetal scan. It was 35 degrees centigrade and my husband's charity cricket game was cancelled due to the extreme heat. We melted in the house together, where it was impossible to stay cool even inside with the curtains down and the windows closed. I froze a bottle of water, placed it in front of a fan and sat with a dampened tea towel over my enormous stomach as my daughter kicked every few minutes and I struggled to sit comfortably. I felt lethargic all day and mainly stayed in bed sipping cold lemon and ginger tea with ice. I ignored the news as it made me anxious, disabled alerts from all the social media apps on my mobile and tried to finish reading a novel.

Ahead of my due date, I received a home visit from the maternity team, which was the only time that anyone came to see me. Chris reminded me of a school matron, firm and no nonsense but also warm and kind. She took a tour of the house to see how organised I was for my baby's arrival and seemed relieved that I had everything in hand in the nursery. When she met Henry she gently probed as to how he was getting on, and I was interested that she was covertly assessing him and what level of support he would provide as the expectant father. I was surprised that she stayed with me for over an hour and didn't make me feel like she was clock watching. She had a cup of tea and asked me how I was. My recent appointments had only been for scans in the hospital and the majority of my other health meetings had been online, so it was reassuring to have someone check up on me in person and not just to ask about my baby. I was grateful to have had this home visit, but I soon became aware from other pregnant friends that they had not been offered the same service. There appeared to be a postcode lottery and any continuity of care was the exception, not the rule.

Chris recommended that I enjoy the remaining time I had left at home, focus on self-care and prioritise getting some rest before labour. She stressed that I should get the house as ready as I could, so I did jobs that I never usually got around to like cleaning the fridge and restocking dried foods in the cupboard. That weekend, Henry and I sat down to watch the UEFA Women's Euro final at Wembley Stadium. The Lionesses won the match against Germany and for the first time, I thought that women's football had cut through with the public to become a mainstream sport. I joked that I would get a Lionesses poster for our daughter's nursery as I wanted her to grow up to be a strong feminist too and believe that she could do anything. I listened to the full stadium chant 'Three Lions' and 'Sweet Caroline' as they spurred the players on and we watched the exciting game. It felt good to be distracted.

CHAPTER FIVE

RESIGNING IN HOSPITAL

I sat in Stafford's County Hospital with my community midwife Stacey for our first meeting. I was thirty-six weeks pregnant and she was doing my regular check-up to monitor my baby. I liked her straight away – she was calm, practical and listened compassionately when I shared my phobias of needles and the sight of blood. I refused to have any new blood tests and asked her to refer to my notes in my previous records, which she did. Instead, we discussed my birth plan, which had been prepared by my previous NHS trust down in London.

It was 5.30 p.m. and I was tired after a busy day in the constituency. I'd come from my office to go through that month's casework. That morning, I'd had a call, in my role as trade envoy, on attracting investment into the UK, virtually met with clerks in Parliament to discuss my handover notes for the select committee I chaired for the overseas aid watchdog known as ICAI, and I'd spoken to my whip about the concerns that veterans of the armed forces had raised with me about supporting the government in the upcoming tricky Northern Ireland Bill. The bill controversially proposed to end legal proceedings concerning Troubles-related conduct and provide conditional immunity from prosecution for those who cooperate with investigations, conducted by the newly established Independent Commission for Reconciliation and Information Recovery. I then managed to speak to the Refugees Minister about the Ukrainian refugee scheme in Staffordshire.

The temperature was 18 degrees and I felt hot, sticky and exhausted. I was only four weeks away from my due date – which, coincidentally, was also my thirty-seventh birthday – and my belly felt like I had a hot water bottle inside that I couldn't get out. I wanted to go home, lie down in the dark in front of a fan and get some sleep. I climbed heavily up onto the examination chair for her to check the baby. Stacey got her stethoscope to feel our daughter's heartbeat but couldn't find it. I could feel her rising anxiety as she called a colleague to help to double check.

'Your daughter's heartbeat is skipping a beat,' she said.

My husband's phone pinged with a BBC News alert. Henry interrupted to show me, saying, 'You might want to hear this.' He read out the news that Rishi Sunak and Sajid Javid had quit Boris Johnson's Cabinet. The Chancellor and Health Secretary had said they no longer had confidence in the Prime Minister to lead the country. I began to feel a wave of panic. I had been considering resigning as the PM's trade envoy for weeks, fed up with having to defend his behaviour during Covid, especially since the report into lockdown parties during the pandemic in Downing Street had been published. I believed that the public rightly expected competence from the government and we had become a laughing stock since the PM had been fined by police for rule-breaking in No. 10. It had become impossible to defend the government in private or in public and it shocked me how Boris had trashed his leadership and our party when just a few years earlier, he had won the biggest majority at a general election since Margaret Thatcher's victory in 1987.

Our midwife interrupted my train of thought. 'Henry, I think you should drive her to the hospital immediately,' she said. 'Don't wait for an ambulance to blue light her. It will take too long to get to Royal Stoke.' She explained that an irregular heartbeat was serious and that in the worst-case scenario, I could end up having an emergency Caesarean that evening to get the baby out. This was my top fear and the one I had spent months trying to avoid; the headline in my birth plan said that I wanted to avoid medical interventions. I focused on my breathing as I walked to the car park, aware of the pressure of the baby on my bladder, as I considered my options. I was intensely worried about the baby and whether she would be OK, but I was also extremely stressed about the news that was unfolding and my heart pounded as I thought about what to do.

I was furious with Boris, especially as I had always supported him as Prime Minister and had campaigned for him twice as Mayor of London. The final straw was that Chris Pincher, one of my fellow Staffordshire MPs, had been accused of sexual misconduct, and it had become increasingly clear that Boris had known about previous sexual misconduct allegations against him when he had appointed him to his government role.

I was no longer prepared to support the PM. It was clear when I spoke to other colleagues that the scale of rebellion against him was increasing. We had also just lost two by-elections within a week in Tiverton & Honiton and Wakefield, and I hadn't forgotten how we'd been treated when pressure had been put on us not to suspend fellow MP Owen Paterson. Paterson was found to have broken lobbying rules by the parliamentary standards commissioner, but us Tory MPs had been whipped to support an amendment to the commissioner's recommendations that would set up a new committee to investigate standards, which threw into question the values of public life that were expected of us as MPs. The situation had become untenable. The previous week, before the midwife appointment, my husband had driven me to my constituency office to discuss options for resigning with my manager James. We agreed that enough was enough and that if any senior government members were to resign then I would follow them.

Only a month earlier, Boris had won the support of the majority of Tory MPs in a confidence vote, despite serious misgivings about his leadership by many of us, which meant that technically he was immune from another challenge within the party for another year. At the time of the vote, the Whips' Office had rung me to rescind the long-term slip I had been given for my final weeks of pregnancy, which had given me permission to miss votes as my remote 'proxy' vote would not kick in until after the birth of my daughter. Frankly, the Whips' Office reminded me of bullying prefects in a dysfunctional boarding school. As I was so close to my due date, I outright refused to get on the train back to London, taking the calculation that they wouldn't remove the whip from an MP who was nearly eight months pregnant. In the end, 149 of my colleagues voted against the Prime Minister, but even then Boris tried to spin it as a win. Given I had abstained in the vote of no confidence in my party leader, I had to turn my telephone off to ignore calls from journalists asking me to comment.

As Henry drove me to the large university hospital in Stoke-on-Trent, I thought about whether I needed to resign that evening before I possibly ended up in theatre. Given I had requested a general anaesthetic in an emergency scenario, there was every chance

RESIGNING IN HOSPITAL

I wouldn't be in any fit state to be making decisions the next day, which could be too late. I called James in the car to get his view. First, I would need to submit my letter of no confidence in the Prime Minister to the 1922 Committee, but I was on my way to the hospital and not able to get to a computer. James offered to go back into my office after hours. For weeks the whips had been watching the chair Sir Graham Brady's office for signs of any of us submitting letters of no confidence, which was pointless when we could text him directly. I ignored the rush hour traffic en route to the hospital and typed out notes on my telephone.

The Maternity Assessment Centre was on the second floor in the hospital. It was full of mothers in the queue ahead of me and the wait would be several hours once triaged. It was now dinner time and there was no food in the wing, only a drinks machine. My husband got me some water and we sat down on the uncomfortable plastic chairs to wait to see the consultant. No one checked on us. I felt faint, very stressed and I sweated profusely in the stuffy room, which had no windows open despite the July heat. I hadn't even got my hospital bag with me, as I wasn't expecting my daughter to arrive early. Meanwhile, the political context was certainly not helping to calm my baby's irregular heartbeat.

In my letter, I wrote:

Dear Sir Graham,

I am writing to inform you that I no longer have confidence in the leadership of the Prime Minister.

As a loyal member of the Conservative Party, I have always tried to support the government, but the current situation cannot continue.

As one of the Party's new female MPs, and a member of the

Women and Equalities Select Committee, I take allegations of sexual misconduct very seriously. To learn that the Prime Minister chose to elevate a colleague to a position of pastoral care for MPs, whilst in full knowledge of his own wrongdoing, shows a severe lack of judgement and care for the parliamentary party. I was shocked to see colleagues defending the government with assurances that have turned out to be false. This is not the way that any responsible government should act.

As an activist myself, I know that those people who ultimately take the fury from the public are our hard-working volunteers and local councillors, who often end up paying the price for these failures. I think that we need to draw a line under the current debacle and get a grip on government on their behalf, as well as, most importantly, the country.

I would therefore ask that you add this letter to the others I am sure you have received, which are calling for a vote of no confidence in the Prime Minister.

Writing the letter in the hospital waiting room as my husband paced up and down, not knowing if we were going to have our baby any minute, was surreal. I sent it to James and he put the text on my letterhead and signed it on my behalf. I emailed and texted a scanned copy to Graham and felt relief to have finally done it.

It was a high-stakes game. I knew I could be throwing my political career away after more than a decade of hard work and campaigning to become an MP. I was committed to doing my job in the constituency, but I knew I needed to resign from the government. The previous day, I had reconsidered whether I would even want to stand for a second term as an MP after the parliamentary security team had come to our constituency home to install panic buttons and an alarm. Threats increasingly concerned me when I became pregnant. I paced around the waiting room, tried to monitor my baby's kick count and considered whether her movements meant she was behaving as normal. I constantly needed the toilet and hid in there to make another call to James to discuss the next steps.

I drafted another letter, this time to resign, which was a variation of the no confidence one that I'd sent Graham and set out why I no longer supported the PM. After 10 p.m. I tweeted a screenshot of my letter and sent the link to friendly journalists. I was only a backbencher with no public profile, unlike Rishi and Sajid who were Cabinet ministers, but I hoped that my name would add to the trickle that might become a flood and force the PM to do the right thing and stand down. I breathed a sigh of relief that both letters were done, but the stress of the night was far from over.

The nurse came out and finally called my name, which meant I was going to be seen by the consultant after waiting several hours. It was not someone I recognised. The team on shift were all new, so they didn't know anything about me or my baby. I was hooked up to the baby monitor machine, which was attached uncomfortably around my stomach. It beeped eerily and drew scratchy lines on a graph that charted my daughter's heartbeat. The paper printed on a continuous roll and sounded both menacing and disconcerting. I calmed my breathing down and focused on what was happening in the noisy and stifling ward with only a thin curtain around my bed for privacy. I could hear everyone next to me and no one else seemed to be aware of what was happening within the government. I wondered, not for the first time, if my job was too all-consuming and whether constantly having to choose between work and my family would make me a bad mother. Was I being selfish trying to be an MP and a mother and have it all?

I was terrified that our daughter was going to come early and I didn't want to end up on the operating table. I didn't feel prepared for her arrival at all, and I reviewed my day, thinking about whether I should have gone to the office or attended any meetings. Perhaps I should have finished unpacking the nappy items I had bought instead? Or made a changing table zone? Or focused on buying food for the freezer? It was too late now. I could only watch and listen to the monitor. The wait was agonising and I resisted the urge to check the social media apps on my phone. I wondered if colleagues had seen my letter and what my Conservative Association would think.

Eventually, the consultant reviewed my chart and reassured me that my daughter was going to be OK. Her heartbeat had calmed down and they were not going to need to get her out urgently that evening. Henry and I were hugely relieved. I was asked to come back the next day for another scan to check how she was doing and I was referred to the foetal medicine team. I felt relieved but completely exhausted as the pressure of the day caught up with me. We drove home and I couldn't wait to be back in my bed. Suddenly, I was too tired to read the news or care if the government had imploded.

CHAPTER SIX

LEADERSHIP ELECTION

The next morning, I woke up and instantly panicked that I had resigned too early. There was one story on every front page: the Prime Minister was battling to cling to power and Downing Street was in chaos. Boris was said to be on the brink as ministers quit. 'Can even Boris, the greased piglet, wriggle out of this?' screamed the *Daily Mail*. 'Johnson hanging by a thread as Sunak and Javid walk out' cried the *Daily Telegraph*. However, so far only ten of us had resigned. The Solicitor General, Alex Chalk, had left government half an hour after me – we hadn't spoken, I found out from social media – but no one else had taken the leap. I wondered if I'd jumped too soon, as I was only the ninth MP to do so, but I knew deep down it was right to do. I didn't know how the PM could save his premiership after two of his most senior Cabinet ministers, the Chancellor and Health Secretary, both of whom I respected as colleagues, had resigned within ten minutes of each other. Boris was rattled and tried to fill the growing gaps on the front bench. He had lost control of the party and I didn't know how he could carry on like this. His behaviour as our leader was reflecting badly on us all. My local Conservative Association members seemed to think differently and that Boris could do no wrong. A number of my councillors still supported him and did not understand why I had resigned.

I tried not to obsessively read the news and to focus on my baby, but it was hard. No one called me from the hospital the next day about my foetal medical scan and I was not booked in for an appointment. When I chased, I was told there was no space for anyone to see me in the clinic and to try again the next day. Last night's experience in the hospital had been a wake-up call that my baby could arrive any minute, so I kept calling. At last, Dr Young agreed to fit me in between cases the following day.

I decided to focus on getting organised for the baby and cancelled all meetings in my diary. All the stress and excitement of my job and the developing news wasn't helping anything, and I constantly worried about my daughter. I was concerned that the stress of my work was affecting her health. Was it worth being a politician if it was going to impact so negatively on my pregnancy? Had the pressure from work resulted in her heart skipping a beat? What if something happened to my baby? What if I was forced to have an emergency Caesarean when I was so opposed to medical interventions? I was terrified that something might happen to either her or me.

I watched BBC News live to see what was happening down in London. I felt very isolated up in my constituency, unable to attend meetings of the 1922 Committee with other backbench MPs or my One Nation caucus of moderate centrist Conservatives. I realised how crucial it was to be on the parliamentary estate to speak to colleagues during votes or drink with colleagues in the members' tearoom. Friends, family members and Conservative members began texting me to ask what was going on, but I didn't know anything more than they did. I kept track of the number of ministers resigning, which steadily increased over the next twenty-four hours to an unprecedented number. There was no longer a functioning government. Finally, I saw the lectern with no government logo appear in front of No. 10 and I knew Boris was finally resigning. I could barely believe it. It had taken three days of resignations by government ministers for him to step down. I watched his typically flamboyant and unapologetic speech and I was relieved and worried at the same time. It was right for him to go but we were now leaderless in increasingly dangerous and uncertain times.

My next thought was that I hoped that former Defence Secretary Penny Mordaunt would run, so I texted her to ask her to stand and told her that she had my full support. She added me to her WhatsApp group named 'Greater' and I joined the colleagues supporting her bid. Former Cabinet minister Andrea Leadsom was running her campaign along with the MP Craig Tracey. I was in Stafford and there was only so much I could do, so they asked me to call MPs I knew to find out who they were supporting in the race and to gather intelligence on them.

My pitch to them was that Penny was best placed to win a general election, as she was the strongest campaigner and she had won her seat from Labour. I believed in her values and had witnessed her competence. I had supported Penny for many years since she had first helped me as a candidate and agreed to mentor me as a new female MP. We had also worked together when she was International Development Secretary and I had reported to her as trade envoy when she was International Trade Minister. It was going to be tough to keep seats like mine in the next general election and hold together the electoral coalition we'd had in 2019 of Leave-voting ex-Labour seats with our traditional Conservative heartlands. I agreed to write an op-ed to publicly endorse her when she was ready. I knew we had to get it published before my baby arrived, so I spoke to her immediately about talking points before heading to my pregnancy yoga class.

Early on, Penny was the clear favourite with the public and polling showed that she was the candidate that Labour feared most. I'd watched her at the despatch box and seen at first hand her hold the Chamber's attention as they listened to her every word. She was a great communicator and brilliant on her feet. I believed she was the only one who could unite the party as both a high-profile Brexiteer and compassionate Conservative.

As she edged towards the final two, hostility around her leadership campaign increased. I was dismayed that colleagues started to attack her or misquote her views, such as those on gender, to represent her unfairly in the press. The other teams were desperate to stitch Penny up and take her out of the race, and the leadership campaign became increasingly nasty despite us trying to play fair. I was shocked by the level of personal attacks on Penny, which left all of us on her campaign team feeling bruised. I didn't agree with negative campaigning and I believed that nasty smears would only backfire on us as a party. She had run a positive and clean campaign of which I was proud. I had found the relentless pace of the race exhausting and I felt trapped at home, unable to go far in case I went into labour, having to make do with making leadership calls in our garden. It was tough not to be down in Westminster with everyone at such a crucial moment and to be so removed from the action.

A fortnight after I'd resigned and now two weeks into the leadership campaign, I attended my next appointment with Henry at the Women's Health Centre in County Hospital, Stafford. I felt calmer given our baby's heart rate had been normal during the past two scans and I remained keen to have midwife-led care during labour.

Stacey discussed options during birth with me, including pain relief, being mobile in labour and foetal monitoring and referred me to a professional midwifery advocate (PMA). She sent me home aware of the early signs of labour, with emergency contact numbers to call, and explained that at forty weeks I would be offered a membrane sweep if I hadn't naturally gone into labour, which we hoped would not be necessary.

That week, back at home, I fielded calls from different leadership teams who tried to persuade me to defect and join them. Parliamentary private secretaries in my intake would ring on behalf of different candidates with their pitch, but I kept my powder dry and didn't declare who I was supporting. Meanwhile, Penny set up daily meetings in her parliamentary office to discuss her campaign and agreed that I could dial in remotely from Staffordshire. I sent in the latest intelligence I had gathered to her team, including questions she might get asked at hustings organised by different Conservative groups of MPs.

The following week, I published an endorsement on social media and I was assigned more MPs I personally knew to canvass them before Penny called them directly. Given that I represented a Leave constituency, I lobbied them by arguing that it was vital that the party had a Brexiteer in the final two. #PutPennyOnTheBallot began to trend on Twitter and she generated good momentum in the press and with colleagues. We all regularly discussed her latest polling and refined her strategy and policy announcements over the next fortnight. It was intense and felt odd that I was the only member of the team working virtually.

Later that week, I went to the GP surgery in Eccleshall to collect my MAT B1 certificate, which I needed to confirm my proxy vote, and settled down to watch the first leadership debate. I was so exhausted that I fell asleep on the sofa before the end. Newspapers reported that Penny had performed well in the debate with a confident performance. I was very excited when Penny got down to the final three; I was cheering at the television as I really believed she could win and become our party leader.

I kept my fingers crossed as I watched the final ballot be published on our WhatsApp group and then make national news. It was devastating. Despite everything we had done, Penny had failed to make it to the final two. I felt completely dejected and that we had lost a huge opportunity to rebrand as a party. The two final candidates to be presented to our membership would be Liz Truss and Rishi Sunak. I knew one thing straight away: I was not going to endorse anyone publicly now that she was out of the running. Instead, I was going to focus on my baby's imminent arrival.

CHAPTER SEVEN

OVERDUE

My due date – my birthday, 4 August – was fast approaching. I began to feel anxious about how I was going to cope looking after a newborn baby while still being elected as an MP. Margaret Thatcher had famously only needed four hours of sleep a night, but I couldn't function well without at least six hours, preferably ten. How was I going to manage months of sleep deprivation while never being completely off work? One of the challenges of being a politician was that I was not entitled to regular maternity leave, given that I was an elected representative rather than an employee. It was ironic that as lawmakers we set policies that businesses had to follow but that we did not follow ourselves. The number of women who had given birth while an MP remained low. Many of my female colleagues fell into two camps: those with adult children or those without children at all. The only process that seemed to have been thought about in detail was how I could continue to vote. The proxy system, where I could vote remotely via a colleague, meant that I didn't have to travel from Stafford to London for six months, but the reality was that I would be unable to take regular maternity leave as an employee would in any other business.

I tried to obtain a copy of a maternity document from Parliament to read our policy for new mothers, but I couldn't easily find one. Alicia Kearns, a friend in my intake who'd recently had a baby, suggested I read her evidence to the Procedure Select Committee and I noted that she had also stated that official guidance was hard to find. I contacted the committee chair, my constituency neighbour Karen Bradley, who was sympathetic to new mothers but confirmed that there was no maternity guidance for MPs written down in a single place. She suggested instead that I read relevant speeches and reports, such as those from the Women and Equalities Select Committee on a gender-sensitive Parliament, chaired by Maria Miller, to work out the policy.

I did some research and found that a number of Labour colleagues, such as Harriet Harman, had publicly raised concerns about the lack of maternity leave for MPs and had campaigned to make Parliament more family friendly. I was horrified to read reports of other colleagues' experiences, such as Tulip Siddiq, who had delayed her planned Caesarean due to a close Brexit vote. I knew how lucky I was to be elected when the government had a large majority, but I was conscious throughout my pregnancy that if I needed any time off before the birth or after the first six months, in the event of complications, then it would be at the discretion of the whips to pair me with another MP and I was entirely at their mercy – nothing was guaranteed. The only person who had obtained a small increased budget to employ a proxy member of staff was Stella Creasy, but she had talked about how they still could not represent her in the Chamber, in meetings with ministers or attend select committees on her behalf. Stella had also taken her thirteen-week-old son, who she was breastfeeding, into a debate in Westminster Hall and been castigated by the Speaker for breaking the rules. I became more aware that there were certain parts of my job that would not be undertaken if I did not continue to do them, even while I was supposed to be on maternity leave. The shocking truth was that Parliament was not fit for working mothers in the twenty-first century and had avoided the modernisation that had taken place in other workplaces in the UK.

I spent the final days of my last trimester attempting to rest, avoiding the scorching summer heat and planning with my team what they could cover for me. We agreed that they would contact me in the first six weeks only with urgent matters and preferably by text message. If I needed to sign anything off, my office manager James would come to my constituency home. I assumed that I would be in a fit state, both mentally and physically, to continue to represent my constituents, apart from suffering from sleep deprivation.

My daughter was active daily and frequently kicked me, which caused me to double over in surprise, but nothing happened to indicate labour. My mother and my best friend Harriet drove up to Stafford with my toddler goddaughter on my birthday to celebrate. We kept it low key with a simple lunch at home. It was the first time I had seen any family or close friends in several weeks; it was a relief to speak freely and not have the constant filter I always had with constituents.

Every day, Henry went to work at his local estate agent and I sat at home waiting for our daughter to arrive. The days felt endlessly long – until 7 August, when I was sat on a bench outside the church next to our house and felt a gush to signify my waters had broken. I took a photograph to send to my midwife to show the size of the stain and sniffed it to ensure that it was not urine. I felt deeply anxious about going into labour, despite all the preparation I had done.

I called Henry at work and he rushed back to drive me into Royal

Stoke hospital. I was referred for a pelvic examination to check my cervix, which took place in a cold, brightly lit room. Henry was not allowed in with me, which surprised me given we were out of Covid restrictions. It was not clear to me why not.

I reluctantly clambered onto the table on my own and heaved my large belly up. I had no idea what to expect, and without any explanation the nurse inserted a large, duck-billed plastic speculum to force open my cervix. The procedure was very painful and I felt like a slab of meat being inspected by the butcher in a refrigeration unit. Afterwards, I felt bruised inside my vagina from the brusque manner in which the examination had been carried out. The nurse told me in a bored tone that nothing had been noted on the speculum, which surprised me. Feeling like I was not being listened to, I requested an additional liquor volume scan to check the amniotic fluid levels surrounding my baby, as I didn't think this was correct. I also called my midwife Stacey, who was immediately more compassionate and said it sounded exactly as if my waters had broken. She wondered if the hole in the amniotic sac was at the top, which was rare but meant the hole could reseal and stop leaking and I was unlikely to develop an infection. It was unclear what to do, so they sent me home from the hospital and the waiting began again.

The next day, 8 August, which was now four days past my due date, Liz Truss texted me. I was surprised it had taken this long for her to ask to speak with me, given that Penny Mordaunt was out of the race. I had worked for Liz directly in my role as trade envoy and had reported to her in the Department for International Trade, where I had found her awkward and often difficult. Her manner was frequently jarring and she came across as overly ambitious. I thought she often oversold her brief, took credit for the work of others and posted excessively on social media, planning ahead for her future leadership campaign years in advance.

Early on in my parliamentary term, she had come up to Stafford to visit National Farmers' Union members and discuss their view that our new trade deals were undercutting British farmers. While I appreciated having a visit by a Cabinet minister to my constituency, the roundtable did not go as I'd hoped. She sat in a Staffordshire farm kitchen, sipped from an Emma Bridgewater mug and completely batted away their genuine concerns. I came away with the impression that although she was always on top of the brief, she seemed to have few social skills and little empathy with colleagues or constituents. Her leadership pitch to me on the telephone was short and unexciting and she didn't bother to reference Stafford or my personal priorities. I was not impressed, but to be polite I told her that I would also be speaking to her opponent to be fair to both contenders.

Rishi called me a few days later to ask for my support in the contest. I was on tenterhooks waiting to be booked in for induction now that I was overdue, so I refused to take any other calls bar the hospital, but I wanted to hear directly why he wanted to be our Prime Minister. Unlike Liz, Rishi was personal in his approach and wanted my input on how we could move on from Boris and get back to the business of serious government. I knew Rishi reasonably well and liked him, but I pushed him on how he would govern differently and what his priorities were.

Although I was already likely to support Rishi over Liz, we had clashed repeatedly in the past over our views on foreign aid. In 2021, I had challenged him over an amendment to the legislation for a new science agency, the Advanced Research and Invention Agency

Bill. Through the amendment, rebels had forced an unexpected vote on reversing cuts to the aid budget that the government had announced the previous year. I had been opposed to cutting our overseas aid budget from 0.7 to 0.5 per cent of GDP and had made these views known to him and the PM privately. Prior to being an MP, I had visited numerous aid programmes around the world and seen first-hand the impact our development programmes had in reducing global poverty. I had serious concerns about the damage the reduction in spending would do to the UK's international reputation. So, while I believed that Rishi would make a better leader, I disliked the pressure he had put on me to support the government in this crucial vote.

Rishi reminded me that he had taken the time as Chancellor to meet with me one on one to discuss the amendment, after I had spent weeks in private meetings with Foreign Office ministers and No. 10 making the case for the government not to make the cut. At the time, Rishi told me the best he could do was agree to a clear roadmap back to the target when public finances were in a better shape after the pandemic. This last-minute concession, ahead of the vote, had been a relief and I was thankful that the opposition of myself and other vociferous colleagues, such as Andrew Mitchell and Anthony Mangnall, had managed to contain the cuts to only 0.5 per cent of GDP. We had been fighting considerable opposition within the Conservative Party, including other colleagues who were demanding a complete cut in overseas aid or a reduction of the budget to 0.07 per cent. Rishi had referenced me in his closing speech at the despatch box for my constructive work with him on the bill, as he appreciated how difficult the vote was for me. But I had not forgotten how upset I was with the government at the time and how annoyed I was that I'd been told my opposition to the cuts made it increasingly difficult for me to ask for money locally for constituency projects while also making the case for spending money abroad.

I had learnt that politics was a game of influence and favours, and Parliament often reminded me of the history books I had read about the royal court surrounding the king in medieval times. Now Rishi had called me asking for his support in the leadership race, it was time to cash in my credit. I wanted to know what he would do to support me in Stafford, as I felt I had supported him on a difficult piece of legislation and now it was his turn. He listened to my strong opposition to HS2, which directly affected my constituency, and said that he was willing to take another look at the viability of the project. He agreed with my concerns about the proposal to send huge number of asylum seekers to Stafford and suggested that I met with a Home Office minister about the site. He also offered me a reception in Downing Street with the development sector, after I pointed out that previous Conservative ministers had not been willing to engage with the charities delivering our aid programmes. I told him I would think about it, but it was already clear to me that he was heads and shoulders above his rival.

* * *

I had little understanding of what might happen if our daughter didn't arrive when she was due. Induction of labour was not something that was covered much in our antenatal classes or referred to in appointments with my midwife. I was led to believe that the baby would come naturally when she was ready and likely around her due date. From one week overdue, I began to worry for my daughter's safety, as the likelihood of something going wrong had increased significantly. The hospital offered me a Caesarean, but I declined as I was keen to have the natural birth that I'd been led to believe I could have. The two options I was offered were either a C-section or induction of labour, nothing else, and I had very little understanding of my rights as a mother. I researched online recommendations for how to naturally start labour and I tried them all: having sex, hot baths, eating spicy food, pineapple and medjool dates, drinking raspberry leaf tea, breast stimulation, reflexology, rocking on a fit ball, and climbing the stairs multiple times a day in our house. Nothing worked.

On my husband's forty-first birthday, now eleven days overdue, I refused to go anywhere more than a short drive from the hospital. So to celebrate, instead of going further afield to the Peak District, Henry and I went to visit the stately home Weston Park at the edge of my constituency, on the border with Shropshire. I waddled around the seventeenth-century hall in Weston-under-Lizard and admired their art collection, including the portraits by van Dyck, horses by Stubbs, coastal scenes by Vernet, and the Victorian library with thousands of books and furniture by Chippendale. I frequently sat down and borrowed the volunteer guide's chair for a rest.

After a tour of the grand house, we went on a long walk around the ornamental lake in the parkland that had been designed by Capability Brown. This was when I felt my first contractions, which were like someone had squeezed a metal ring tightly around my stomach. The tightenings were painful, but I was excited. This was it, I was finally going to meet my daughter! And after nine months, I was also desperate to no longer be pregnant, get my baby out and reclaim my body for myself.

I began to time the contractions, but they seemed a long time apart, with around fifteen or twenty minutes between each of them.

I did not know that the start of labour, the latent phase when my body began to prepare for my baby to be born, could take days instead of hours. The contractions were uncomfortable, rather than excruciating, and did not last long or occur too frequently. The NHS website said that I should call my midwife or maternity unit only if I was having three or more contractions every ten minutes. I was disappointed – maybe she was not coming as soon as I thought. We headed home to monitor the situation. After a few hours, the contractions fizzled out and nothing happened. It became clear they'd been Braxton Hicks contractions. I spent the next day watching the news for updates about the leadership election. The wait was agonising, and I felt like my life was on hold.

I developed terrible backache over the next few days and constantly went to the toilet, obsessively looking for signs of losing my mucus plug as a signal of the start of labour. I also felt like I had the worst period pain of my life, in addition to feeling the pressure of my baby as she pushed down on my cervix or my bladder when it was full. Henry and I went for a long countryside stroll to attempt to 'walk the baby out'. We got lost with bad reception and had to escape through a cornfield to outrun a herd of cows, which still brought no result. I got sporadic painful spasms across my belly but nothing else, despite trying everything to encourage labour. I went into the hospital for a membrane sweep, where the midwife inserted her fingers into my cervix and swept her fingers around inside me in another painful examination that was recommended to try to stimulate labour. I repeated my request to avoid a medical induction. My daughter was not keen to come out into the world yet and I preferred to wait.

After my due date passed, my fears for the birth grew and I decided to visit a women's natural health specialist in Newcastle-under-Lyme, which I was lucky to be able to afford. Amanda was a former midwife from Royal Stoke who specialised in complementary therapies for fertility and maternity. I booked my first ever reflexology session with her in her quiet, relaxing private clinic near Brampton Museum. I was desperate to find something that would make me calmer before the birth. I felt extremely agitated after two failed, highly invasive membrane sweeps.

I tried to focus on the warm light from the Himalayan salt lamp and the pregnancy artwork on the walls. She talked me through relaxation techniques and worked on my feet to stimulate my pituitary glands as my body was so tense. Normally I was ticklish and struggled to have a pedicure without fits of laughter, but this time my soles felt tender, as if she was pressing hard on a bruise even though the pressure was gentle, and I unexpectedly burst into tears. Amanda gave me tissues and gently asked me what was wrong. She listened patiently as I told her about my fears of childbirth, induction of labour and having an emergency Caesarean. I had never met her before, but she immediately made me feel calmer. She asked if I was subconsciously holding my baby in due to fear of the birth and we talked about learning to let go. I went home with a custom essential oils blend with clary sage, lavender and two drops of frankincense, which I added to a warm bath. That night I slept better and felt more centred.

CHAPTER EIGHT

INDUCTION

TRIGGER WARNING
The following pages contain graphic descriptions of traumatic birth, which some may find distressing.

My midwife told me that I would be induced by fourteen days overdue at the latest, so I kept my hospital bag packed, excessively tidied the house and made sure everything was ready for our baby's arrival. I was told to be ready from 7 a.m. for the hospital to call and book me in for induction on the same day. I tried to remain patient as I paced around the house expecting the call at any time, but I waited all day and no one contacted me. I tried calling and was repeatedly told that they had no room for me. The next day was the same. This time I called the ward every hour for an update, but often there was no answer, or when the shift changed the new staff on the front desk had no notes of my previous attempts to try to book myself in to be induced.

After two days of waiting, I had still not been booked in for induction, so I panicked and called my PMA Judith to get her advice. I had been referred to Judith by the Lotus maternal mental health service in Staffordshire and I had liked her immediately when I first met her in the Maternity Assessment Unit (MAU), as she was gentle, kind and explained at our first meeting how she was there to support my care and be my advocate in hospital. She helped me with breathing techniques to keep me calm and discussed distraction therapy to manage my anxiety. I had found it increasingly difficult to navigate the labyrinthine nature of the NHS with its many different services, so it was very helpful to have a real person with a mobile telephone number that I could call.

When I rang her to say I had not been called in for induction she was shocked, especially as she had seen my name written up on the board. She offered to go up to the ward and ask for herself what was happening, which reassured me straight away. Within twenty minutes I had a telephone call back, which invited me to come to the hospital. My husband left work early and drove me back to Stoke-on-Trent. I arrived at the hospital wearing a grey maternity nightie, complete with buttons down the front and back ready for labour, in my sheepskin slippers and clutching my water bottle to stay hydrated.

It was late afternoon on Thursday 18 August 2022 when I was finally admitted into the induction ward alongside several other women. I was put onto a bed with a thin purple curtain to pull around us for privacy. It was hot with no air conditioning and the sterile bay was tiny, with space only for a small upright chair for my husband to sit on next to all the medical equipment. I requested a fan as I sipped Lucozade and snacked on fruit, nuts and fizzy Haribo sweets that I'd brought with me from home. I put on the playlist of calming music I'd been encouraged to put together in my antenatal classes, but it was hard to hear the music through the grunts of pain from the other expectant mothers on the ward as they groaned through

INDUCTION

contractions that were still too far apart to have them admitted to the labour ward. I was frequently strapped up to the CTG (cardiotocography) machine with a turquoise stretchy band around my swollen stomach as they tried to record my daughter's heartbeat, which meant I wasn't allowed to be mobile. I felt trapped and it was disconcerting to be stuck there for so long. Finally, once my tests were concluded, they brought me a fit ball and encouraged me to rock back and forth, offered me some water and I was allowed to run a hot bath, which I used to distract myself every few hours throughout the night.

My first speculum examination took place on my own, in a room with strip lighting that was more like an interrogation cell in a prison than a hospital. I was taken in without Henry, despite my asking for him to attend, and there were two other people in the room who did not introduce themselves but just watched. No one explained to me what was going to happen. The midwife didn't introduce herself either, just asked me brusquely to lie down on the bed and thrust a huge vaginal speculum, which looked like a pair of large plastic pliers, inside me to examine my cervix. The examination was highly invasive and painful; I felt like I was being raped and I immediately burst into floods of tears and began to whimper like a wounded child. I was given no proper pain relief, bar gas and air, and struggled to breathe Entonox through a plastic mask over my nose and mouth, which did nothing for the pain and served only to provide a distraction.

Once back in my bed, I was not checked on for several hours. Around 9 p.m., I was informed by the midwife that they would need to put a pessary inside me to induce labour, as my cervix was 'closed' and it needed to be pumped with hormones to open it. I was extremely agitated and insisted that this time my husband came with me for whatever the procedure was. Once more, I was not informed what would happen next. They asked me to lie down on the bed with my knees open and inserted a pessary, which looked like a small, flat tampon, into my vagina to slowly release the female hormone prostaglandin to 'ripen my cervix'.

The objective was to try to start my labour spontaneously, but it failed and I spent another long six hours waiting for something to happen, feeling like a caged animal in the induction ward. I was given another pessary at 1.30 a.m. The medical staff repeatedly told me I had failed to dilate, and all the language used to describe the process was negative. I was hungry and very tired, having been awake all night. Judith was the only person during my stay in hospital who regularly checked up on me and was the only healthcare professional that I had met before. It did not feel that anyone else on the ward was that invested in my welfare, as the hospital staff changed every eight hours and became a rotating shift of disinterested nurses who did not know my name. There seemed to be zero continuity of care and I realised that the other women around me did not have an equivalent advocate on their behalf, as they had not accessed specialist mental health services before birth.

It was Friday morning when I had another painful vaginal examination, and by lunchtime they decided to give me a third and final pessary. Afterwards, I finally began to have painful contractions. It felt like my stomach was being squeezed tightly, as if a Tube door was being repeatedly trapped on me. However, the contractions were sporadic and not frequent enough for active labour to begin. I had now been in hospital for nearly twenty-four hours, confined in the tiny bay with my husband, who was doing his best to keep me calm and divert my attention. I was desperate to go outside and persuaded them to let me go on a short walk in my nightie into the park opposite the hospital. It was a relief to have the sun on my face and to get some fresh air, which helped me to relax and feel calmer, as I found the ward stifling and stressful. I was convinced my daughter was finally on her way, so I was devastated at the evening round to hear another midwife report to me that I had only reached a 2 centimetre dilation of my cervix.

Finally, at 12.40 a.m. the medical team insisted on the 'artificial rupture of membranes'. I didn't know what this opaque medical terminology meant, and the midwife explained that they would manually break my waters to encourage my womb to contract for labour to begin. She inserted into my vagina a small instrument with a hook on the end to make a hole in the amniotic sac, which released the fluid surrounding my baby. It gushed out all over the table.

The whole process had become like a nightmare and I was losing touch with reality from the pain and exhaustion. I wanted to go back home and crawl into bed to sleep, as it was now the middle of the night again and I had been awake for two days. At 3 a.m. I finally started to develop contractions that started off as two every ten minutes, but I was still not in active labour. I did not think I could take much more, and I felt like an animal trapped in an abattoir. It was only then that I was moved into my own room for some privacy. I gritted my teeth in agony and crushed Henry's hand as I was told to breathe through the pain. I was unable to move whenever I was hooked up to the CTG monitor, but the rest of the time I paced around the room as it felt better to be on the move than stuck in the bed. Henry fell asleep next to me in the reclining chair as I walked in circles with only darkness to look at out of the window.

My agony and exhaustion increased, and time began to blur so much that I barely noticed that it was now 5 a.m. and time for another dreaded vaginal examination. I was told witheringly that after so many hours in labour, induction had failed and I was still only 2 centimetres dilated. The midwife told me I would now be pumped full of hormones with an oxytocin drip to increase the contractions and make them more frequent.

This was my worst nightmare. Knowing that I would now have to have an IV line with a cannula put into my hand filled me with absolute terror. When the senior anaesthetist arrived, I was relieved that she took the time to read my notes and listened to my husband explain about my needle phobia. I was so agitated that I could not bear to watch as they put the cannula into the vein in the back of my hand, and I began to shake from head to toe and sob. Henry tried to calm me down by talking to me as if to a child and stroking my back. Afterwards, he wrapped my hand in a turquoise pashmina so that it looked a large candyfloss, which meant that I could no longer see the needle. But my hand throbbed incessantly and I could feel the drip of the drugs as they infiltrated into my bloodstream, the sensation of which made me feel faint. The medical staff increased the dosage almost every thirty minutes to force my contractions to increase and shock my body into an artificial rhythm. I began to dissociate from my body, and it felt as if I was watching myself from above down on the bed writhing in pain.

The morning shift arrived at 8 a.m. and I was handed over to more new staff that I didn't know. The midwives who checked on me continued to berate me for 'failing to progress'. I could not take much more; my body and mind were nearly at breaking point. It was now Saturday morning and the inducement had started on Thursday afternoon. I insisted on more pain relief. I also needed to rest, so I agreed to an epidural now that my contractions had increased and my body was struggling with the pain. They handed me a leaflet on

INDUCTION

the risks of the procedure, which I was no in no fit state to read. My signature slid off the page as I tried to focus on writing my name.

The medical team sat me down on the side of the bed and opened the poppers on the back of my nightie, which was covered in sweat. I tried to concentrate on looking out the window at the concrete wall opposite as they inserted the epidural into my lower back. I sat as still as I could and tried hard not to shake too much, as I was deeply scared that they might paralyse me accidentally if the needle slipped. They slowly inserted the long needle and it felt like I had been stung by a hornet. Afterwards, I whimpered and lay down, turned on my side with my huge belly protruding off the bed and tried to hide the hand that was hooked up to the IV. I was on the verge of hysterics and I did not know how much more of this I could take. I was also overcome with exhaustion, with my body continuing to have painful contractions. Henry was shattered too and dozed off on the hard floor, sleeping next to me on a mat with a blanket and pillow brought from home.

I must have fallen asleep, as all of a sudden it was nearly midday. I had not eaten properly for nearly two days, so I requested some food and someone brought me tea and hot toast with butter. I wolfed it down and recovered a tiny bit more energy before being reattached to the CTG to check my baby's heart rate again.

So far, everything during my labour was the opposite of what I had expected. I had wanted a water birth in the midwife-led unit, but now I was being told that my daughter was close to coming out via an emergency Caesarean as my body had 'failed' me. I was required to undergo yet another vaginal examination, but this time the midwife's tone was different, more urgent and animated. It was 12.50 p.m. and I was finally fully dilated. They told me I had gone from 2 to 10 centimetres in the time I was asleep. I was in shock and I struggled to hear what they were saying due to the acute pain I was in. My contractions were now four in ten minutes and I had strong urges to push, which felt like straining on the toilet.

An hour disappeared. It felt like my mind was separating from my body and I no longer knew what was real or unreal. I could barely hear the midwife tell me that my baby's head was now visible. I felt my daughter's skull push my cervix open, and without any conscious thought or shame, I emptied my bladder and bowels. The sensation was nothing like I anything I had felt before; it was as if I was trying to squeeze out a watermelon through a space the size of a lemon. My daughter was now very low down in my pelvis and the contractions tried to expel her out. It was raw and elemental and I began to hallucinate that I was a cave woman giving birth millennia before. I felt her head thrust out of me and became aware of the extraordinary sensation of my baby being half in and half out of me, with my body feeling like I was being split open from the inside. The epidural dulled the pain, but I could still feel the contractions pulse through me and hear the midwife urgently tell me to keep pushing. She could see that I was exhausted and running on empty; there was a risk that the baby would get stuck. She told me that I was nearly there and that I needed to summon all of my energy and push like I had never done before in my life. I gritted my teeth, grunted and let out a guttural scream as I pushed my daughter out completely and felt her little body rip through me and out into the world.

PART II

BUILDING A MOVEMENT

CHAPTER NINE

MY BIRTH TRAUMA

TRIGGER WARNING
The following pages contain graphic descriptions of traumatic birth, which some may find distressing.

My daughter was delivered at 3.27 p.m. I shook uncontrollably, with chapped lips and matted hair. Tears ran down my face as they took her away to wash off the blood off and ringed her foot like a bird with a tag labelled 'Baby Clarke'. I heard her cry out and I knew she was alive. There seemed to be blood everywhere and I tried not to look at the stained sheets, which they rushed to change.

The medical team handed my daughter to me and I felt an instant rush of love and tenderness towards this extraordinary 8 lb 4 oz of pure beauty and innocence. She did not magically crawl up my chest, as the NCT class had led me to believe, so the midwives put her on my chest and for a few minutes I held her, feeling broken but also completely elated, amazed that I had given birth. My body had cleaved; I was one person but now I was miraculously two. I had never felt such complete exhaustion in my entire life. My body and mind felt bruised and broken and so I tried to concentrate on the warmth from my daughter's skin and inhale her sweet smell. I truly forgot everything, including the cannula still in my hand, as my husband and I hugged as a family of three, agreeing to call her Arabella. We were completely wrapped up in the joy of meeting our daughter.

I did not notice initially that I was still bleeding. Suddenly, the replaced sheets were red again as I began to haemorrhage. Everything became a blur as Henry called out for help. The midwife said something was wrong and suddenly the room was full of people. I heard someone say that I'd lost 700 millilitres, which was a concern and more than usual, and that I needed to be prepped for theatre. My daughter was taken away from me and I felt her loss as if my arm had been cut off. My legs were covered in blood and I started to feel faint. It was an agonising thirty-minute wait to be transferred to theatre to stem the bleeding. I was in complete terror of going into theatre so I requested a general anaesthetic, but it was rejected due to my earlier epidural. I refused to go in without Henry and the medical staff finally agreed that he could come in once he had cleaned and put on scrubs, as the need for surgery was so urgent.

I was wheeled away from Henry and suddenly I was on my own. I put an eye mask on to hide from the bright lights and the many people who prodded and assessed me. The trolley bumped into the walls and I was slid on to the operating table, where I lay whimpering and bleeding out. My consciousness began to fade in and out and I was so stressed I thought I might have a heart attack there and then. Henry was finally allowed in; he held my hand throughout and tried to reassure me. I shook from absolute terror as they stitched me up.

Time lengthened and hours stretched into days. I was convinced that I was going to die and that I would never see my daughter again. For over two hours, awake in theatre, the only thing that stopped me from blacking out on the operating table was the desire to see Arabella again. I was barely awake and I kept my eyes tightly closed. Henry was my lifeline, and I clung to his voice while the nurses took away huge cotton pads soaked with blood and the surgeon's needle and thread went back and forth, up and down, as they sewed me back together inside. I gripped Henry's fingers and tried to ignore the chilling sounds of beeping machines and the low, worried murmurs of the medical team. My consciousness faded as trauma took over and redacted my memories, burying what was happening to me deep inside my consciousness.

I only half heard when a more senior surgeon was asked to step in and finish the stitches, fixing the extensive damage between my anus and vagina. It was complete chance that the surgeon on duty that afternoon was local resident Dr Nitish Raut, and it reassured me to hear his kind voice as someone I recognised. He distracted me by speaking about the recent leadership hustings with Rishi and Liz in Birmingham, and the references to politics kept my sanity from slipping completely.

The operation was completed and I was transferred to the recovery ward. My daughter had been born nearly three hours earlier and I still had not seen her properly; no cot was brought in and no one took the time to update me on what had happened to her when we were separated. I was kept in recovery for several more hours with concerns over a spike in my temperature. They checked my pulse until I was considered stable and I signed some more paperwork that I did not read, my name blurred on the page. I was told they were going to take my bloods as I had a possible infection. I lay on the trolley bed, a dead weight with my arm hanging out as the nurse took six test tubes of blood. I was so tired and woozy that I could not move; I just lay there unable to care any more. My body shut down and my blood and needle phobia was overridden by a combination of exhaustion and the potent cocktail of drugs I had been given.

It was past 10 p.m. on Saturday when I was attached to another IV, this time for antibiotics. The lady who came to check up on me nonchalantly referred to the fact that I'd had a C-section. I screamed at her to read her notes and do her fucking job. I wanted to know where my daughter was. Had something happened to her and they hadn't told me?

I was transferred back to Ward 205, where I lay in the hospital bed exhausted and broken, feeling bereft. I rang the emergency bell and, very agitated, repeatedly asked to see Arabella and for my cannula to be removed from my hand. Henry was ignored when he tried to advocate on my behalf. It was midnight, the staff had changed and I did not recognise anyone who had looked after me that day. My vagina began to throb with stabbing pain, and I was aware of the strangest sensation of feeling both shredded and stitched up inside. I requested more medication, but the midwife told me that she was busy. In a dismissive voice, I was told that she may not be able to give pain relief to me when I asked, given that she had twenty-eight other patients to look after. No one in the hospital offered us any food. I fell asleep eventually, with my exhausted husband lying next to me on the floor as he tried to do the same.

I woke up and suddenly my daughter was there, lying in a transparent cot next to me. My hand was still hooked up to the IV with cables attached and I had a urinary catheter in. My legs felt heavy and frozen in place from the epidural and I could not move my feet. I was devastated that I could not pick my baby up to finally hold her properly. I watched her sleeping instead. She looked so peaceful as she gurgled, wearing a small peach knitted hat that fitted snugly over her tiny head. It was not the hat with pink hearts on that we'd brought in my hospital bag, and I realised it must be one that the midwives had put on to keep her warm. She was in a white and pink onesie and I could see there was a minuscule drip in her small hand, attached to a splint so she could not pull it out. She was so small and calm and I loved her completely. I wanted desperately to walk over and pick her up, but I couldn't move, so I asked Henry to do it. I lay on the bed immobile as he brought her to me to hold and wept as the three of us were finally together again as a family.

It was only then that I noticed how completely exhausted Henry was by the whole ordeal. I could see that he had reached the edge of his tolerance and was in no fit state to look after me or our baby without some help. He had been awake since the start of my induction, three days earlier, and was extremely stressed from our experience in the operating theatre. He went outside to call my mother to update her on her new granddaughter and what had happened. It was late on a Saturday night, but she got straight in the car and drove more than two hours to the hospital. On arrival, my mother swapped with Henry so he could go home to sleep and she stayed to look after me. Her introduction to Arabella was changing the heavy meconium nappy, which looked like black tar. My mother, who was in her late sixties, stayed with me that night in the hospital room, sleeping on the hard upright chair under her coat.

At 1.30 a.m. I was finally brought a hot meal, which disintegrated on my fork and seemed to have no calories left in it. The hospital food was mushy, tasteless and barely suitable for a starving dog. Instead, I ate little bites of plain brown bread like a sparrow and sipped water from a cup, which I found difficult to hold while hooked to the IV.

I dozed on and off while Arabella slept. Eventually, my epidural wore off and I could shakily move my legs. At 5 a.m., I requested to have my catheter removed. The only thing I was able to concentrate on was my need to go to the toilet. My body no longer seemed to be under my control and I couldn't get any bodily functions to work properly. I was given advice not to become constipated, which made me anxious and I became terrified to eat as that meant I had to open my bowels. They gave me lactulose to help avoid constipation, but the dosage seemed too high, as excrement kept running down my legs. When Henry returned, he carried me to the bathroom to use the bedpan, where I passed urine and blood. He lifted me to the bath and hosed me down with the shower. I was desperate to feel clean, but I constantly bled all over the floor of the room and saw faeces run everywhere. Henry gently held me upright on the toilet and I felt weak and ashamed every time I replaced the thick maternity pads in my pants to soak up my blood.

I could not bear to look at the drip still in my hand, which had been in there for days, and I became so distressed by the IV line that I could barely concentrate on anything else. I also wanted to be able to hold my baby properly and try to do skin-to-skin contact. At 8 a.m. the day shift began again and a nurse came to top up my antibiotics. It hurt when the cold drugs were pumped into my hand, so I yelped and asked them to slow down. The whole ordeal stressed me out and my anxiety soared. I was determined that they take it out and I insisted that they change me over to oral antibiotics. Arabella was distressed by her cannula too and moaned and pulled at her tubing. The nurse had to cover her small hand in a white baby sock to protect it.

I was so overwhelmed by the pain in my own body that it was difficult to think about Arabella's needs too. I left it to my mother and husband to look after her, and they did everything as I could not dress her, change her or hold her properly to feed. I was unable to sit up on my bottom and I felt completely incapable of looking after myself, let alone a baby, and wholly dependent on others. I felt completely broken and spent and everything was difficult. This was not how I had imagined my first few days with my daughter to be. I felt like a total failure.

Henry swapped again with my mother. He went home to get more sleep and she went to get lunch. Left alone, Arabella began to scream next to me. I pressed the emergency bell for help, but no one came. I felt completely helpless that I could not look after myself or her. After a long time calling out repeatedly, a nurse entered the room. She took one look at me lying pitifully on the bed and told me, 'Not my baby, not my problem.' Then she walked out and left me there. I had never felt so vulnerable and alone. When I told Henry he was outraged and reported her to the ward manager, who sheepishly gave us a verbal apology. The next few hours became a repetitive blur as I tried to rest, and my mother and husband alternated shifts to change Arabella's nappy, feed her and rock her to sleep.

Finally, I was moved to the midwife-led unit where I had originally planned to have my water birth. That now seemed a lifetime ago. There were more people around, but the ward seemed understaffed. It was only after I'd had my IV removed that they sent a senior midwife to try to help me breastfeed, but Arabella could not latch. I tried every fifteen minutes, but I started to flag and feel disheartened when I couldn't manage it and my daughter became increasingly distressed after being forced to attempt it so many times.

The midwife resorted to manually pumping my breasts to start colostrum production, but Arabella was starving as I was unable to produce enough to feed her. Henry had to drive to the nearest supermarket in Stoke-on-Trent to buy pre-made bottles with sterilised milk in to feed our daughter. My energy was spent from induction and labour, and I was in pain each time they manually massaged my breasts and eked out more colostrum. I persevered but only managed to produce two syringes of golden colostrum from my right-hand breast, which was excruciatingly painful. The ward staff were dismissive about my inability to feed her, and I felt mortified whenever Arabella came off the breast and instead had to sip formula milk hungrily from a small plastic cup. I was exhausted, but I could not sleep properly given that my baby needed to be fed every couple of hours around the clock. Hours slipped by. I tried to rest when she did, but it was hard to fall back to sleep, with the air punctured by her cries and heavy breathing. Eventually, a student midwife called Tilly was sent to help me. She was kind, patient and compassionate, unlike some of her older colleagues. Tilly explained to me more about breastfeeding and helped me to try different feeding positions, given the damage to my perineum. She had the most luck getting colostrum into the purple syringes to be fed to Arabella, and I was grateful to her.

The next morning, the doctor came to check on me and said I would have a follow-up appointment with the specialist clinic for my obstetric anal sphincter injury of a third-degree tear. I did not understand what this terminology meant and I was so tired that I could barely listen to his advice on how look after my stitches and keep them from getting infected.

I had been in hospital for so many days that I had lost all sense of time. I could barely keep track of my constant pain relief, so I kept a medication list in my diary and became obsessive about tracking the timings of when I took codeine, ibuprofen, paracetamol and antibiotics. Whenever I felt the painkillers wearing off it was like being hit by a train, so I learnt to press the emergency buzzer at least thirty minutes before the four-hour window came around again, knowing it might take a long time for anyone to come. The staffing levels seemed low for a busy week in the summer holidays. Once, a woman came in and told me off for pressing the button to ask for pain relief. She was angry and complained that she was in a ward with fifty-six patients, twenty-eight babies and only four staff, which left me feeling humiliated.

I did not want to be trapped in the hospital any more. I found it impossible to sleep due to the constant noise and I became hyper anxious that no one cared about me there, apart from my family, and that I had become only a number, not a name. Now I was out of theatre and in the recovery ward, it felt like I no longer mattered because I was out of the danger zone. My mother was exhausted after several nights in the hospital without a bed, so she braved the two hours' drive back home. While she was gone, I tried to focus on small things like letting Arabella lie quietly on my chest and sipping Lucozade to slowly get back some strength. I wanted to be back home in my own bed with soft pillows, privacy when I went to the toilet and trees to look at in our garden rather than a concrete car park. I wanted to eat something other than congealed mush.

It was only on Tuesday, my sixth day in hospital, that I was finally discharged. That week, a message was left on my voicemail from a local resident who complained that they could not have a face-to-face surgery appointment with me. They referenced that I had had my baby nearly 'a whole week ago' so I should be available to them as their local MP. I was shocked; I was in no fit state to see my immediate family, let alone a member of the public. My office manager James stepped in to deal with constituents who were angry to be speaking to the 'organ grinder and not the monkey'. I refused to hold any surgery appointments and delegated casework to my team. I was in no fit mental or physical state to speak to anyone and I could not think about work in any capacity. All I wanted to do was go home, crawl into my bed and finally get some sleep.

CHAPTER TEN

HOME

I had a shower and changed out of my nightie for the first time in a week to put on proper clothes. I felt better wearing a blue and white flowery maternity dress, suitable for the warm and balmy day, knowing that I would soon be home. Henry packed up all my stuff to head down to the car. Arabella looked so tiny when he put her in the car seat to carry her outside. I walked very slowly down the ward corridor, into the lift and down to the entrance. It was agonising to walk. I could feel the stitches inside my vagina and the rubbing of thick maternity pads to stem my heavy bleeding. Henry struggled to fix the cumbersome car seat into the back seat but managed to click it into position. Sitting in the car was immediately painful as I was unable to get comfortable; it was clear that I could not put any weight on my bottom at all. I sat on the seat next to Arabella, wedged my pillow behind me, perched on the edge of the seat and clutched on to the head rest in front of me. I was completely exhausted from this short attempt to walk from the bed to the car. I watched my daughter sleep the whole way home with her head slumped over to one side.

On arrival, Sheryl, a reassuring former midwife from Yorkshire, was waiting to help for a fortnight as I was unable to look after Arabella on my own. I was too exhausted to think about my daughter on top of my own recovery. I had never met Sheryl in person before, but she immediately made me feel calm. We had raided our unused summer holiday budget and all of our savings to book her and I knew how incredibly lucky we were that we could afford some help. She took charge of our baby and Henry helped me upstairs to the bedroom, which took me a long time, step by step, as I inched my way there. It was such an effort to get up that I knew that I would not be going back downstairs any time soon.

The next few days were a haze of broken sleep and grogginess from the medication I had to take daily. It felt incredible to be home, but I was too shattered from the surgery to leave my room and I had no energy to look after Arabella. Once I had crawled into bed, I wanted to stay there for weeks and rest completely until I was fully recovered. But my daughter was on a feeding routine and even with help, I still had to get up to try to breastfeed her every two to three hours. Sheryl carried my daughter into my room multiple times a day and attempted to help me breastfeed, but I could not get her to latch and I yelped as she bit on my nipples with her hard gums, which caused them to bleed.

I was unable to pick up Arabella without help and I could not sit on my perineum. I also had literally no idea how to look after a newborn baby. I felt constantly weak and tearful and I could not bear to look at the gouge in the back of my hand where the cannula had been taken out, leaving a bruise. Arabella had a matching dark purple mark on her hand.

I left our bedroom only to painfully inch my way to the bathroom and back. I decided not to risk the stairs yet, so Henry had to bring me food every day in bed. I had all of my meals on a tray propped up by pillows. I was ravenous after the disgusting, nutrition-free hospital food. Much of the first few days at home were a blur, but I remember that Henry went to the local supermarket and bought me an incredible array of foods that I hadn't eaten for months during pregnancy, including blue cheese and salami. The grazing platter tasted more sensory and delicious to me than the amazing three-course lunch we'd eaten at our wedding.

I relied on my husband completely to look after me. He prepared my meals, did the washing, kept the house tidy, helped with feeding, changed Arabella and sat with her to do skin-to-skin contact. I could do nothing for myself but attempt to sleep, eat and recover. I was too tired to even feel shame that I was not capable of looking after our daughter. I didn't read or watch television, but I never once felt bored. I just lay there trying to rest and sleep when I could. When I wasn't doing that, I spent hours being hypervigilant, watching my daughter's chest moving gently up and down and constantly checking she was still breathing. I didn't want to let her out of my sight, but I was too tired to stay awake all day.

I constantly needed the toilet and it was impossible to hold anything in. I often didn't make it to the bathroom in time and excrement and urine ran all over the floor. I bled everywhere, with a constant, heavy period that seemed to never end and which caused me deep embarrassment. I began to think I might never be able to leave the house again. I obsessively wrote everything down in a notebook to keep track of my medication, including lactulose and different painkillers at varying times, on top of Arabella's feeds and nappy changes. Henry had to inject me with a large needle to prevent blood clots as I was too terrified to do it to myself, which left bruises up my legs. I felt constant jabbing pain in my abdomen, like I was being stabbed repeatedly, which made me wince and wheeze and my brain struggled to concentrate on anything at all. My medication often wore off long before the four-hour cycle came back around for another dose, so I would intersperse codeine with paracetamol and ibuprofen in the intervening hours to try to get me through. I was concerned by how addictive codeine could be, but without it I could not sleep at night due to the pain.

It was a struggle to get through each day, but Arabella was beautiful and I was so relieved to feel a strong bond with her, despite us being separated so early on and for so long in the hospital. Her fluffy dusting of sandy hair had the unique smell of a newborn baby and when she snuggled up to me on the bed, I could feel her warm body against mine. I still could not feed properly, but I attempted skin to skin and let her lie on my chest while I lay naked on the bed. I found every attempt to breastfeed very frustrating and when Arabella screamed with hunger, I would have to resort to giving her formula again instead. My milk took several days to come in as my body was so traumatised by the birth and I could only express milk out of one breast. I was also unable to sit properly after surgery, so she couldn't latch. Sheryl was very patient with me and at each feed we tried again, but I was exhausted and still barely any milk was coming out. She suggested that we order and rent a hospital-grade Medela pump to help stimulate milk production.

The antenatal classes I had attended led me to believe I would be able to naturally feed my daughter with ease, so breast pumping made me feel like a failure as mother. I wore a 'hands-free pumping bustier', which was a black stretchy bra with two holes in it. Plastic bottles were attached and I was then hooked up to the bright yellow machine, which was a double pump that attached to my breasts with suction cups for around twenty minutes at a time. I felt like a cow being milked at a dairy, which was painful and humiliating.

I had to sit near a plug so that the machine could be plugged in at the wall, which made me feel constantly trapped. I was unable to do anything else while I was attached to the pump, which mimicked a babies' sucking rhythm and tried to stimulate milk production. I could not bear for anyone to see me like this and I resisted any visitors. My nipples soon became sore – and all this for the tiniest amount of milk, sometimes only 20 millilitres, to come out.

I tried to persevere with breastfeeding, lying down or resting my daughter on a breastfeeding pillow around my stomach, but it became increasingly painful as my nipples began to crack. Nipple cream helped, but it was impossible to recover and heal because each time a feed came around the pain intensified when my daughter tried to latch on to me with her gums, chomping down on my tender breasts. It became too uncomfortable to wear anything other than a large baggy T-shirt, maternity leggings and a breastfeeding bra. Arabella slept next to me in her woven Moses basket and I watched her obsessively to check that she was all right. I began to panic that I was not feeding her enough breastmilk and had deprived her of vital antibodies, which meant she would get ill or develop a weak immune system. But triple feeding her through breast pumping (which made me feel hungover), attempting to feed her on the breast and bottle feeding her formula to top her up, in addition to sterilising all her baby equipment, drained me completely. It was very time consuming and often took one and a half to two hours to complete each round.

No one had met Arabella bar us and my mother, and I put off my in-laws coming to visit for as long as I could. I sent a short text with a photograph of her to close family, but I had not seen my siblings or any friends since coming out of hospital and I did not feel like seeing or talking to anyone. I felt numb and I was not ready to acknowledge the shocking truth of what had happened to me. I just did not know how to feel or process it at all. Henry looked after me as if I was a child and helped me to regain my strength. He made me post-partum specialist herbal recovery teas and brought me chicken soup, fenugreek and vitamin C tablets. I looked anaemic with unnervingly pale skin due to heavy blood loss, so he made me spinach salads and brought me glasses of water with liquid iron in it to replenish my low levels. After a fortnight at home, I began to feel even more exhausted between the adrenaline of labour and surgery wearing off and the constant waking for feeds in the night, which meant that I never truly slept.

My brain felt tight all the time, like it was candyfloss wrapped in clingfilm that pressed down uncomfortably on my temples. I was extremely tired, which meant I had a constant headache. I also felt stir crazy being trapped in my bedroom, having not gone downstairs once to even make a cup of tea. I would stand at the top of the stairs and look down, desperate to go out into the garden to have some fresh air, but it was too difficult and painful to walk back down. I missed having a lift and a bed that would recline from pushing a button in hospital. I felt exhausted, even though my day mainly consisted of basic, repetitive tasks.

The only medical appointment I was invited to in those first few weeks was for Arabella, not me. Within a few days of the birth, she was given an appointment at County Hospital in Stafford to screen her for any health conditions. It took the whole morning for us to drive there and feed her in the car before the appointment. I slowly shuffled in pain, acutely aware of my vaginal stiches, while I pushed the pram to the ward at the other end of the hospital. A healthcare professional pricked my baby's heel to collect a few drops of blood to test, which made her cry, and not once did anyone ask how I was or check on my mental or physical health. The same occurred at my six-week check-up with my local GP. The appointment was only fifteen minutes long and all the questions were focused on my daughter. The only reference to myself as the mother was the final question. I was asked if I suffered from postnatal depression, which was posited as a yes or no question as she ticked the relevant box on a form and I was told I had only one minute left of the appointment.

I tried to focus on small achievements at home, and one of my earliest good memories with Arabella is when she had her first bath. Until her umbilical cord fell off we sponge bathed her with cotton pads, so the first time she went in the bath was with Henry holding her on his chest while we gently washed her. I could see her alert and intently exploring the world around her. The water seemed to reassure rather than scare her and she lay on my husband peacefully. I completely trusted him with Arabella and did not feel the anxiety that I usually did if anyone else held her. The memory is partly tinged with sadness that it was not with me, as I couldn't yet be submerged in the water due to my stitches, but it was a wonderful moment of calm after the drama of the previous few weeks. We finally felt like a proper family of three.

It was a huge shock when Henry's paternity leave ended after two weeks and he had to go to back to work, leaving me on my own all day with our daughter. It also coincided with Sheryl leaving us, once our budget had been depleted, which meant that I was now home alone all day with Arabella. As often as he could, Henry would pop home at lunchtime from the office or stop by briefly between property viewings with clients.

Nevertheless, I felt intensely lonely and overwhelmed. I had no idea how to look after a newborn baby and I was exhausted from sleep deprivation. It was a daily struggle to get through the day. I didn't watch the news and I ignored messages from constituents or anything related to work, as simple tasks took me a long time and my brain often felt like it was processing at half the speed, like I was wading through treacle. It felt like a huge achievement when I could hold my daughter by myself, stand up for a few minutes or manage to wash my hair without assistance from Henry holding me up in the shower. It was also an endless, repetitive cycle to sterilise her baby bottles and keep on top of her dirty clothes, which had to be washed daily. There was barely enough time in a day to do anything whether Arabella was asleep or awake. I felt trapped in a constant loop of newborn baby jobs with no rest for myself and barely even time to reply to a text message as I never had a free hand.

I began to obsess about the fact that my proxy vote would end at exactly six months and that I needed Arabella to sleep through the night before then, as I could not imagine going to back to work full time if I was still getting up for feeds. I attempted the 7 a.m. to 7 p.m. baby sleep routine recommended in Charmian Mead's book. My pregnancy journal listed my schedule, with other household jobs and pain relief added in, as:

- 7 a.m. – Wake up, feed baby (breastfeed, bottle feed, breast pump).
- 8 a.m. – Change/wind baby, sterilise baby bottles. Baby awake time. Daily injection and take lactulose and paracetamol. Shower, breakfast.
- 8.30 a.m. – Baby sleep, attempt to sleep myself!
- 9 a.m. – Antibiotics.
- 10 a.m. – Feed baby (breastfeed, bottle feed, breast pump).
- 11.30 a.m. – Baby sleep, do baby washing.
- 12.15 a.m. – Lunch, take baby outside to garden in pram? Baby awake time. Take lactulose and ibuprofen.

- 1 p.m. – Feed baby (breastfeed, bottle feed, breast pump).
- 2.30 p.m. – Baby sleep, attempt to sleep myself!
- 4 p.m. – Feed baby (breastfeed, bottle feed, breast pump).
- 4.30 p.m. – Baby awake time. Tidy up and sterilise baby bottles. Take paracetamol.
- 6.15 p.m. – Dinner, shower, get ready for bed, take lactulose.
- 7 p.m. – Feed baby (breastfeed, bottle feed, breast pump).
- 8.30 p.m. – Take paracetamol and ibuprofen. Sleep.
- 10 p.m. – Feed baby (bottle feed, breast pump), wind baby.
- 11 p.m. – Sleep. Take codeine.
- 4 a.m. – Feed baby (bottle feed, breast pump), wind baby. Take paracetamol, ibuprofen and lactulose.
- 5 a.m. – Sleep.

By 7 a.m. the next day, the whole brutal routine would start again. I often found it impossible to go back to sleep in the middle of the night after I had woken up to feed Arabella and instead lay in bed awake and attempted to rest. It was also difficult to spend any time with my husband, as by the time he came home from work I was already in my pyjamas trying to feed our daughter, agitated and exhausted from the day and ready to go straight to bed before he wanted dinner. I didn't feel like we got to spend any quality time together as a married couple as the days were so relentless and exhausting. I felt that two weeks of paternity leave was nowhere near enough given what had happened to me and the huge amount of help I needed on top of looking after a newborn baby.

CHAPTER ELEVEN

RECOVERY

I woke up one night at home covered in sweat and shaking like I had jungle fever. I was so disorientated that I thought I was suffering from a bout of malaria, as my sheets were soaked through and my nightie was drenched and clung to my clammy skin. Post-partum night sweats were a discomfort that I was not expecting or prepared for post giving birth. No one had told me that they occurred after having a baby due to changing hormone levels as my body attempted to regulate itself. My low oestrogen levels made my body believe it was too hot and cooled itself off by excessive sweating.

The sweats kept me awake in the precious time that Arabella was down and I tried to catch up on sleep. They lasted for over a week and left me more tired and irritable each morning. Sometimes, the hot flushes were so bad that I would need to change clothes in the middle of the night or even strip off the bedsheets. I tried wearing cotton pyjamas or slept with a towel under me to absorb the sweat. We did not have air conditioning, so I slept with a fan on due to the late summer heat, and at night I would gulp another glass of water to avoid being dehydrated. My body felt like it was on strike and could not take any more.

I also knew that everything was not right with me physically post-birth when I struggled to control myself going to the toilet. The doctors in the hospital had given me a laxative to keep my bowels from getting constipated but had not explained to me why in detail. I knew that lactulose was a stool softener, but it was only when I researched it online that I found out that this was to prevent my anus stretching and my stitches coming out completely or not healing properly. The label on the bottle advised to take 10–15 millilitres twice per day. It was also advised that I eat fibrous foods and stay hydrated with lots of fluids for at least six weeks. I was also concerned because the codeine tablets I had been given had a side effect of constipation and so the drug needed to be avoided in the longer term, in addition to concerns about the risks of becoming addicted to the pills. The only relief was that there seemed to be no concerns about the codeine impacting the breastmilk I was pumping for Arabella.

I was constantly needing the loo and it was impossible to control my bowels. I often did not make it to the bathroom on time as it took me so long to painfully shuffle there from bed. I would find faeces streaming down my legs, on top of the heavy bleeding that leaked onto my clothes and onto the floor. One morning, Henry found me passed out on the toilet, pants around my ankles, with Arabella asleep in her cot and a stinking mess on the floor.

Every time I opened my bowels, I was terrified that they would fall out. I was acutely aware of the stitches between my vagina and anus. I began to go through so much toilet paper from the constant urgency that it began to irritate the area. NHS guidance told me to pat the area dry from front to back to avoid passing germs from my rectum to my perineal and vaginal area. I found passing urine excruciating and I had to pour a jug of water over the area to help with the painful stinging. I felt dirty all the time and would excessively clean my hands before and after going to the bathroom and would change my thick maternity sanitary towel every few hours. I ordered Anusol cream to treat haemorrhoids and showered myself multiple times a day to wash off urine, blood and faeces whenever my daughter was asleep. Sometimes I would have to sit on a bag of frozen vegetables wrapped in a tea towel to reduce the inflammation. I forced myself to drink at least 2 litres of water ever day to avoid getting constipated and my anxiety only increased as I realised that my pelvic floor had no control.

The only position that helped me was to sit with my legs up on a toddler plastic step for potty training and keep my knees raised above my hips, which made it easier to empty my bowels. I tried to rest my elbows on my knees and relax by breathing deeply and slowly, but I was becoming paranoid that nothing worked as before. It would take me a long time to go to the loo as I had to try not to strain my bowels. As I could not control my bladder or bowels properly, was unable to control my wind and constantly felt an urgent need to go the toilet, it became impossible to leave the house. I felt completely trapped at home with my baby.

I had been given a leaflet in hospital on pelvic-floor exercises, on which had been handwritten 'third-degree tear', but I did not know what any of this medical terminology meant. I knew only that I was not allowed to have a proper bath until my stitches had healed, which could take weeks, so I would run a warm sitz bath only a few inches deep to sit in, which kept the vaginal area clean and helped my skin to heal. I would sit for as long as I could manage and sometimes only a few minutes passed before it was too painful to continue sitting on the floor of the tub. The bath was the only respite for my vagina from feeling itchy and sore. Afterwards, I would lie on the bed naked to air my stitches every morning for ten minutes. I forced myself to look at the area in a handheld mirror and felt queasy when I could see the ends of white stiches with knots that stuck out of me. I thought that after a couple of weeks they should have healed, but I could see they oozed, looked red and inflamed and were incredibly itchy. I called to book an appointment with my GP at the local surgery within walking distance from our house.

I carefully got dressed in stretchy black yoga leggings in case I leaked blood onto my trousers on the way. I walked incredibly slowly, pushing the pram to get to the surgery, with Arabella lying asleep wrapped in a swaddle, with a hat on to keep her warm. My appointment was only ten minutes long and the doctor was more interested in asking after my baby. I asked her to check my stitches, but she told me that was not her job and that I needed to drive half an hour to A&E at Royal Stoke and queue to be seen again. She was polite but seemed busy and told me she didn't have access to my medical notes about my third-degree tear as it was a different computer system to the hospital. I wondered how this was even possible when both the surgery and hospital were in the same county and only thirteen miles apart in Staffordshire. I felt upset and let down as it did not feel like anyone cared about my recovery; the focus was always on my baby and never me. It seemed that the NHS had forgotten that they had two patients, not only one, since I had given birth.

The last thing I wanted to do was return to the same hospital where I had given birth, but it seemed I had no other choice. Henry drove me once again to Royal Stoke, but this time with Arabella in the car. It was a strange experience to be back there with our baby. As we parked near the maternity wing, I was flooded with memories of induction and the horrors of giving birth. It was too much to think about and I was fearful about setting foot back inside the hospital as I felt very emotional to be there. The trauma was too recent to process.

It was also the first time we had returned to the MAU since Arabella's heart had skipped a beat on the night I had resigned earlier in July. So much had changed since then. On the previous visit, I had spent the hours waiting to be seen writing my resignation letter and expecting to have an emergency C-section. This time around, I also had to feed Arabella and attempt to rock her to sleep in the busy reception, surrounded by pregnant women with huge bellies waiting to be seen. The wait was several hours and no one cared that I was there with a newborn baby. When I was finally seen, the doctor told me the stitches hadn't healed properly but refused to issue me with antibiotics. I was sent home and told to buy more of my own painkillers from the chemist on the way home.

It was only when I attended the perineal clinic at Royal Stoke that I finally felt like anyone was checking up on my physical health. The specialist Nicole was the first person to make me feel like she cared, confirm that my symptoms were normal after a serious birth injury and talk me through how to help my body to recover. She asked me some difficult questions to input into her computer about my health. It was the first time anyone had brought up sex with me. It was the last thing on my mind given I had stitches in my vagina, heavy daily bleeding and was unable to go properly to the toilet. She offered me some free sachets of lubricant to alleviate any pain once I was ready. I told her I could not even use tampons yet, let alone think about anything else up there ever again and I didn't know how I would have penetrative sex ever again after such a traumatic birth.

Nevertheless, Nicole reiterated how easy it was to get pregnant again before even having my regular period. She went through my concerns and asked me in detail about my incontinence issues. She referred me to the poo chart and told me to keep track of each time I emptied my bowels. I was stunned to hear that my body would not return to how it was completely before the birth and that, although my bowel movements would likely improve, my pelvic floor was weakened for the rest of my life and would likely worsen with the onset of menopause. I was not ready to accept my new body in its damaged physical state and that it would likely be like this for ever.

When she asked me to lie down on the hospital chair with my legs up for a vaginal examination to look at my tear, even though her manner was kind and compassionate, I felt invaded and promptly burst into tears. She gave me a glass of water, calmed me down and asked what was wrong. I told her of the history of my long labour and the huge number of vaginal examinations I had undergone during induction, each one increasingly painful. She agreed to look from the outside only and to do a check by sight this time around until I felt more comfortable for her to feel inside the sensitive area. She agreed to see me again in a few weeks and arranged for me to see her, rather than her colleague, at the weekly morning clinic for some continuity of care. I went home feeling in safer hands and that she would and could help me.

To aid my recovery, I decided to try to focus on doing some simple, normal activities that were a gentle way to get out of the house without overdoing it. Shopping for food seemed the easiest option. Since the birth, I had mainly lived off delivered frozen meals or let Henry lead on cooking, which I usually enjoyed. I hadn't driven for several weeks and taking Arabella to a large supermarket, only a few miles away, seemed suddenly like a huge undertaking.

It took me a long time to dress my daughter and get her into the car seat, as I struggled to pick her up on my own and fix her in. I sat on my new doughnut cushion to keep my perineum lifted up while sat in the driving seat, as it was otherwise too uncomfortable, and drove the first mile to the superstore slowly. I panicked every time I saw a tractor or a fast vehicle and I felt paranoid about having my daughter in her car seat facing away from me as I was unable to see her. I pulled over in the first lay-by to check on her, convinced that she was going to stop breathing and concerned that it was dangerous to take her out of the house in case something bad happened, but she was completely fine and had already fallen asleep with the hum of the car. I drove the next mile very slowly and allowed cars to overtake me. I felt sure now that the seat belt was blocking her airways as I couldn't hear her even though the radio was off, so I pulled over again at the entrance to a farm driveway to check her. Again, there was nothing wrong. I felt so alert and hypervigilant towards her all the time that it exhausted me.

We parked in the supermarket and as I took her out of the car seat, I realised that I didn't know how to hold her and carry a shopping basket at the same time. She was too small to sit in a shopping trolley in the fold-out toddler seat. There were no newborn seats that I could see to lie her in flat on top. I couldn't use her pram as it was too heavy for me to lift from the boot and assemble on my own and it hadn't occurred to me to bring the baby sling with me – Henry usually walked with her in it, as I found Arabella too heavy to carry until my stitches healed. I could not think how to carry my baby and several bags of shopping at the same time. A mundane activity now seemed a daunting and impossible task. It began to bucket it down with rain and I burst into tears in the car park as I realised I could not even do something as basic as shopping for essentials alone. I drove back home with nothing to show for it and felt mortified. I was so embarrassed I did not even mention it to Henry and asked him to get food for dinner and more nappies on his way home from work.

I became obsessive about cleanliness in our house in a way that I was not prior to my traumatic birth. Before having my baby, I was messy and would leave dirty plates stacked by the sink and old *Sunday Times* newspapers and *Country Life* magazines strewn around the house with piles of paperwork and post on the dining room table. However, in the months after giving birth, I became obsessed with the house being tidy and clean, as it was the only environment I had complete control over, and I began to exhibit symptoms of OCD.

The moment Arabella went down for her nap, every few hours, I would start to clean our house. I would start with the kitchen and wipe the surfaces clean multiple times, first with water, then with disinfectant and dry it all with a tea towel, which I would then put in the wash. I would repeat this multiple times throughout the day, which would take up much of the time that I should have been resting when Arabella was asleep. Henry would come back from work and make a cup of tea but before he had even put the empty mug back down, I would hover and take it off him to put in the dishwasher. I became paranoid about breadcrumbs by the toaster and began collecting them individually to make sure none were left. Changing Arabella's nappies of bright yellow poo, which frequently stained her sleepsuits multiple times a day, would freak me out. I would rinse my hands again and again with soap until they would become dry and red and found myself putting on a daily wash with Napisan to keep her clothes and muslins clean. I would also spend hours folding her tiny clothes to put in her nursery chest of drawers or reorganising her changing table station with nappies, antiseptic cream and wet wipes, even thought it was already tidy. Despite all this, I failed to notice that I was not my usual self.

CHAPTER TWELVE

UNEXPECTED NEWS

I did not feel physical or mentally well, so I was incredibly relieved that the Speaker had previously arranged for me to vote via proxy for six months after birth so that I could continue to represent my constituents. I had designated my constituency office manager, James, to be my official representative for the duration, although it soon became clear that the system for new mothers in Parliament had not been properly thought through. While I could vote remotely, James was refused admittance to MP-only briefing calls on policy, ministers would not speak to him about casework and he was not able to sign everything off, including significant changes to the office budget, without me. No one was able to represent me in the Chamber to ask a question on an urgent local issue, speak in a parliamentary debate or attend a select committee meeting on my behalf. This meant that despite having to recover from major surgery and the stress of looking after a newborn baby, I was never truly off duty throughout my entire 'maternity leave'.

I pulled out of local events I'd planned to attend such as the Eccleshall Show, as I couldn't walk. I was terrified of not being near the toilet in case I had a mishap in public and I was in no fit state to be seen out with my baby. I felt guilty, as I knew how important it was to be seen locally and the annual fair was in my proposed new constituency, now that the Boundaries Commission had redrawn the map for Stafford for the next general election. It felt a struggle even to manage to vote by post for Rishi Sunak as leader of the Conservative Party.

There was always an urgent work call where I was told they would only speak to the MP. Less than a fortnight after I was discharged from hospital, the police and crime commissioner called to tell me that my local police force was being put in special measures and that I needed to put out a reassuring statement to the public. I was used to working in a busy, high-pressured environment, but now my brain barely functioned as I tried to process all of these important pieces of information. I relied on James completely to take charge and to follow up on anything important. He was critical to running my office, despite the challenges of working yet more hours while also trying to manage his local farm with his own small children. I valued his honesty and competence and I was exceedingly grateful when he stepped up to help me, far beyond his job description, for months while I recovered.

During those first difficult few weeks, I had to learn to ask for and take help and to be reliant on others, so I could prioritise my physical and mental health. I felt lazy every time I lay down on the sofa to close my eyes for a few minutes when my baby was asleep. It was a new challenge for me to learn to rest and recuperate and not to constantly work. Westminster had become an addictive bubble where the daily thrill of breaking news and world events, which buffeted us from all sides, had made life too manic. This had run my energy down to rock bottom already before my daughter arrived.

UNEXPECTED NEWS

Arabella was nearly three weeks old when, on 5 September, we watched Sir Graham Brady announce live on television the result of who had been elected as the new leader of the Conservatives. To my horror, the right wing of the party's membership had triumphed and Liz Truss had won. I despaired as I thought the party was unelectable under her. The following day, as our new Prime Minister she travelled to Balmoral Castle to meet the Queen. Liz looked far too smug in their official photograph and I inwardly groaned that she would lead us into the next general election when she had none of the charisma needed to run a campaign and I failed to agree with most of her policies. The next day, the Queen cancelled a meeting of the Privy Council on health grounds, but I didn't think anything of it. I focused on feeding Arabella and getting precious sleep when she was down for her naps.

On 8 September, I watched a sombre bulletin of the early evening BBC news with Huw Edwards, saw that the flag was flying at half-mast at Buckingham Palace and noticed that he was wearing a black tie, which was highly unusual. I was completely shocked when he announced the death of the Queen. I felt intensely sad. Even though I had never met her, only observed her at the state opening of Parliament while I watched from a few rows back, I was in awe of her commitment to public service throughout her life. It felt like a monumental moment in our history, and it was incredible to think that Liz had been Prime Minister for only forty-eight hours while this was happening. I was contacted immediately by my clerks as the chair of a select committee and told all government business and parliamentary activity would cease given that Operation London Bridge was underway, which was the funeral plan to announce the Queen's death, period of official mourning and details of her state funeral. I delegated duties for the committee I chaired on the overseas aid watchdog, the Independent Commission for Aid Impact, to my fellow Conservative MP Richard Bacon.

I finally felt able to spend my days downstairs after a fortnight of spending almost all my time in my bedroom, but I found it too painful to go up and down the stairs more than once a day. Instead, I spent each day on the ground floor so I could watch the unfolding news on the television, attempt to breastfeed Arabella and sleep on and off on the sofa in the sitting room.

The period of national mourning began, which continued until the day after the state funeral. On the first day, death salutes fired across the UK and the new King Charles addressed the nation. Stafford Borough Council, as the local authority, invited me to the proclamation ceremony, when the town crier made the public announcement on the steps of the Shire Hall, but I felt too exhausted to attend. It was noticed that I was not there as the local MP. I also failed to attend the local service of thanksgiving at St Mary's Church as I did not feel able to sit through two hours of a service in public, given it was so uncomfortable to sit on my perineum and I was still in recovery from such a long labour and major surgery. Instead, I asked Henry to drive me into Stafford for a few minutes to lay some flowers of remembrance to commemorate Her Majesty outside the church. We sat outside in the car so I could feed Arabella afterwards and then headed home. Despite this, I received complaints from residents and councillors that I had not bothered to attend the church service.

It began to cause me considerable stress and agitation that I was being criticised for not doing my job as the local MP. I knew what a huge moment it was in our history, and I felt shame that I was seen as absent from my duties. No one knew yet, bar James and my immediate family, that I had also suffered a traumatic birth and spent so many days in hospital. So, when the Speaker invited me to the historic ceremony at which the king would address both Houses of Parliament in Westminster Hall later in September, Henry and I discussed what I should do. Arabella was only a few weeks old and I was meant to be on maternity leave, but realistically it was impossible to be off given the exceptional circumstances we were in. We had had yet another change of government and the unexpected death of our monarch in quick succession, and the public looked to all of us in public life for stability and leadership. I could not walk very far due to my stitches, so public transport and my usual trip down on the train to Westminster was not an option. It was also going to be uncomfortable for me to travel too far, given my ongoing issues going to the toilet and the fact I was unable to sit for too long on my damaged perineum, so my mother offered to collect me in the car from Stafford and drive me to London and back so that I could attend.

Henry agreed to look after Arabella and bottle feed her. Technically, his paternity leave had ended, but his employer made an exception. I pumped as much milk as I could and put storage bags in the fridge and freezer for him to use. I borrowed an Elvie pump from a friend in my NCT group to continue to produce breastmilk while I was away to keep up production. I needed to pump regularly, as if I was with my baby every few hours, but I had no way to keep the precious milk. I threw it away at the petrol station and was gutted as I watched it disappear down the toilet. I brought my doughnut cushion to sit on in the car, wedged with pillows so that I could keep any pressure off my perineum.

It was the first time since the birth that I had been separated from Arabella, and I felt incredibly anxious about leaving her. My OCD symptoms continued and I checked in on her constantly, watched the live stream of her video monitor on my mobile and called Henry to have regular videos of her awake to show me that she was fine. I was very grateful to him that he was able to step up and look after her so well on his own.

I didn't fit any of my regular clothes post-birth, as my stomach had not yet shrunk back to its usual size, so my mother lent me her long black coat plus a smart hat. I put make-up on for the first time in weeks and tried to look my usual self, but I couldn't hide my exhaustion. It felt like a lifetime ago that I was in Parliament. I had last been in the House of Commons more than two months earlier, when Boris Johnson was still Prime Minister and my daughter had not yet been born. It was a shock as I thought of everything that had happened since: my traumatic birth, recovery from surgery, sleep deprivation, trying to care for a newborn, the government in constant crisis and now a state funeral when I did not feel like myself either emotionally or physically.

My mother dropped me off right in front of Black Rod's entrance and I walked slowly, taking my time, to Westminster Hall, which was the oldest part of the Houses of Parliament. I felt the history when I stood under its impressive timber roof, enclosed by high stone walls, built all the way back in 1099 by the son of William the Conqueror. The doorkeepers directed me to my seat up at the front with the other VIPs, but I'd forgotten how long Westminster Hall was, at nearly four cricket pitches end to end, and I didn't feel able to shuffle up the aisle past so many people at an event being broadcast live on television. I explained the situation to the Serjeant-at-Arms, who found me another seat in the final row right by the exit in case I needed to leave at any point to urgently find the toilet. I carefully sat on my doughnut cushion, my Elvie pump and my prescribed codeine in my handbag, and looked around. The air felt electric. There was low-level but respectful murmuring of conversation as we waited for our new king. I could see hundreds of Members of Parliament and peers sat in front of me and government ministers starting to arrive. A few colleagues smiled or waved at me, but mostly they were wrapped up in the grandeur and solemnity of the occasion. No one seemed to have noticed that I had been away for so long and no one congratulated me on my new baby.

A claret-coloured Rolls Royce flying the Royal Standard with no number plate on it arrived in the courtyard. Suddenly, I could see behind me the Prime Minister, Leader of the Opposition and the Speaker as they welcomed His Majesty to Parliament. King Charles III looked impressive dressed in a mourning suit with a black tie and the Queen Consort wore a matching dress with a huge pearl necklace. I sat on the inside seat of the back row and he smiled at me as he walked down the aisle. Everyone was silent in the presence of our new king. To the fanfare of trumpets, they made their way up to the top of the steps and sat in two adjacent thrones of gilt and silk. I reflected that the late Queen had met hundreds of thousands of constituents in her lifetime, likely more than all of the MPs who sat in the hall combined had ever met within our elected terms.

As the hall emptied, my immediate thought was how far it was to walk to the nearest bathroom so I could empty my bowels, change my adult nappy and take my next dose of medication. I could feel the heavy painkillers wearing off. Some of the female MPs in my intake spotted me, gave me a hug and asked how Arabella was. They noticed that I looked pale and exhausted. While I was grateful to see them, having felt so isolated up in Stafford, I didn't feel able to tell anyone about the birth and I knew this was not the appropriate moment. They invited me to join them for drinks in the Smoking

Room, but I didn't feel able to walk upstairs and pretend to be sociable when I was anxious to return home. I missed Arabella intensely; it felt like I had a missing limb and I constantly wanted to check on her. I was also finding it harder to produce breastmilk when I was away from her. So, I left quietly as Big Ben tolled above me.

CHAPTER THIRTEEN

GOVERNMENT IN CRISIS

On Monday 19 September, the period of national mourning came to an end and parliamentary and government business resumed. On Friday that week, the new Chancellor Kwasi Kwarteng announced the mini-Budget. There had been no consultation with colleagues and I had no idea what he was going to say bar what was trailed in the news. I watched his speech live and was shocked to hear announcements of a huge range of tax cuts, which included abolishing the 45 per cent rate of income tax and the proposed Health and Social Care Levy, cuts to stamp duty and the basic rate of income tax, and a cancellation of National Insurance and corporation tax rises. He concluded by telling the House of Commons that he would pay for this package of measures through extra borrowing. I was furious. Why were they making tax cuts for the wealthy a priority now when my constituents faced a cost-of-living crisis? This would only reinforce the view of us as the party of the rich. He had no mandate from us as Conservative MPs to make these announcements, but we would still be asked to defend the government's position regardless. The moment he finished his speech, the financial markets began to react badly and the pound fell to its lowest ever rate against the dollar.

Within ten days, new Prime Minister Liz Truss was forced to reverse the abolition of the 45 per cent income tax rate. However, it failed to stem our slide in the polls or the markets, and the situation became untenable. Our MP-only WhatsApp groups became silent, which was always an ominous sign, and many colleagues refused to do broadcast interviews to defend the government. I did not attend the Conservative Party Conference for the first time in years, glad to have a genuine reason for avoiding both the hostile press and annoyed members.

Liz finally replaced the Chancellor with Jeremy Hunt, which filled me with relief as he was a former businessman, astute and sensible, who I rated highly and who had helped me on numerous occasions. Jeremy immediately reversed many of the decisions made in the mini-Budget. I was so tired from overnight feeds that I struggled to read the news, but I forced myself to keep abreast of what was going on as I felt the weight of expectations from constituents to be on top of my brief, despite being off with my baby. The mood in the party continued to darken. I received an unsolicited call from a former Cabinet minister who sounded out my views on Liz and her premiership. He told me that the men in suits would come for her soon and that she was on a knife edge from being removed.

The newspapers in October made for grim reading as the party became locked in infighting. The Home Secretary Suella Braverman resigned and was replaced by Grant Shapps after she admitted to breaking the rules by sharing official documents on her private email. I distracted myself by booking a babysitter and preparing for our first night out in Stafford since Arabella was born. She was now two months old and I finally felt ready to leave the house to try to regain some sense of normality. Macmillan, the national cancer charity, were holding their annual big fundraising dinner in Staffordshire later that month and I was keen to support them with some local friends.

However, that morning Labour tabled a vote on fracking, which meant that I would have to vote on the government's plans even though I had long been opposed to shale gas extraction and residents had written to me frequently to share their concerns about lifting any restrictions. I called my whip to let them know that I would not be supporting the vote, and over the course of the day my opposition was escalated up the government. By mid-morning, I received a call from the parliamentary private secretary asking me to change my mind and sounding out my views in more detail. I reminded him that this went against our manifesto and that we had pledged in 2019, on a platform that I ran on during the election, that we would not support fracking. I was concerned that our new leader seemed to have a very different stance from Boris on the environment. I was a member of the Conservative Environment Network and I didn't believe that fracking was either safe or viable in the UK. It worried me that Liz was committed to expanding oil and gas drilling in the North Sea. Our reliance on fossil fuels risked losing our hard-won leadership on the issue.

By lunchtime, the department's whip had called me with a more threatening tone. Then a junior minister attempted to explain why fracking was a good policy that would result in better energy security. By teatime, it was the Business, Energy and Industrial Strategy Secretary Jacob Rees-Mogg MP who called me. He was my uncle by marriage and now a Cabinet minister. We got on well, but we often disagreed on policy as we sat in very different wings of the Conservative Party. I was a member of the centrist One Nation

Conservatives, who had joined the party under David Cameron's leadership and his banner of modern compassionate conservativism, whereas Jacob was chair of the European Research Group and an arch-Brexiteer. Jacob was very polite as he rang to explain that he proposed to lift the 2019 moratorium on fracking. It was the only telephone call that day where I was asked about Arabella and how I was doing after giving birth, and he was kind and sympathetic as I briefly updated him on the situation. Jacob told me the Chief Whip had asked him to tell me to vote with the government that evening. However, he didn't attempt to change my mind but only noted my opposition down on his spreadsheet.

I got ready for the black-tie event by putting on a smart evening dress for the first time in months and doing my hair and make-up. It felt good to get dressed and out of my milk- and vomit-covered yoga pants and T-shirt, which had been my usual daily attire. But within an hour, the deputy Chief Whip called me and cut straight to the point. The tone turned nasty and bullying. I was told that the vote was now considered a confidence vote, which meant it was a test of loyalty to the government. In no uncertain terms, he told me that I would lose the whip and be kicked out of the parliamentary party if I didn't vote with the government, which meant I would have to sit as an independent and likely not be able to stand again at the next general election for the Conservative Party. This would be the end of my political career.

I hadn't previously spoken to the new deputy Chief Whip and this was the first time he had ever called me, so I was shocked. I held firm and told him I still opposed to fracking and did not agree with the policy. After the call, I texted him:

I'm deeply disappointed that this was made a confidence vote.

This does not foster good will with backbenchers like myself. I remain opposed to fracking and will vote in any future motions on this accordingly. I have serious concerns about the direction of travel of this government and our competence on the economy. And I do not appreciate being put in the position of either voting against our manifesto or losing the whip. Saying that we need to do much better is an understatement.

I knew from previous experience opposing HS2 that it was important to hold out right to the wire, as if enough colleagues opposed the government, it was possible they would back down. However, as a new MP, I hadn't appreciated how serious a confidence vote was and the lengths the government would go to. As I got in the taxi to the event, I received a text message back from him that reinforced the message: 'This is not a motion on fracking. This is a confidence motion in the government.'

I watched the debate on my mobile using headphones for privacy as we headed to the Macmillan gala. Several MPs said openly in their speeches that they planned to rebel with others set to abstain on the motion. The Climate Minister Graham Stuart got to his feet and retracted what I had been told by the deputy Chief Whip. He stated at the despatch box that the decision had been reversed and that the vote was no longer a confidence issue. I breathed a sigh of relief. But there was confusion on the benches and I watched as the parliamentary private secretary handed a note to the minister on the front bench, who seemed to be contradict himself again. It was a minute before the vote and it was still unclear what the exact situation was. With a heavy heart, I texted my whip to vote on my behalf with the government, as I was not in any fit state to risk losing my job.

The Government won the vote by a majority of ninety-six and the BBC began to report that Conservative MPs had been bullied and manhandled into backing the government. Video footage posted online showed chaotic scenes in the voting lobby as the whips tried to get my colleagues to oppose Labour's motion. The Speaker ordered an investigation into the incident and angrily said that members should be treated with courtesy and respect. I couldn't have agreed more, and I hoped that anyone who had bullied and harassed us would be disciplined. I was outraged that MPs had been intimidated into voting with our party.

I hid in the toilet at the gala to read social media reports that the Chief Whip Wendy Morton had left government. It was a complete shambles. The Prime Minister had lost control and I knew then that she could not lead us into the next election. I watched my colleague Charles Walker give an irate interview on live television from the House of Commons after the vote, where he called what had happened 'inexcusable' and 'a shambles and a disgrace'. He stated what many of us felt but were not prepared to publicly say. I said nothing at the dinner and tried to avoid discussing politics with constituents.

The next morning, Liz Truss stepped down as Prime Minister after an embarrassing fifty days in office, which meant she was the shortest-serving PM in British history. This triggered the second Conservative leadership election within four months. I despaired at the state of the party and I never truly trusted the Whips' Office again. From then on, I asked Penny Mordaunt and George Freeman to alternate being my proxy during the rest of my maternity leave, instead of the deputy Chief Whip, to ensure they voted how I wanted.

Rishi subsequently won the ballot and was elected as our new leader after Penny pulled out of the race. I hoped that the result would finally end a tumultuous period in British politics and that he would now unite the party and country as we faced profound economic challenges. Stability, competence and professionalism were key as we looked towards the next general election.

CHAPTER FOURTEEN

CHEQUERS

During my maternity leave, I received abuse in person, on the telephone and via my staff. This ranged from 'She had the baby in August and I pay her wages; tell her to get back to work' to 'You can't be an MP and want to go off and have children'. Another resident said, 'This constituency needs a hard-working MP who doesn't just take six months off when she fancies it.'

The local Conservative Association also kept inviting me to events during my maternity leave and putting pressure on me to attend. I particularly offended the older, retired male members who seemed to have a chauvinistic attitude and clearly didn't like having a new, younger, female MP after having had Sir Bill Cash represent them for decades. They frequently conveyed their annoyance that I was not able to attend evening events, such as the Harvest Festival supper, and they deemed that choosing to feed my daughter and do bathtime and bedtime was an excuse, rather than a crucial job for any new mother with a newborn baby. I found their behaviour completely unacceptable and in another workplace, they might have been pulled up for breaches of the Equality Act.

I found it astounding that in political life, sexist comments or jibes were often ignored and the always-present, on-demand nature of being an MP was seen as simply part of the job with no allowances made. It also seemed deeply ironic that while we claimed to be the party that espoused family values, members viewed having a newborn baby as an MP to be an unwelcome distraction. On top of this, I was in possibly the one job in the country where I had to work throughout my maternity leave anyway.

When I tried to send James to local events as my representative, he was told, 'I demand to see my MP, not a junior secretary.' There were certain things he also couldn't attend on my behalf, and it was immediately apparent that Remembrance Sunday in November was one of those occasions. I knew that laying my wreath was non-negotiable in a military town – Stafford was home to the Beacon Barracks, which I was hugely supportive of – and that I would have to be there with our veterans and serving personnel, despite not being well. It was one of the highest-profile events in my constituency calendar, attended by several thousand people, where the public turned out en masse for the parade of local groups in support of the local Signal Regiments and Tactical Supply Wing Unit. I was very concerned about standing up for so long outside in the rain, as I was still bleeding heavily every day and didn't have access to a toilet for over two hours to change my maternity pads. I took extra codeine to get through the pain throughout the outdoor service and asked for a seat or fold-up chair but had my request refused.

My daughter was now ten weeks old and I had been up all night every few hours to feed her, so I was exhausted. I could not take her to the service as it was too cold and I could not risk her crying during the wreath-laying ceremony or the bugler playing 'The Last Post'. So, my husband came into Stafford and stayed with her in the car nearby so that I could feed her straight away when we were finished, as she needed milk every two hours. All I wanted to do was crawl into bed to get some sleep and warm up, but I was not able to go straight home after the service. It had been several months since anyone had seen me publicly in the constituency, so my team strongly advised me to go to the official lunch with the mayor and Stafford Borough Council, which meant that Henry and Arabella had to come too so I could feed her. I was broken and I did not feel in a fit physical or mental state to be seen by the public or to be making conversation with civic leaders and other dignitaries, but I knew I would be criticised if I wasn't there in person as the local MP.

The female councillors made a beeline for me and fussed over my daughter, and it was nice to see some friendly faces who cared. But then I saw all the other local politicians and dignitaries jostling for position as they each tried to bend my ear on a different issue. The council was concerned that the Home Office wanted to requisition the old site of Staffordshire University for a huge asylum seeker site on the edge of town. The hospital complained that free lateral flow tests from the government had ended and ambulance waiting times were too high. Residents asked me about the autumn booster programme of the Covid vaccine for vulnerable groups. I was urged to tackle school waiting lists that were too long, especially for children with special educational needs. I heard how businesses were still struggling to recover since the pandemic and how the high street was in urgent need of more investment. I was given an update on Staffordshire police being in special measures. Farmers raised concerns about winter flooding and protecting their crops. The list went on and on. I struggled to focus and digest all the information coming at me like incoming fire after so little sleep. My brain was so tired and only processed information very slowly. It felt like I had been intellectually downgraded from a new iPhone to be replaced by an old brick Nokia 3210. I made it through the day, but I was completely drained afterwards. Later, a constituent contacted me to complain that I had not bothered to lay a wreath in their village, even though it was at the same time as the main service in Stafford. I was too fatigued to reply to them.

The following day, I took Arabella to our neighbouring town of Stone to shop for basic supplies. We went down the aisles looking for baby formula in Morrisons when my telephone rang on a withheld number. This usually signified a government minister or civil servant calling from a department, so I nearly didn't answer given that my office was meant to dealing with all work-related issues. The lady told me in clipped tones that it was the Downing Street switchboard and that the Chief Whip wanted to speak with me. I rushed out of the supermarket, leaving my trolley stacked with goods in the aisle, and waddled back to the car to find some privacy.

I had never spoken to the Chief Whip, Simon Hart, before. When he called me, he was friendly and businesslike and got straight to the point. He told me the Prime Minister would like to appoint me as the parliamentary private secretary (PPS) at the Department of Business and Trade, where I would be working for the Secretary of State Kemi Badenoch and her team of junior ministers. Arabella gurgled in the background and I shushed her to be quiet so I could hear what he was saying. I was surprised, given that I had publicly endorsed Penny in the leadership election and worked on her campaign. He referenced that I had resigned from the previous Johnson administration and had supported the PM over Liz. I had also never voted against the government. Loyalty rather than competence seemed to be key. I was amazed that Downing Street had thought of me at all, given I had been away from Parliament for several months due to my maternity leave and the fast nature of politics meant that out of sight frequently meant out of mind.

The role was unpaid but meant that I would become the eyes and ears of my ministers in Westminster, report back to them what colleagues thought, help head off potential rebellions on votes, support them in the Chamber for debates and legislative committees and organise their surgeries with fellow MPs, among other duties. Becoming a PPS was often seen as a stepping stone to becoming a government minister as I would get to attend the weekly ministerial meetings where they discussed and agreed policies and thereby shadow their work at the department. It was the first time I had been asked, and I was immediately flattered but concerned about the practicalities. I was not expecting a promotion and thought that I would most likely only be given my old trade envoy to Kenya job back. I politely asked the Chief Whip what was happening with my previous role and asked if someone had been appointed. He said no one had yet taken over the brief. I pointed out that I had done multiple trips to Kenya on behalf of the government and held relationships with senior politicians and businesses there after doing several years of negotiations to progress our trade deal.

I reminded him that Arabella was not even three months old yet and I was not coming back to Parliament until February the following year. I was concerned that the Whips' Office would expect me back in the Chamber immediately and I knew there was an important third reading debate and vote coming up the following week on the Trade (Australia and New Zealand) Bill. It would be tricky to defend the government's trade position in this department when I represented a farming community, and I briefly wondered if I was being offered the job to keep me quiet. However, the Chief Whip made the point that he was aware of my background in international affairs and that the PM thought the department's work would be of interest to me.

I counter-offered Simon's proposal and asked if it would be possible to have my old job back as Trade Envoy and be PPS simultaneously. I reminded him that I would not be back in Parliament in person for another three months until my proxy vote had ended. There was a sharp intake of breath and the line went quiet; it was a bold request for a young, new MP and I realised I might have gone too far. But he chuckled and told me he thought it might be possible to do both, although I would need to be issued with formal guidance from the Permanent Secretary on my remit as the roles were both in the same department. I was acutely aware that I could not make the decision without speaking to my husband first – the role affected him too, as my workload would only increase. I told the Chief Whip I needed to go home and speak to Henry about it and discuss the childcare implications. He sounded annoyed and surprised that I did not accept the job on the spot but agreed that I could let him know by the following day. If not, then the offer was off the table. He hung up and left me to decide.

Arabella was hungry so I rushed home to feed her and ask Henry what he thought. He was supportive and told me I should accept both jobs and that we would find a way to make it work. I texted Simon to accept and then Kemi to confirm, who I did not know well and, truth be told, found quite formidable, but I had always been impressed by her work ethic, ability to be frank and track record in getting stuff done. She seemed, like Michael Gove, to be one of the few ministers who had genuinely delivered in her brief and had a clear idea of what she wanted to achieve in government and how to do it. I told her that I was still physically recovering from the birth and would not be able to attend any in-person meetings until my daughter was six months old. I explained that I was feeding Arabella every three hours and that she was not yet sleeping through the night, so I did not think I could be that helpful until then. I was relieved at her reply. She welcomed me to the team and told me not to worry about anything until I was back from maternity leave, seeming unconcerned that I was unable to help straight away. Thankfully, I knew that she had one of my Red Wall colleagues, Alex Stafford, already supporting her. I asked her if I could tweet that I was joining her team when I got back from maternity leave, but she told me to stop checking social media and take some time off. It was good advice. I laughed when she replied again to tell me I was worrying too much. I felt much more confident about going back to work only when I was ready.

I tried to focus on my physical and mental recovery and not to do too much else, but it was hard to ignore the constant streams of WhatsApp messages in different MP chat groups. Ministers constantly plugged their departments' announcements, colleagues clogged up my feed with queries on policies, campaigns sent me briefing notes and fellow MPs wrote draft group letters to lobby me on different issues. I felt exhausted from the lack of sleep and resentful that my routine as a new mother was relentless.

I did not like to admit to friends or family that I also found looking after a newborn baby boring and repetitive after the buzz of Parliament. I did not anticipate that one of the hardest things about maternity leave was being away from all my colleagues. The physical separation of being in Stafford and away from London was difficult and isolating, and I felt anxious that I was not down in Westminster doing the job I was elected to do. It was hard to gauge what was going on only by listening to the news or reading text messages and emails.

* * *

I was delighted when, out of the blue, I received an invitation from the Prime Minister inviting my husband and me to Chequers, the PM's country residence, for lunch. I called No. 10, explained that my daughter was still only a few months old and asked if they could accommodate her too. Henry had never before been to an event with the PM, having turned down the opportunity to visit No. 10 previously as he was not that interested in politics, which I found refreshing. But even he could not resist the chance to visit the sixteenth-century manor house and, as an arts graduate, to see its renowned picture collection.

We drove to Buckinghamshire into the depths of the Chilterns and nearly missed the entrance as it was so hidden. Immediately we were surrounded by armed police and they examined our identification and called ahead to check we were expected. I was also excited to see the house, which had been a country retreat for serving Prime Ministers and was never open to the public. It felt steeped in history and like we were walking in the footsteps of many world leaders. We drove to up to the red brick and stone mansion and saw that there were only a handful of cars parked outside, which confused me. I was expecting a large event with all of my Conservative colleagues, as Boris had previously hosted a similar event as a garden party for all the new MPs elected in 2019, which I'd been unable to attend. As we got Arabella out of the car, I began to worry that we had got the timings or date wrong.

We went into the Great Hall with its dark wooden panelling and impressive artwork, including a portrait of Charles I by van Dyck and white and blue Chinese vases. I recognised the room from photographs of Theresa May as she negotiated her failed Chequers plan.

Then I saw the Prime Minister, who walked towards us and hugged me warmly. He welcomed us to the house and took the time to meet our daughter for the first time, wishing us congratulations as new parents. It felt very strange to be in there with Rishi and my family, especially after the trauma of the past few months. I caught up with some colleagues that I had not seen in months and it was wonderful to catch up with friends like Siobhan Baillie. I was relieved to see she had brought her toddler and baby too.

We went through to the dining room and I could now see that it was only a small group of us, fewer than thirty, who had been invited for brunch. I felt quite star-struck when I was seated next to the Prime Minister's wife, Akshata. I had not met her before, but she was lovely and warm and put us all at ease. We discussed the challenges of being a new mother and she related to how tough it was having young children with a political career. I alluded to the fact that I had had a difficult birth, but I did not feel that I could share too much. Instead, I told her that I was looking forward to being back at work soon and joining my department in my new role. As a businesswoman, she was clearly very astute and began to ask me about my local hospital and what support I'd had during the birth and afterwards. Arabella sat on my lap and I tried not to let her throw food on the expensive thick carpet as she constantly tried to grab the cutlery or items off my plate and wriggled around. I was worried that she was going to cover Akshata in scrambled egg or accidentally knock over my fine bone china cup of tea, so I passed her to Henry to feed her some milk in a bottle.

Halfway through the meal, Akshata swapped seats to move on to the next table and the Prime Minister came and sat down next to me. The table went quiet and everyone waited to see what he had to say and why we were really there. It became apparent that it was more of a social than a work event. He mainly wanted to thank our families who'd supported us during the previous difficult few years. I was very touched that he had taken the time to reach out to our partners, who rarely got acknowledged for their roles. I knew that I couldn't have got through the general election or multiple challenges, including being elected during the pandemic and being pregnant as an MP, without Henry. He was often shy at group events, so I smiled when I saw him talk animatedly to the Prime Minister despite having never met him before.

Afterwards, we were offered a tour of the collection in the famous Long Room. Arabella babbled in her pram, which was too unwieldly to take around the house, so I said I would stay downstairs and look after her. To my astonishment, Rishi stepped forward and said he would look after her. Everyone was silent to see what I would do at the unexpected offer. As the Prime Minister held out his arms to take her, I was momentarily lost for words. I asked if he really did not mind and he reminded us that he had two daughters. I passed him Arabella, who smiled in her tiny red dress with white tights and kicked in the air. Henry leant forward and said with a straight face, 'Prime Minister, you might need a muslin.' He draped the cloth over Rishi's shoulder so she didn't vomit all over his tailored blazer and crisp white shirt. Our baby was no longer than his forearm. The other guests all laughed as they observed the comical situation. We could scarcely believe that the Prime Minister was babysitting our daughter, but Rishi waved us off and we nervously headed upstairs to see the rare antiques, books, memorabilia relating to Oliver Cromwell, paintings by Churchill and other priceless works of art. I was most astonished by a small ring, which was one of the few surviving pieces of jewellery belonging to Elizabeth I, taken from her finger when she died. It was made of diamonds, rubies and mother of pearl set in gold, with a secret compartment that contained a portrait of her mother, Anne Boleyn. The collection was not open to the public and the items were rarely loaned, so it was a huge privilege to see them.

We had been at least twenty minutes, and I was worried about leaving Arabella downstairs without us. Suddenly, a man burst into the room and told me that she was crying so I rushed back down the oak staircase and found the PM with my daughter, who he bounced up and down in the air as he tried to distract her. It was the most unlikely scene and I was amazed that he hadn't pawned her off to an aide. She calmed down when I picked her back up again and nestled her on my chest. It was the first time I was left alone with the PM, so I thanked him for offering me the job as a PPS and said how surprised I was that he was keeping the role open for me for several months. He replied that having a baby should be no barrier to career progression. He seemed delighted to have offered me a job in a department where I was genuinely interested in the brief and could help the government at the same time. I was relieved and impressed and I reflected that his predecessor would have been unlikely to do the same.

The group returned and I asked where we could change Arabella's nappy. The housekeeper sheepishly admitted there were no baby-changing facilities at Chequers. Nonplussed, I asked if there was somewhere else that I could use and she offered up one of the side rooms that was sometimes used as an office by the PM. We went through to a plush office with fragile Chinese lacquer tables, porcelain and rows of hardback books. I put Arabella's changing mat down on the carpet and changed her nappy, terrified that she might have done an explosion that would leak all over the floor. It was a reminder of the day-to-day realities of being a new mother, despite the grandeur of the surroundings. Nevertheless, I felt buoyed about going back to work after reconnecting with my colleagues and I looked forward to returning to my job in Westminster.

CHAPTER FIFTEEN

RETURN TO WORK

My proxy vote ended in mid-February, exactly six months after I gave birth. It had been a lifeline for my recovery not to have to attend late-night votes in person while I didn't feel well enough to work the very long hours that the House of Commons demanded. I was also very upset at the thought of having to leave my daughter five days a week to return to work full time. I had assumed that Arabella would go to the nursery in Parliament, which the previous Speaker, John Bercow, had brought on site to finally bring maternity provision for MPs into the twenty-first century. However, I was stunned to discover that she was unable to get a place. The nursery manager told me the waiting list was over a year and that only siblings would be prioritised. I pointed out to her that pregnancy was only nine months, so the waiting list was longer than the gestation period for a baby. The whole situation was absurd. Every parliamentary passholder was eligible to use the facilities, which included hundreds of staff and potentially thousands of people. I was shocked to discover that even a contractor working in a government department in Whitehall was eligible to use the parliamentary nursery as long as they had security clearance on the estate, despite its small size and limited spaces in their baby room. The entire premise of the nursery had been to help new mothers who were also Members of Parliament, due to our unique role, unusual working hours and requirement to vote late at night, which meant that we were frequently unable to leave the House of Commons and had to always be within a few minutes' walk of the voting lobby.

Out of 650 MPs, only a handful of MPs then had a newborn baby so it had not occurred to me that my daughter would not get a space. I had no idea what we were going to do as a family. My proxy vote was going to end and I was expected to be back in my new department and start my new job, while also continuing to represent my constituents. I was acutely aware that I would be unable to visit or feed Arabella if she was at nursery anywhere other than in Parliament. She was so tiny that she could not even sit up unaided, and I had to hold her on my lap or watch her at all times as she lay down on the floor and tried to roll across her mat. At six months, she was completely helpless and needed to have everything done for her. Only Henry and I knew her routine intimately and when she needed to be fed, soothed, burped over my shoulder after a feed or settled to sleep by rocking her in my arms.

It seemed ironic that Parliament wrote the laws that businesses were expected to follow on maternity policy but which we failed to follow ourselves. There seemed to be very little consideration made to working mothers, which no doubt contributed to the lack of female representation in Parliament and therefore, by extension, our democracy itself. I wrote to the Speaker to express my concerns and asked him to revisit the rules for MPs with newborn babies and ensure that they were prioritised to use the on-site nursery so that other colleagues were not left in the same situation in the future.

As we could not get our daughter into the parliamentary nursery and given Henry had taken a new job in Stafford, we decided that I would go down to London during the week and therefore be separated from my family.

I felt helpless, angry and deeply sad about the situation. I felt I was abandoning my daughter after everything we had been through and that I was not ready to go back to work. I needed another few months at home to focus on recovering fully from the trauma of her birth. I also wanted to be there to protect and nurture her during that critical first year of life. We were both exhausted from months of sleep deprivation and I had no idea how Henry was going to manage such a long week without me. We did some viewings of nurseries in Staffordshire, but our local site had been rated 'poor' by Ofsted and the good or outstanding nurseries told me I should have put her down on the waiting list when I was pregnant, so I became increasingly alarmed by the whole situation. Arabella had only slept through the night a few times, after I had rigidly stuck to her 7 a.m. to 7 p.m. routine, and I worried what Henry was going to do when she had sleep regression. How was he going to be able to get up to feed her in the middle of the night and manage a full day in the office? It seemed impossible to leave them both and I began to develop severe anxiety about going back to work.

One morning, I burst into tears and told Henry I was overwhelmed. I found that the worst part about being an MP, after the abuse and threats, was being forced to work every week in two locations, in both London and Stafford. I did not know how we were going to be a family when we were being compelled to live split lives, several hours' travel apart. I had championed our government's policy on the Start for Life programme and the importance of a child's first 1,001 days. Instead, I was going to have to do the complete opposite and leave my baby without her mother for most of the week at only six months old.

Henry listened as I explained my concerns about leaving Arabella and we talked through our choices, which were limited. There seemed to be only one option left to us: that he quit his job so we could move back to London, remain together and travel together back and forth to the constituency every week as a family. He committed to look after her while we tried to find part-time alternative childcare. I felt a huge relief and knew straight away that it was the right and only thing to do. It wasn't a completely perfect solution – we had made our main home in my constituency in our lovely three-bedroom house in the countryside, which we loved and had filled with all our favourite things, including the books, pictures and furniture that I had inherited from my father, and now we would be moving back to a tiny one-bedroom flat in London. Regardless, I tried to focus on the positives and not to think about the added stress of commuting more than three hours each way every week with a baby.

We agreed that I would also write to the Speaker and request an extension to my proxy vote since I was still attending the perineal tear clinic and having regular hospital appointments for my birth injury. The rules had recently changed to accommodate illness and injury, due to the absurd situation of MPs like my colleague Tracey Crouch, who had talked movingly about her experience with cancer and being unable to attend Parliament to represent her constituents in important debates while undertaking chemotherapy, due to the rigid proxy rules. I was relieved that the rules had finally been updated to be more accommodating, but I felt embarrassed about asking for help. It felt like I had admitted failure and I questioned whether I was letting both my family and my constituents down. If I spent time at work then I felt guilty not being with my baby, and if I spent time with Arabella then I felt guilty about not working. I lay awake at night thinking it was impossible to be a good mother and an MP at the same time. I also knew I would be creating a precedent by asking to have my proxy vote extended and it would be on the public record if it was granted. I rang my surgeon, who wrote to the Speaker and confidentially detailed my traumatic birth and resulting third-degree tear. It was the first time I had told anyone outside of my immediate family. I hoped that journalists would not notice or ask too many questions, as I did not feel publicly ready to talk about what had happened to me in the hospital. I felt ashamed of my birth injury and the daily physical and mental scars I still battled every day.

* * *

My first Monday morning back in Parliament after the birth of my daughter felt strange. It was by now late February and the last time I had been back at work full time, Boris Johnson had been the Prime Minister and I had been the trade envoy to Kenya. It was like nothing and everything had changed.

The first thing I noticed was how untidy my desk was, so I began to neatly tidy away the old Post-it notes covered in spidery writing and six-month-old newspapers from when I had last been there. As I compulsively straightened the edges of the piles of printer paper on my shelf, I began to realise the stark contrast between my pre- and post-birth selves and how obsessed I had become by cleanliness and tidiness. Consumed by my return to work, I pushed the thought away, but it lingered in the back of my mind as I went about my day.

I caught up with my team and debriefed on the week ahead, looking at debates I wanted to speak in, planning ahead for my next constituency surgery, identifying select committee briefings I needed to read and reviewing the daily deluge of invitations and press requests. I decided I would prioritise meeting with the Levelling Up Minister about Stafford Borough Council's bid for our flagship Stafford Station Gateway project, join a group meeting of Midland MPs to discuss concerns about immigration, attend the Downing Street roundtable on violence against women and girls, pop into drinks with Penny in her office, dial into the special briefing on Ukraine with the former US National Security Advisor, support the Foreign Office Minister as a PPS in the debate on humanitarian support for the recent earthquakes in Syria and attend the 1922 Committee of Conservative backbench MPs. It was only my first day back and already the to-do list looked overwhelming and ambitious, especially considering my brain was running at half-capacity due to lack of sleep.

At lunchtime, I headed over to the Department for Business and Trade to attend my first departmental meeting with Kemi Badenoch and her junior ministerial team. I was parliamentary private secretary alongside my colleague Alex Stafford, another MP in my intake who had already been in the department for several months. I went into the Old Admiralty Building, the former headquarters of the British Navy and the building where Winston Churchill had worked as First Lord of the Admiralty. Despite the display of modern art from the government art collection, which was housed in the same building, I felt the history that seeped through the place as I navigated the myriad of corridors to find the meeting on the first floor. I met her secretaries and was ushered into her private office along with ministers Nigel Huddleston, Nus Ghani, Lord Johnson and several special advisers.

It was the first time I had ever sat in on a government meeting and seen how a department was run up close. I was now in effect the unpaid assistant to a team of government ministers, and I saw immediately why becoming a PPS was seen as the stepping stone to being promoted to the front bench, as I now shadowed them in their roles and had become their eyes and ears in Westminster. I was invited to attend private meetings with our department's Cabinet minister and hear her set out her priorities to her team, discuss the political implications of policies and work out how to practically deliver on our manifesto commitments. I soon became aware of divisions with No. 10, rivalries with other government departments, the volume of submissions to their red boxes, spending fights with the Treasury and negotiations ahead of the spending review and the Budget.

It was my job to act as a conduit between my ministers and backbench MPs. A crucial part of this role was going into the tearoom to listen to colleagues and spending more time around Parliament to pick up gossip or any concerns about our department's work. I was now bound by the ministerial code and was viewed as part of the 'payroll' vote, which meant I was expected to vote with the government in all divisions and I would be fired if I couldn't support them. I was now unable to speak in debates affecting my department – on business and trade – and had to avoid making criticisms that might embarrass the government. Instead, I would sit behind the minister at the despatch box, carrying messages between the civil servants and the minister as they fielded questions or responded in debates. I remained on the Select Committee on International Development, but I would have to recuse myself when we scrutinised the work of my department.

Kemi welcomed me to the meeting and asked me for my weekly update as PPS. I laughed nervously and said that given it was my first day, I didn't yet have one. I found her intimidating, but it was refreshing to see a minister with a clear sense of what she was trying to achieve in the time left of the parliamentary term. It helped that her ministers clearly respected her and chose to be helpful. They all worked hard and, as they went through their respective updates, I was impressed at their energy and the sheer volume of work each of them had undertaken on top of representing their own constituents. I did not envy their diaries; the pace looked relentless, with meetings scheduled every thirty minutes from early in the morning until late at night on top of debates in the Chamber, prepping for committee hearings, international travel, conferences and regional visits to see other MPs and local businesses.

At the meeting I was tasked with setting up my first tearoom surgery, which involved arranging private meetings between colleagues and ministers to try to head off the likelihood of public acrimony in the Chamber, which was televised live. I was sent off to recruit and plant friendly parliamentary questions. Before I left, I explained to the team that I was coming into Parliament only during normal working hours and that I would leave each day by 5 p.m. now that my proxy vote had been extended by the Speaker. This meant I could get home to feed and bath Arabella and not have to stay late for votes while I was still recovering from surgery. They seemed surprised, so I alluded to the fact that I had spent time in hospital post-birth but didn't choose to elaborate. I knew I was creating a new precedent by moving from my maternity proxy to an injury proxy, the first MP to ever do so, but I was happy for it to be on the public record, as I was conscious that Parliament desperately needed improving when it came to pastoral care. I felt that no one looked after us as people and we were seen only as politicians to be mocked and abused. Nus Ghani, one of the ministers, came up to me after the meeting and asked if I was really doing OK. She was pleased to see I was taking care of myself and told me to let her know if I needed any help. Before I left, I asked Alex to attend the evening PPS meeting with the deputy Chief Whip later that evening to update them on the work of our department.

I rushed back from the departmental meeting to the House of Commons to undertake my oath. Unlike the rest of my colleagues, I had not yet sworn my allegiance to His Majesty the King – the Speaker had granted me special dispensation to do it on my return to Parliament. I was ushered up to the front to swear fealty to the new monarch. The Chamber went very quiet as colleagues saw me walk up to the clerks by the despatch box and place my hand on the King James Bible to give my oath. I felt very conspicuous doing so alone. Michael Gove gave me a smile as I walked past him on the front bench, welcoming me back. It marked an important moment of my return to work and I felt like I was now finally able to properly represent my constituents. However, being in the Chamber also made me anxious. I had to bring my doughnut cushion with me to sit on the green benches to relieve pressure on my perineum, and I kept the specialist pillow in a canvas bag as I was embarrassed to show colleagues what was inside. I also constantly worried about the lack of toilet facilities for women near the Chamber or about having flatulence in public.

On Wednesday, my fears were amplified when I attended my first Prime Minister's Questions (PMQs) since my return to Parliament. I was terrified that I would be unable to control my bowels properly. What would happen if I had to run out to the toilet in the middle of speaking live in front of the cameras and microphones, which picked up even the smallest noise, hanging above me in the Chamber? I had asked the Speaker in advance to pick me, as I had an urgent local issue to raise and I hadn't spoken in the House of Commons for months. My question concerned the government's proposal to relocate approximately 500 single male asylum seekers to Beaconside in Stafford. I had received a huge number of objections from constituents and I was going to hold a dedicated surgery to meet with more residents who opposed the plan that week. I asked the Prime Minister to meet with me urgently to discuss it. In reply, Rishi Sunak welcomed me back from my maternity leave and agreed that I would meet the Home Secretary. It felt bizarre to be back in the heart of Westminster where no one knew about the traumatic birth I'd been through, bar the Speaker, and I breathed a sigh of a relief at delivering my question without anyone being aware that I was still in recovery.

That night, running late, I called Henry as he was doing bathtime with Arabella so I could watch her on the screen and say goodnight. She turned away from the camera and ignored me completely, punishing me for being away from home. The next morning, I tried to give her a cuddle in my suit before I went back to work, but she pushed me away and began to sob hysterically as I left for the office. It was heartbreaking and I felt crushed that I was having to prioritise work over my family.

By the time it was Friday, I was exhausted from my first week back and being in the relentless bubble of Parliament. Arabella had only just begun sleeping through the night and I was depleted from months of sleep deprivation. My brain found it hard to process information and I was unable to remember basic things. My memory had become so foggy that I now had to write everything down on Post-it notes on my computer and desk, always kept a notebook with me to keep track of my growing to-do list and took copious notes in meetings. I had also become obsessive about my diary and set up a traffic light system to code meetings in a way that I had never done before my traumatic birth. I couldn't wait to be back in our proper home in Stafford to finally get some fresh country air and escape Westminster.

CHAPTER SIXTEEN

FRIENDS AND FOES

My husband, daughter and I took the train back up to the West Midlands on Friday morning so I could attend my constituency surgery. I spent the next few hours being shouted at in back-to-back appointments about the proposed asylum seeker centre. The fact that I had just raised it at PMQs and set up a meeting with the Home Secretary did not seem to quell their anger. Then I headed off to Stafford College to meet the principal and some students and open the new skills and innovation centre, which I'd actively championed to get the necessary funding from the Department for Education. I'd had such a busy week that I didn't give too much thought to my parliamentary candidate readoption meeting that evening at Stafford Conservative Association. It was usually a short meeting with the executive committee where I would give an update on my time as their local representative.

So, after a busy day in the office and out on visits, I went home to give Arabella a quick cuddle and feed her a bottle of milk. She'd only just turned six months old and I was conscious that I had barely seen her all week and now, once again, I was missing her bath and bedtime routine to head out on a Friday evening. I loved holding her on my chest and breathing in her sweet smell. I stroked her soft hair and felt her breathing fall in sync with mine.

She sobbed as I left her and I was once again grateful to my husband for looking after her so I could return to work. As I got in the car, I promised Henry that after campaigning on Saturday in support of my council candidates, who were up for re-election in May, we would finally spend the whole day together on Sunday. When I arrived at the 7 p.m. meeting at our association offices on Castle Street, there was a small group of around thirty people. I said hello to several councillors I knew well, many of whom I had not seen properly for months due to my maternity leave, but the rest I didn't recognise. The boundaries were changing significantly in my constituency, as Stafford was being merged with part of my constituency neighbour Bill Cash's area in Stone, and I assumed they were the representatives of the villages that were moving across to me if I was lucky enough to be elected again at the next general election.

I gave my ten-minute speech to update them on what I had delivered since 2019, including record investment in our town, increased funding for mental health provision and schools, high street regeneration, tackling flooding and resolving more than 10,000 pieces of casework from residents. I also answered questions about how I would run my campaign. We had chosen to live locally as a family in Stafford, as it was important to me to be part of the community. I took my role as the MP very seriously and did not, unlike some colleagues, have a second paid job, so that I could focus solely on my representative duties. Everyone cast their ballot and I had a cup of lukewarm, weak tea with some members and caught up on their news as we waited for the votes to be counted.

The chairman of Stafford Conservatives and a representative from Conservative Party headquarters went to the front of the room to announce the results. The room went quiet as he announced that I had lost by a handful of votes. I was astonished. I fought back tears in front of everyone in the room as the news sunk in. I was the sitting MP and I had been deselected by my Conservative Association only four days after returning from maternity leave. My key supporters were as gobsmacked as I was, but I could see the chairman and deputy chairman struggle to contain their delight. I knew immediately that it had been orchestrated and that they must have used the previous six months that I'd been off to plan the whole thing. I remembered now how my association had tried to hold my readoption meeting while I was still on maternity leave and were annoyed that I had refused to attend until I was fully back at work.

I discovered later that I had been right and there had been a co-ordinated campaign to remove me. The hostility towards me went right back to my original adoption meeting as the parliamentary candidate in 2019. I recalled how the deputy chairman had refused to shake my hand on the night I had been selected, as he had endorsed a different local candidate to win, and had walked out after I won. My detractors told members that I'd been parachuted in by No. 10, despite my husband's family connections to Stafford, and I constantly faced criticism that I was not a local candidate even years into my term.

I could barely believe this was happening. I wondered why I had given up my interesting and well-paid job in international affairs to run for elected office, only to be treated like this by my supposed colleagues. I felt particularly gutted about everything we had been through as a family. Henry had sold his house, quit his job and moved to Stafford for us to have our main home up in the new constituency and I had chosen to transfer my maternity care from London to Staffordshire to ensure that I could be a local mum. The chief criticism was that I was not seen out and about enough locally as the MP. While there was no doubt a grain of truth in this – and I admit that, bar Remembrance Sunday, I didn't attend work events on Sundays as I chose instead to prioritise my family – members also seemed to have forgotten that 100 days into my term we'd gone into our first Covid lockdown and that I'd spent the first half of my term working in a pandemic before then having a baby.

I immediately decided to fight back against the decision, as I thought it was absurd that such a tiny group of people (around thirty) out of a constituency with more than 76,000 residents could decide whether I stood again at the next general election. I put out a statement on social media saying I had requested a full ballot of the entire membership of several hundred local Conservatives, so that they could be asked if they wanted to keep me or not. If the majority of my membership decided against me, then that was another matter and I knew that if I lost the second, wider ballot then I'd have to accept the result and bow out as their parliamentary candidate.

I contacted a former journalist to help me rebut the smear campaign against me and reached out to several colleagues to ask them to support me. The first was Theresa May. I did not know our former Prime Minister well, as I'd not been elected during her premiership, and I always found her quite formidable. But the week after it happened, I ended up sitting next to her at PMQs and I summoned up the courage to ask for her help. To my relief, she was supportive and got straight on the telephone with No. 10 and the party chairman after I explained to her how I was not able to contact my members to update them on the situation and ask for their support while my opponents, given their roles on the executive committee, had access to the Stafford Conservative Association membership list. It was clear to me that they were misusing their access to relevant databases. Several members complained about my treatment to Conservative Party headquarters, which was reported in *The Times*.

My political mentor Penny Mordaunt, then Leader of the House, also offered her support straight away and agreed to come up to Stafford. She drove me up to the constituency from the Conservative Party's away day conference and we discussed tactics in the car. She was dismayed at how I'd been treated and spoke at a fundraiser for me at Sandon Hall in front of my association members, ostensibly to help raise campaign funds for the local election campaign while also helpfully reminding them that while I was down in London, I was still working hard to represent them in Parliament. Penny also credited me for the millions in investment that I'd brought into Stafford to support key local projects. The instigators of my deselection still had the audacity to attend the event, which was held in my father-in-law's house, but when they realised that they were far outnumbered by my supporters, they hid at the back and slunk out early after the speeches.

The Education Secretary was also keen to offer help. I'd known Gillian Keegan for many years, since before she was elected, when I was a new parliamentary candidate and she was the director of Women2Win, which tried to recruit more female members for the Conservative Party. I rang the association to say that I'd been offered a visit from a member of the Cabinet and asked them to organise an afternoon tea for our members. My chairman refused outright, so I found another venue at the beautiful Orangery Ingestre where we had a full house. I was grateful that Gillian also took the time to visit Stafford College with me. I was shaken that a few members of the local party executive committee were so opposed to me that they would even snub a Cabinet visit for their members to try to ensure that I did not win the wider ballot of members. However, the show of strength for me from senior politicians helped and I won the second ballot convincingly.

I was relieved but deeply wounded by the personal attacks on me and my character. The final straw had been when my chairman commented to the political blog Guido Fawkes that my failure to be readopted as the candidate was due to 'widespread and long-standing dissatisfaction' with me as the MP. I knew that there had been mutterings about my failure to fully work during my maternity leave, but this was news to me. I'd also heard reports of a councillor who complained that I'd not been out campaigning in their ward straight after my daughter's birth, who'd commented publicly that 'surely I could distribute leaflets from the pram'. I was mortified and upset, but I refused to be cowed into giving up my job.

I discovered that I was not the only MP to face deselection and it had happened to several other colleagues, most of whom were also women. I called my good friend Sally-Ann Hart, MP for Hastings & Rye, who'd faced the same humiliation, to give her encouragement that she could also win her wider membership ballot. We were both appalled at how easy it had become to deselect sitting Members of Parliament, especially given the Conservative Party had struggled to recruit and retain good female candidates.

The whole experience was bruising and I didn't feel equipped emotionally to deal with what had happened to me, especially after everything I'd been through in the previous months. I seriously considered whether my job was worth having or if it would be better to accept defeat and find something else that was less stressful to do, where I could make more of a difference and have a better balance between work and family life.

CHAPTER SEVENTEEN

BREAKING THE TABOO

As an MP, it was often difficult to see progress being made locally or to point to any visible proof that I was making any difference to my constituency. One of the few times was setting up the Stafford Network for Mental Health during the Covid pandemic with St George's Hospital, after seeing how badly my constituents were affected by repeated lockdowns. From my surgery appointments, I'd realised that there was not enough support for residents suffering from mental health issues, so I began a three-year campaign to secure extra funding for local services. I relentlessly lobbied the rotating door of various ministers through different government reshuffles, bombarded them with questions in the Chamber about the issue, raised it frequently in debates and doorstepped them in Parliament. I was pleased when the minister wrote to me to confirm I had successfully raised new funding from the government to improve our mental health provision in Stafford.

I was delighted when St George's Hospital, who had supported my mental health campaign from early on, invited me to visit again after my maternity leave, this time to see the new Crisis Assessment Centre, which the additional funding would be spent on. On the suggestion of the NHS Trust's chief executive, Neil Carr, I also visited the parent and baby unit, known as the Brockington Unit, to meet some mothers who were experiencing severe psychological mental health problems during pregnancy or early motherhood. It was the first time I had heard the term 'post-partum psychosis' and I was dismayed to hear from mothers about the serious mental health issues that had developed after they had given birth. They told me about symptoms including hallucinations, delusions, manic behaviour and confusion. I have never forgotten the mother who told me that during her psychosis, she'd gone around the ward offering her newborn baby to healthcare workers, saying that it was not her baby and could they take it away.

It was heartbreaking to hear stories of their difficulty bonding with their babies or of being separated from their partner and families when they entered the unit for a period of weeks or possibly months, especially when many of them had no personal or family history of mental illness. I was shocked to hear that suicide was the leading cause of direct maternal deaths between six weeks and twelve months after birth. I could see that the hospital had made a huge effort to make the unit as homely as possible by decorating the wing more like a hotel and providing baby toys. The fathers also told me how distressing it was for them to see their partner go through a psychotic episode, and about the challenges of attempting recovery in such a specialist psychiatric unit, but how pleased they were to have an integrated model of care in Stafford.

I had not yet spoken about my traumatic birth to anyone publicly and I wondered if experiences like mine could bring on such psychosis. That night, I went home to do some initial research and discovered that this was indeed the case. I found online that there were only nineteen mother and baby units (MBU) in England. I looked up what happened if they had no space and was stunned to find out that mothers would be admitted to a general psychiatric ward in a hospital until an MBU became available.

I had no background or expertise in healthcare at all, given my interest had always been foreign affairs, so I felt intellectually out of my depth. And I knew from my unsuccessful lobbying to reopen the 24-hour A&E department at Stafford's County Hospital how complicated and technical NHS policy was, so I didn't feel confident that I'd be able to make any difference on improving maternity provision, but I felt compelled to try. My experience so far was that government departments were difficult to influence, ministers often worked in siloes, even on cross-cutting issues, and the Department for Health and Social Care often seemed to focus on numbers in a spreadsheet rather than the real people behind the statistics. However, I felt strongly that as a politician and as one of the few female MPs to give birth while elected, I had a responsibility to find out more about mental and physical health support for new mums and at least ask the questions to the right stakeholders in government to find out the answers.

I spent the next few weeks doing research in the evenings while waiting to vote, reading pertinent NHS documents in the House of Commons Library and making a list of relevant organisations or people to reach out to for advice. The first group I came across was the Birth Trauma Association (BTA), who had an active Facebook group of over 18,000 members. I sent an email to their chief executive Kim Thomas asking for a meeting after Easter. I also went for lunch with my good friend and former colleague at the Coalition for Global Prosperity Eleanor Shawcross, who now served as the head of the No. 10 Policy Unit, to get her advice on what I was planning. I knew her before I was elected and she was one of the few people

I trusted in politics. She was extremely bright and more analytical than me about policy, and she also understood the challenges of being a mother of young children while working in the never-ending hamster wheel of Westminster. Thankfully, Eleanor was immediately supportive of my proposed campaign to improve maternity provision in the UK. At lunch, I half-jokingly took my calendar out and put a fictional date in the diary for a birth trauma event in a year's time, around International Women's Day, which I hoped the Prime Minister or at least the Health Secretary would attend as the speaker. It seemed like a long shot and highly unlikely to be achieved, but it buoyed me to talk to someone who took my ideas seriously.

That April recess, I went on my first trip abroad since Arabella had been born, as a UK delegate at the Council of Europe. I sat on the busy committee for migration and displaced persons, and I was conscious I had missed multiple meetings due to my pregnancy and subsequent maternity leave. The issue of how to deal with both refugees and migrants had got much thornier in the previous few months due to an influx of desperate people crossing the Mediterranean. All countries across the European Union were stretched for resources and had failed to agree on the way forward. I wanted to report back to the Foreign Office on these international discussions and update countries in the Council of Europe on the work of the Homes for Ukraine scheme in the UK, which had been successful in housing families in my own constituency. When I rang their clerks, I was surprised at how encouraging they were about me coming to France, given Arabella was only eight months old. They were extremely accommodating and offered for Henry to come too, so he could look after her while I was speaking in the chamber or representing the UK in committee meetings.

We took the Eurostar to Strasbourg and arrived at our hotel to find a cot and a kettle to make her baby formula in our room on arrival, in addition to the coffee machine that was more usual in France. Henry and Arabella were both given security passes to come into the Palais de l'Europe with me and the clerks offered for her to sleep in UK chair Ian Liddell-Grainger's office during her nap times. They also invited my husband and baby to the opening reception for the plenary session at the European Parliament. The difference from the British Parliament in accommodating children for a political delegation felt striking. I didn't feel like I had to choose between being a mother or a politician but that I could do both. It felt like I was finally able to do my job properly and simultaneously not neglect spending quality time with my family.

The following week, I returned to Parliament for another demanding term. I maintained a hectic and tiring campaign schedule across Stafford and the surrounding villages ahead of our local elections and dealt with the backlog of constituency surgery appointments since my maternity leave. In the first week of May, the whole country was excited ahead of the coronation of the King and Queen at Westminster Abbey, which was the first to be held in nearly seventy years. The coronation lunch held in my constituency was a good opportunity to celebrate with residents and recover from the shock of polling day, when only the day before we had lost control of Stafford Borough Council to a coalition of Labour and independents. I was hugely disheartened to see our excellent leader, who'd given more than twenty years to the party as a councillor, be ousted by the Greens in his ward, along with many of our excellent cabinet members who'd fought with me for funding and to deliver so many other local projects. I knew they could not have worked harder to get re-elected but had been let down by national politics and our party's leadership. The local election results did not bode well for my own future general election campaign in Stafford, which was a bellwether seat.

* * *

When Kim from the Birth Trauma Association came to my parliamentary office for our first cup of tea that May, she confessed that she had been surprised to hear from me, as she could see that I was a backbench MP who'd not been an active campaigner previously on maternity care. She was also unclear as to the purpose of our meeting, given that I'd not been too forthcoming in our brief correspondence, although she was clearly happy to meet any parliamentarian who'd taken an interest in their work. Kim was amazed when I shared with her the story of my traumatic birth and then peppered her with questions about birth trauma. She patiently explained more about the issue and introduced me to the basic facts. Some 30,000 women a year suffered from post-traumatic stress disorder due to birth trauma and the MBRRACE UK report, which looked into maternal deaths, had shown that black women in the UK had a much higher risk of dying in pregnancy in comparison to white women. As Kim shared with me some horrific stories of birth trauma, it became clear to me that this was a wider issue that the public and Parliament didn't seem to be talking about enough or doing anything to address. I asked her to send me a copy of the BTA's submission to the government's Women's Health Strategy consultation and the 2020 safety of maternity services inquiry. We also agreed that she would bring in a group of affected mothers to meet with me in a month's time, so I could hear their experiences first hand. I didn't realise then what a turning point this would be in my career as an MP.

One month later, on 7 June 2023, Kim brought ten mothers to meet me in the House of Commons along with the BTA's founder, Maureen. The women were Rachael, Chloe, Alice, Eleanor, Neera, Neya, Gill, Susan, Katie and Leone. It was the first time I'd met any other women who had also suffered from birth trauma. To be honest, I was scared to meet them in case it triggered flashbacks of my own traumatic birth, and I didn't know what to expect or say in our meeting. It felt like I had nothing specific to offer them but the chance to listen to and hear their stories, and I didn't know if that would be enough. I felt the weight of their expectations, given that they were meeting a politician and clearly thought I could do something to help them.

I booked a small room in Parliament for us to meet for an hour and began by sharing my story to break the ice and allow them to feel that it was a safe space to speak. It felt strange to be telling the most intimate details of my life, including anal incontinence, heavy blood loss, challenges breastfeeding and recovery from surgery, to a group of complete strangers. But I found it cathartic to finally speak about my experience in a way that I'd only done to my therapist, as I hadn't felt able to tell friends, family or colleagues.

An hour flew by as I listened intently to their harrowing experiences, which included both physical and mental examples of birth trauma. I was shocked as Neera told me how she'd had a post-partum haemorrhage and lost 7 litres of blood, which went unrecognised as a result of poor communication and a lack of training on symptoms in non-white patients. She shared with me her experience of emergency surgery and five nights in the ICU, with poor aftercare and no follow-up psychological support, which resulted in ongoing physical challenges and post-traumatic stress disorder. Another mother, Chloe, shared with me her story of baby loss, and after listening to so much grief, I unexpectedly burst into tears. I had never cried at work before and I was surprised at the impact that hearing their experiences had on me. They were surprised, but immediately I was offered a hug and I could feel everyone in the room wanting to support each other. I knew I could not ask them to finish until they had all completed sharing their stories, so I refused to leave the room until everyone had had the chance to do so, nearly two hours later.

As we finished the discussion, I asked for the mothers' views on how to improve maternity care, surprised to hear that the BTA was not regularly invited to meet with politicians interested in improving NHS care or to speak directly with health ministers. Their advice for the Prime Minister included increased trauma-informed care, more listening to patients, better access to pain relief, more post-birth services for mums and the use of appropriate language and support for partners. It was clear that there was a postcode lottery across the UK, given their experiences of care appeared to be so different. I sensed that several of the issues they faced were to do with either policy failures within their hospital trusts or a lack of funding or prioritisation by the government. I didn't feel expert enough on the topic to understand all the medical references and terminology they shared with me, but I took copious notes to look it all up later in the library.

Improving maternity care within the NHS seemed such a huge campaign that I didn't know where to begin, but I also knew something had to be done to address the situation. I had no idea where to start and I thought it was unlikely I could make much difference given I was not a minister, but I was prepared to try. I knew the best chance I had was if I could find support across Parliament and, most importantly, from the opposition benches.

CHAPTER EIGHTEEN

RECRUITING UNLIKELY ALLIES

I began to research parliamentarians who had spoken on birth trauma in the House of Commons. I found many references to maternity services, heartbreaking stories of baby loss and miscarriage and many examples of poor postnatal care in different health discussions, but I was surprised not to find a single debate that had been dedicated solely to birth trauma, which in a thousand years of our Parliament seemed extraordinary. The only MP who seemed to have referenced birth injuries in detail was the then Labour politician Rosie Duffield, MP for Canterbury. I came across a debate on perinatal mental illness in 2018 in which she'd spoken, and I was struck by this passage in her speech:

> We do not discuss post-natal truths enough in the UK. Women will sometimes share with their friends the gory details of their experience of giving birth, but we rarely ever see in the print media, on TV, or in films what happens after a baby is born. If the fairy tale does end when Cinderella weds her prince, as most fairy tales do, it most certainly has ended by the time Cinderella has entered her third trimester and is waddling around the palace.

Nobody wants to hear about Cinderella's third-degree tear, the fact that her boobs leak, the possibility that she may experience incontinence, or the fact that, even though she has a wonderful, healthy baby in her arms, she just cannot stop crying. But fairy tales are out of date and so is the fact that we do not talk about perinatal experiences – both external and internal experiences – with the honesty we need.

I'd met Rosie briefly before, due to our work with the National Farmers' Union in support of Back British Farming Day and through campaigning to support our local farmers and tackle food shortages during the pandemic, but I didn't know her well. We'd also spoken on a panel together, back when I was a parliamentary candidate, for the cross-party 50:50 campaign to elect more women. However, Parliament made it hard to build alliances with members from different political parties. Even the tearoom outside the Chamber of the House of Commons, where we ate and drank while waiting to speak in debates or votes, divided us into tables by our political parties. The government's MPs sat at one end beyond the tills and the opposition at the other. It remained unusual to have close friends from across the aisle and the left often viewed us 'nasty Tories' with deep suspicion. I had found it disappointing how often select committees broke down along party lines, which I'd observed at first hand on the Women and Equalities Select Committee. The Chamber had been designed with the central aisle between the two front benches of the government and opposition to be the width of two swords. As a result, we sat opposite each other in rows rather than in a circle as with other countries' parliaments or the United Nations. Our political system was designed to encourage and entrench division, rather than unity and consensus, but I didn't believe that politics should be so tribal.

I texted Rosie to say that she was the only MP I could find who had mentioned a third-degree tear in a debate and asked to meet up with her to discuss birth trauma and speak about potentially doing some campaigning together on this topic. She replied immediately to say she was happy to help and asked if I was OK to talk about my experiences publicly, given how stressful it could be to talk about something so deeply personal in Parliament. I was struck by her concern and knew straight away that she was the right Labour MP to have approached. Her comment also made me realise that I needed to talk about my experience sooner rather than later, so I could create a platform to help other affected women.

We met for a coffee in the glass atrium of Portcullis House. Everyone could see that I was meeting an opposition MP, and I had a few sideways looks as I shared with her my experiences and the reflections of the mothers I had met via the BTA. It was apparent that there was so much we could do together. I knew that I could recruit some Conservative politicians who'd campaigned on related issues such as baby loss, premature babies or mental health support for mothers, but it was essential that we had members of other political parties join us to ensure our campaign had cross-party support, and I was keen to have some male MPs join us too. We agreed to set up a new all-party parliamentary group on birth trauma the following month if we could recruit enough politicians. I offered to deal with any administration from my office and we talked about whether I should do an interview with a national newspaper to share my story and to launch our campaign. I decided to go with *The Times*, which I read every day and I knew could help put birth trauma on the news agenda. I assumed that if they ran my story it would be a tiny piece buried at the back of the paper, given I was only a backbench MP with no national profile.

After my meeting with Rosie, I headed to the Speaker's study for my first ever meeting with Sir Lindsay Hoyle. I had written to him to raise the lack of space in the nursery for Members of Parliament with babies. He agreed to see me and brought with him the head of the parliamentary estate to hear my concerns. I began by thanking him for my proxy vote and explaining what a lifeline it was for new mothers who were MPs. I then told him how ludicrous the current nursery situation was, with MPs not getting precedence to use the baby room and every passholder on the entire parliamentary estate being eligible to apply for a handful of places, and how I had been told that the waiting list was a year. He was struck by my comment that I'd have had to put myself down on the waiting list before I even knew I was having a baby! Lindsay listened intently as I went on to explain how if I'd had Arabella with me in Parliament, I could have picked her up after nursery and taken her with me through the lobby to vote while she was still so young.

My key argument was that the entire reason that Parliament had built a nursery, under the previous Speaker John Bercow, was to help MPs like me with late-night votes and the specific need to be within a few minutes' walk of the division bell. However, the nursery was currently not fit for purpose. The fact was that as MPs, our place of work was unique. By being forced to be separate from our babies due to the lack of nursery provision, it meant that as new mothers we were also being restricted from breastfeeding, which went against the government's own guidance to other workplaces. I told the Speaker that it was hypocritical that our place of work did not offer proper maternity leave or indeed follow any of the directions specified in legislation that businesses had to adopt in support of new mothers. Lindsay was angry and surprised to hear this was the case and, to his credit, asked for the nursery situation to be reviewed. It was too late for Arabella and me, but I hoped that raising the issue would impact positively on the next MP who was a new mother and faced the same issue.

* * *

In the first week of July, the senior political correspondent for *The Times*, Geri Scott, came to my tiny office in Parliament to interview me after I had decided to share my story in the hope that it would kick off my campaign to reduce birth trauma by improving maternity care. It was my first interview with a national newspaper and I was terrified to speak to a journalist with such reach. I was scared to speak about something so deeply personal to me and I worried that I would say something that I would later regret. I was also conscious that anything I said would be read by my daughter when she was older.

When the day came, I was relieved to find Geri to be professional, compassionate and a serious journalist. She pressed record and asked me to tell her what had happened in my own words. For nearly an hour we went through the specifics of my birth and the lack of postnatal care afterwards, and I shared my distressing experience of being in labour, being rushed into emergency surgery and the birth injury I had suffered. I told her about meeting other affected mothers from the Birth Trauma Association and how they had spurred me on to try to make a change. I had no idea if what I said was of much interest. I knew it certainly wasn't breaking news and was unlikely to be a long piece, given the volume of domestic and international issues the newspaper needed to cover and the daily government announcements that dominated the news grid. I mostly felt relieved to have got through the interview without crying, as it felt emotionally distressing to relive the trauma of what had happened to me yet again. There was no guarantee that the editor would run the story, but I hoped that they might on a slow news day.

I woke up that Saturday morning, sleepily turned my telephone on to check whether it was time to feed my daughter and was suddenly bombarded with notifications. It seemed *The Times* had published my story. I turned the light on, opened their app and was stunned to discover my interview on their home page, entitled, 'I was ignored after traumatic birth – no mother should experience that'. I tweeted the article link and announced that the following week we would launch a cross-party birth trauma group in Parliament to help address the issue and to ensure that all mums got the support they need.

I was gobsmacked when the post quickly racked up nearly half a million views and was shared with comments by many other leading politicians. The Labour MP Jess Phillips wrote, 'Had to have a transfusion after my first birth & be placed in intensive care after my second. I agree we should look at how we deal with birth trauma. Like with violence against women I'm always shocked that the amount of trauma women are expected to endure isn't zero.' The chair of the Women and Equalities Select Committee Caroline Nokes wrote that she was 'really pleased to support this new initiative from my colleague', while Penny Mordant shared that 'sometimes the biggest difference you can make is because of something you've been through'. Energy Secretary Claire Coutinho posted that she was proud of me 'for turning her own traumatic experience into a force for good for other mums to be. Important work.'

Many other MPs shared my interview, including multiple members of the Cabinet, and hundreds of comments were posted below my article, with women sharing their experiences of birth trauma or poor maternity care. I was completely overwhelmed at the scale of support. I bought a copy of the newspaper and was surprised to see it had been given a full double-page spread, including a photograph of me with my daughter and husband.

My mobile rang. It was a producer from Radio 4 asking if I would go on *Women's Hour*. I had listened to the flagship radio show for years and knew that they could start a national conversation just by referencing an issue. I could barely believe it. I went to the Broadcasting House studio north of Oxford Street, an imposing building in Portland stone lit up with a huge logo of the BBC, and nervously sat in the green room while having a cup of tea and glancing at the papers. While I was backstage, an assistant came up to me to wish me luck given that I would be speaking to the nation via their millions of listeners. I felt my mouth dry up as I thought what on earth to say on live radio. I was ushered quietly into the studio and sat at a microphone with headphones on while waiting for presenter Nuala McGovern to introduce me. She asked me to share my story, so I tried to be as succinct as possible, stick to the basic facts of my experience and to include my headline message that I was launching a new cross-party campaign on birth trauma in Parliament. The interview, which was less than ten minutes, rushed by and I came out of the studio in a daze, blinking into the daylight. I went back to Parliament, opened my inbox and found that hundreds of emails from affected mothers had streamed in. I had numerous direct messages on social media, text messages from friends and more voicemails from journalists and family. I had opened the floodgates in a way that I'd never anticipated.

The following day, Rosie and I hosted the first meeting of the All-Party Parliamentary Group on Birth Trauma in Parliament, which ten parliamentarians attended from different political parties. They'd seen my story in the news and were keen to support us. One of them was Labour MP Bell Ribeiro-Addy, who I knew had done a huge amount of campaigning to improve black maternal health and who'd talked about the MBRRACE UK statistics that showed black minority ethnic women were at higher risk of maternal deaths. Helen Morgan, my Liberal Democrat constituency neighbour in Shropshire, was another who came as many of her constituents had been affected by the Shrewsbury and Telford NHS Trust scandal. Many of the MPs who supported the all-party parliamentary group (APPG), such as Cherilyn Mackrory and Alison Thewliss, had either personal experience, constituents who had been directly affected or had uncovered scandals at hospital trusts in their respective constituencies. Several male MPs joined us to include the experience of fathers, such as Mark Pawsey, Darren Henry and Luke Hall. I was grateful to all of them for taking the time to attend.

At the meeting, Kim spoke about what birth trauma was and gave us a few key facts alongside Helen Allott, an obstetrician. Rosie and I were delighted by the turnout and that we had recruited a group of politicians who were keen to help reduce birth trauma. Now we had to find something tangible for us all to campaign on to effect change and I was unclear on what that should be. We decided to launch a survey with Mumsnet over the summer recess to hear directly from women who were affected by birth trauma to decide what to focus on.

On 11 September, we unveiled the results in Parliament with Dr Ranee Thakar, the president of the Royal College of Obstetricians and Gynaecologists, and Justine Roberts, the founder of Mumsnet. The results were shocking. More than half of women (53 per cent) who had experienced birth trauma told us that they were less likely to have more children because of their experience. The majority of women who responded had experienced birth trauma, of whom 53 per cent had experienced physical trauma and 71 per cent had experienced psychological or emotional trauma. The answers showed that women felt healthcare professionals had used inappropriate language during birth that implied failure or blame of the mother; women were not receiving enough information ahead of birth, particularly about birth injuries; women experienced a lack of compassion during labour; notes were not being passed on between hospital staff's shifts; women felt unsafe during their birth experience; and women felt that postnatal care was not up to scratch.

I was most surprised to hear that 19 per cent of women had not been offered a six-week check up by their GP and that nearly a fifth of women who experienced perineal tears were not offered a home visit within two weeks of the birth by a health visitor. The mothers surveyed identified that the key changes needed were to be listened to more by healthcare professionals, to be given appropriate and timely pain relief, to be offered a post-birth debrief as standard, to be offered better postnatal support, to be offered trauma-informed care and that partners should be included where appropriate, which corroborated what I'd heard in my first meeting with affected mothers.

This survey, although basic, gave us the information we needed to tailor our campaign. It was clear there were structural problems with NHS policy within maternity care but also that we needed ministers to both prioritise and fund maternal health. The question now was how to get the government's attention. Kim had told me at the APPG meeting that the New South Wales Parliament in Australia were currently conducting an inquiry into birth trauma, which was the first I'd heard of it. This planted the seed of an idea.

CHAPTER NINETEEN

A HISTORIC DEBATE

The vast majority of MPs were older, white men – certainly not young mothers – and I was dismayed at the often casual sexism I witnessed in Parliament. These demographics meant that women's health was rarely discussed in the House of Commons. So I was surprised when my colleague Kevin Foster, the former Home Office minister, kindly suggested to me that I put in for a backbench business debate on birth trauma. He'd seen my personal story in the papers and reached out to me, recommending that if I could find enough cross-party supporters I could pitch to the parliamentary committee for Chamber time. I decided to put an application in before we broke for summer recess, so that I might get a slot after party conference season. My APPG co-chair Rosie Duffield was my first signature and between us we drummed up the necessary number of parliamentarians. My pitch was simple: in a thousand years of parliamentary history we had never held a dedicated birth trauma debate and it was time that we did. I hoped that by choosing a substantive motion, with a potential division to vote, the committee would be more likely to upgrade my debate from Westminster Hall to the main Chamber.

I had to wait several months before they announced that I'd been selected and that the topic of birth trauma was finally to be debated on Thursday 19 October 2023, a timely coincidence as it came just after Baby Loss Awareness Week. I was elated that the topic had been chosen, but I was also frustrated that the debate would clash with two by-elections, such as in Bedfordshire where former minister Nadine Dorries had recently resigned. I was concerned that not many MPs would come along to attend our debate, given that Thursdays were always quiet and that the elections meant that very few colleagues would be on the parliamentary estate on the day, so I wrote personal letters to anyone who had supported my campaign to ask them to attend.

I spent several days reading about birth trauma and reviewing stories that the Birth Trauma Association had sent me from several mothers before writing my speech. It was the first debate I'd ever led in Parliament, and I knew that this speech would also be the most important and personal one that I would ever give in the Chamber. My motion called on the government to 'take steps to support women experiencing birth trauma'. During my preparation, I also met with leading midwife Donna Ockenden, who was investigating the failures in maternity care at different hospital trusts, to hear more about the concerns of the families she had seen. A few of the groups I'd reached out to and started engaging with, such as the BTA, MASIC, Maternal Mental Health Alliance, Make Birth Better and Mumsnet, also supported me with briefings and first-hand testimony.

So many women had written to me from across the country since I'd spoken about my own experience of birth trauma that I felt under pressure to represent them all and ensure that their views were heard by the government. I took the time to read all of their

A HISTORIC DEBATE

harrowing stories, and I was impressed at how courageous they'd all been in sharing their experiences with me. I decided that I would do my best to try to change government policy and improve NHS care. I knew this would be very difficult, but if nothing else then I could at least raise awareness of birth trauma in the debate.

When I went into the Chamber to open the debate, I looked up and saw around thirty mothers sat in the gallery with my husband, all facing the green benches, which added to my nerves. I felt the weight of their expectations and I was concerned as to whether I could deliver anything for them, given that I was not a minister in the government. The public perhaps didn't realise how little influence I had as a new MP and backbencher, but nevertheless, I endeavoured to use my voice to advocate for them as best as I could. Several female colleagues came to sit in the Chamber around me and I was very grateful for their support, especially from Cherilyn Mackrory, then MP for Truro & Falmouth, who'd led the APPG on baby loss and had given a similar speech about her own difficult experiences. She had provided me with a lot of advice.

The House of Commons was an intimidating place to speak, as the Chamber was surprisingly small and intimate. I tended to sit on the fourth row, in line with the government minister so that they could hear me clearly at the despatch box, but never on the end as there was an unspoken rule that this space was always to be reserved for former PM Theresa May. Microphones hung down above me, and above the Speaker's chair I could see lobby journalists and Hansard about to transcribe everything I said, which was to be on record for ever. The BBC were also filming the debate in case they could clip anything interesting for that day's news. I had never felt so many eyes watching me as I started to speak. My voice wavered as I introduced the debate but slowly grew in confidence. I felt ready and prepared. I had edited my speech multiple times and I was happy with my policy recommendations to the minister on how to effect positive change.

I began to share my personal story of birth trauma. What I hadn't taken into account was how recounting my birth trauma in the Chamber would affect me emotionally. I began to describe what had happened to me while giving birth to Arabella. I described my difficult labour, post-partum haemorrhage, being rushed into surgery, being separated from my daughter and lying on the operating table awake. I shared that it had been the most terrifying moment of my life and that I had thought I was going to die. Suddenly, I burst into tears. It was completely unexpected and I was shocked when it happened. I had always been a very professional person and that I might cry in public, let alone in my place of work, was a total surprise to me. I had given birth over a year before, but the trauma still remained with me after all this time.

I felt relieved when Dame Andrea Leadsom, who was in the Chamber to listen to my debate, stood up to interrupt me, as it gave me a chance to sit down, attempt to calm down and catch my breath. She congratulated me for talking about such a difficult topic and said how important it was that we discussed the terrible experiences that mothers could have. One of my colleagues got me a glass of water and I took a deep breath. I got back on my feet and thanked Andrea for her work on the Start for Life programme where, as the previous relevant minister, she'd led so much of the brilliant work in government for children under two. I continued my story, sharing the aftercare I had received when I suffered a third-degree tear and setting out some key statistics about birth trauma. I managed to get through the next twenty minutes and highlight challenges in maternity care, including several stories of other mothers. I finished with my headline asks for safe levels of staffing in maternity care and for the government to add birth trauma into the women's health strategy.

I made sure to set out some clear requests that the Government could action or respond to, which included recruiting more midwives; ensuring perinatal mental health services were available across the UK; ensuring that a postnatal check-up at six weeks was provided to all mothers by their GP, which would include separate questions on the mother's physical and mental health; improving continuity of care and better communication between secondary and primary healthcare; providing post-birth services nationally, such as birth reflections, to give mothers a safe space to speak about their experiences in childbirth; rolling out the obstetric and anal sphincter injury care (OASI) bundle to all hospital trusts in England to reduce the risk of injuries in childbirth; better support for partners and fathers; and better education for women on their birth choices and risks in order to ensure informed consent. I sat down, both shaken and relieved, and hoped that I'd done enough to persuade the minister that more needed to be done to support women with traumatic births.

I heard the sound of clapping in the Chamber, and when I looked up, I saw that the mothers who'd come to watch the debate had stood up in spontaneous applause. I was very embarrassed and turned red, especially as there was a convention in Parliament not to applaud. The deputy Speaker stood up and firmly asked them all to sit back down, but I could see that she was moved by their response to my speech.

The debate continued with colleagues from different parties, led by Rosie. She gave a compassionate speech about how birth trauma affected her constituents in Kent, local failings in her hospital and her cross-party work with me on the APPG. I was surprised to see two male MPs join the debate and support the motion: Jim Shannon from the DUP and Douglas Ross, a Scottish MP who I didn't know personally. Helen Morgan gave an impassioned speech about her experience of being induced and having an emergency Caesarean. And finally, Cherilyn Mackrory gave a powerful speech about baby loss and her own experience of a stillbirth, which was heartbreaking. It struck me while listening to their speeches how every MP was passionate, supportive and, most unusually, that the debate appeared to have cross-party consensus. In my entire time as an MP, I had never before seen parliamentarians abandon their party lines and come together unanimously on a single issue. It was a powerful and striking moment. The opposition spokesperson for the SNP agreed that we needed to do more to help women affected by birth trauma and the Labour shadow Women's Health Minister welcomed my speech and expressed her admiration of me for sharing my story.

All eyes were now on the government minister. We had been in the Chamber debating the issue for several hours, but this was the key moment. Had we done anything to change the government's mind and persuade them to take this issue more seriously? The Parliamentary Under-Secretary for Health and Social Care, Maria Caulfield, stood up and I held my breath. Before the debate, Maria had met with me several times to go through my policy asks and to hear more about the experiences of mothers who had written to me, but even then she wouldn't commit to anything. She began by thanking everyone who had shared their personal stories. By the time she had personally named each speaker in the Chamber and summed up their contributions, the clock was running down and there was limited time left to hear what the Department of Health and Social Care was going to do about birth trauma, if anything. Finally, towards the end of her speech, she updated us on the progress and commitments the government would make to improve outcomes in maternity care.

I breathed a sigh of relief as she agreed with the importance of preventing perineal trauma in childbirth. But what was she going to do about it? Then she announced that NHS England would that week publish a national service specification for perinatal pelvic health services, which would be rolled across England by March 2024 to end the postcode lottery in service provision. I inwardly cheered when she committed that NHS England would implement the OASI care bundle developed by the Royal College of Obstetricians and Gynaecologists and the Royal College of Midwives.

Maria continued:

> Getting the specification rolled out across the country is an early success for the APPG. I am confident that this new guidance, which will be implemented across maternity units, will reduce the rate of anal sphincter injuries resulting from labour and vaginal births and help to manage such injuries in a much better way when they happen.

She went on to explain how the introduction of these services would broaden the core service offer of pelvic health beyond the existing guidance on care for obstetric and sphincter injuries. I listened and tried to translate everything the minister said in my head into normal English. What she meant was that women like me who'd suffered a birth injury would now get more treatment options and that all pregnant women would get the advice and support they needed to prevent and identify pelvic health problems. I was amazed and delighted. In the nearly four years as an MP that I'd previously lobbied the government, I had never been able to effect change on a policy before. My personal story and my campaigning had finally struck a chord and the minister had announced a change to NHS policy. I suddenly realised what a huge moment this was for our cross-party campaign.

I came out of the Chamber and found that a video clip of me breaking down in tears in the House of Commons had been posted by BBC Politics on Twitter. Suddenly, it was all over social media. It seemed I had broken a taboo by speaking about my traumatic birth so publicly. It was striking how many people messaged me to say that they didn't feel able to talk about it but thanked me for doing so on their behalf. I hugged Henry and the many women who had come to watch the debate. The APPG had shown we could make a difference, but there were many more battles ahead and the government had not yet committed to any of our other key asks. I knew this was not the end but only the beginning of a much longer campaign.

CHAPTER TWENTY

RESHUFFLE

I knew something was up when, on Monday 13 November, I saw footage of former Prime Minister David Cameron arriving outside No. 10. The previous week had been a busy one in Westminster, with the state opening of Parliament, and I was as surprised as the public when the Prime Minister had suddenly reshuffled his team. I had assumed Rishi would do so in a year's time, when we were much nearer a general election, in order to unveil his final team. Downing Street announced that our former PM had made an astonishing comeback as Foreign Secretary and that Suella Braveman had been finally shown the door and replaced by James Cleverly, who would be a less strident Home Secretary. Several of Liz Truss's allies were also let go as Rishi shook up his top team.

I no longer sat waiting for the telephone to ring during reshuffles, as it never did, so instead I watched the trickle of announcements. I was very pleased to see David back at the Foreign Office and the newly elevated Vicky Atkins moved to the Department of Health and Social Care. I thought it could be a huge opportunity for my birth trauma campaign, given that she was a female Health Secretary.

I knew David a little from my time as director of Conservative Friends of International Development and from when I had cheekily asked him to help me prep for my seat selection in Stafford, as he'd stood there as a parliamentary candidate in the 1997 general election before being elected in Witney in 2001. I had visited his home in London, where he'd helped me prepare my selection speech and some answers to tricky questions on local issues, such as HS2. He'd also launched my campaign to be the next MP for Stafford and spoken at an election fundraiser for me at my mother's house. I hugely respected David and I'd joined the party under his leadership, as I believed in his brand of conservatism. I was delighted that our new PM seemed to be bringing back the moderates of our party and distancing himself from the aggressive and right-wing rhetoric of previous ministers on the subjects of immigration, homelessness and policing, many of whom I did not agree with and whose policies I had refused to publicly defend.

November became another busy month. I briefed the International Trade Minister about my recent trip to Kenya for the department, attended a roundtable with the Chancellor Jeremy Hunt and other Midlands MPs, brought the Farming Minister to the English Winter Fair in Stafford and continued to look for opportunities to raise the issue of maternity care in the Chamber. I also found myself bobbing again at Prime Minister's Questions and trying to catch the Speaker's eye. I had written to the Prime Minister's PPS and told him in advance what I wanted to ask, as I knew that a British Prime Minister had never mentioned birth trauma in the House of Commons so this was a huge opportunity to try to get him on the record for the first time. I used the hook of my recent debate and the fact that so many mothers had written to me to ask the PM to meet with me urgently to discuss the issue and to specifically add birth trauma to the refreshed update to the women's health strategy. The Speaker called me, and the Prime Minister stood at the wooden despatch box and responded to my question:

> I thank my Hon. Friend for raising this important issue and for continuing to be a fantastic campaigner on birth trauma. I am pleased that the first ever debate in Parliament was held recently, in October. It was powerful and moving, and it highlighted the significant impact that birth trauma can have on so many women's lives. The Department of Health and Social Care is working with NHS England to make sure we improve maternity care and related mental health care. I will ensure the Health Secretary meets with my hon. Friend so that we can get this right for all the women who are depending on it.

I wasn't expecting him to agree to meet with me and my question was more of a tactic to meet the new Health Secretary on this issue and get birth trauma on her radar early on into her new role, so I was pleased with his answer in general. His words were an important win for the campaign and it was humbling how many mothers emailed myself and Rosie after having seen the question on television, touched to see the Prime Minister acknowledge birth trauma and validate their experiences for the first time.

On top of my healthcare campaigning, I continued to champion local issues in my constituency. My main pledge during the election had been funding to level up Stafford, so I had constantly lobbied the Department for Levelling Up, Housing and Communities for the Stafford Station Gateway project, which was a huge £20 million funding bid. I was thrilled when Michael Gove's special adviser called me to say the Secretary of State was going to come to my constituency to announce round three of the Levelling Up Fund allocations. Stafford had finally been successful and would be showcased as the flagship bid. It was Friday and he was coming on Monday morning to the Midlands to see for himself how the multi-million-pound project would impact on our county town. My husband looked after Arabella so I could do the visit without a screaming toddler accompanying me. I knew Michael reasonably well and thought we had always got on. I rated him as one of our most competent Cabinet ministers and felt that he was always courteous and helpful to colleagues and always on top of his brief. I remembered how he had supported me back in Bristol East and had come door-knocking with me as a parliamentary candidate many years earlier.

We met on a cold, windy morning at the brownfield site on the edge of a busy road behind the railway line in Stafford. Michael made me laugh when he did a back-to-back media round and at the start of every interview thanked me as the local MP and congratulated me for securing the funding. I could see the new Labour council leader, who I'd obtained the money for, squirm each time Michael namechecked me and gave me credit. The project would not be complete until 2040, and I didn't plan on being an MP for that long, but I knew it would help to make Stafford a better place to live and work. I was particularly pleased that Stafford College had got government funding to open a new Institute of Technology, which would be partly built on the gateway site along with partner businesses, as I had championed the project from conception. It was a rare good day and I felt pleased to have genuinely made a difference in my constituency.

* * *

It took nearly two weeks for the government reshuffle to conclude. I'd lost track of the more junior appointments, as I'd been focusing more on my own parliamentary and constituency work. It was therefore a surprise when the deputy Chief Whip called me and offered to move me to be parliamentary private secretary to the Justice Secretary. Even though it was a small promotion, as I'd be working directly for the Cabinet minister, I told him I'd prefer to remain working for Kemi on international issues at Business and Trade. He was taken aback that I didn't automatically accept, but I felt like I didn't know anything about the policy area and my few visits to HMP Stafford had opened my eyes to how challenging prison reform was. This time I did not say no as a negotiating ploy, but regardless, he called me back a few hours later with a different offer. Did I want to join Chancellor Jeremy Hunt's team at the Treasury? I would work directly for his ministers, attend the Chancellor's weekly meetings with the team at No. 11 and join them in the important months of negotiations leading up to our final Budget, where I would see at first hand decisions being made and the submissions to his red box for his comments or sign-off.

I was stunned. The Treasury was the department I had been least likely to join, given my lack of expertise in economic policy, but it was a huge opportunity. Almost every PPS to the Treasury had become a government minister in the following reshuffle and I secretly hoped that this finally meant the Whips' Office had an eye on me for future promotions. I knew it was an offer I couldn't refuse, but I was conscious I didn't want to let Kemi down, so I texted her to be upfront about the situation. She replied to congratulate me on my excellent negotiating skills and that she was pleased to see me going from strength to strength. I was relieved that she was not annoyed with me and I was also happy to follow my current minister, Nigel Huddleston, from Business and Trade to the Treasury.

I walked to Downing Street to pick up my new security pass, waiting for the iconic black door to open and feeling nervous in case it didn't and I was left in front of the cameras on the doorstep of No. 10, which famously had no doorbell to ring. I handed in my mobile phone and attended my first political meeting with the Chancellor. I was introduced to his private office and special advisers, and we debriefed on the response to the recent Autumn Statement. His team included the Chief Secretary to the Treasury, the Financial Secretary, Exchequer Secretary and Economic Secretary, plus his other two parliamentary private secretaries. I could tell that my new department was going to be far busier, given the number of ministers in the Treasury team and the importance of the final Budget ahead of a general election, but I was excited to start a new role. In the back of my mind, I hoped it wouldn't mean that I had to spend longer evenings at work or attend more Fridays in Parliament, as I liked to get back to my constituency each week and I didn't want to eat any more into my already precious and limited time at home with my family. I was also conscious that my birth trauma campaign was increasingly taking up more of my diary, as I learnt more about the issue and spent time replying to families who were sending me their stories.

* * *

I had received hundreds of emails, letters and messages on social media from mothers who shared with me their experiences of birth trauma, after I had spoken about my own experiences and led the parliamentary debate. The response was amazing, but I also found it triggering to read so many stories of birth trauma. I was not a trained healthcare professional and I had been struggling to process my own trauma. Mentally, I felt unprepared to read the deluge of horrific experiences that I had been sent, but I also felt a responsibility to do so after they had so bravely written to me. I had previously been referred to the Lotus service in Staffordshire for psychological support and I began to realise I might need to contact them for further mental health support. When the NHS sent me my regular cervical smear test letter, my first thought was to put it in the bin, as the thought of having another invasive vaginal examination was too much for me. I realised that I still had a long way to go with my own recovery, so I decided to contact Lotus and ask for additional help. I finally felt ready to speak to an expert about my OCD symptoms and the levels of anxiety I felt all the time, which had become the background hum to my life and were being amplified by the intensity of my job and further exacerbated by being separated from my daughter.

My therapist arranged to speak to me on Zoom – a legacy of Covid and presumably budget cuts that meant we sadly never got to meet in person – and I spoke to her for several weeks in a row. I'd book a session during Prime Minister's Questions and take the call from my parliamentary office, as I felt it was the only safe hour in the entire week when I wouldn't have to cancel at short notice, given everyone was always busy listening to what the PM had to say. I was sceptical when she suggested trying eye movement desensitisation and reprocessing (EMDR) as a form of psychotherapy, especially as I'd heard it was a therapy best known for treating post-traumatic stress disorder (PTSD), which I was still convinced that I didn't have. She told me that using the side-to-side eye movements, combined with talking therapy, would help me to process and recover from the traumatic experiences I'd experienced during childbirth.

I still suffered from OCD tendencies and intrusive thoughts, although they had lessened over time. I had significant flashbacks and nightmares of the hospital and I'd often wake up with my hand throbbing from the cannula, even though I was safe in bed at home. I also had huge blanks in my memories about my extended time in surgery, although I had been wide awake. Despite these gaps in my memory, I would still relive the terror I had felt on the operating table.

In our therapy sessions, I watched my white computer screen as a black ball, similar to a pinball in old computer games, bounced across my vision and my therapist asked me to focus on a specific memory, such as having the epidural injection. I flicked my eyes from side to side and followed the black dot as I tried to remember the emotions and bodily sensations from the time that my traumatic events occurred.

I thought the therapy wasn't working until, out of the blue, I burst into hysterical tears at my desk. Memories of my daughter being taken from me flooded back and I was filled with such intense grief that it made me sob. I remembered how I believed that my baby had died as no one had taken the time to update me on where she was for hours after I gave birth. EMDR made me relive the memory, but it also helped me to process and archive it so that it became less negative and traumatic. It was almost like I was watching myself on a DVD, or sometimes looking down on myself from above at a distance, rather than being the person to whom the trauma was occurring. I was finally removed from the event and no longer processing it in real time, as if the trauma was still happening to me.

I had thought I was fine until we started the therapy appointments, but it became clear that the traumatic memories had been buried deep within my psyche, which explained much of my hyper anxiety and agitation. The therapy helped me to store traumatic memories again so that I knew they were now in the past and not the present. After weeks of this, I felt better able to process my own experiences and I noticed that my OCD symptoms had significantly reduced. I remained neater and tidier than before my traumatic birth, but I was no longer distressed by mess in the way that I had been in those early days. I felt that I could now better focus on helping the women and families who had written to me asking for my help.

I had my meeting with the new Health Secretary, Vicky Atkins, who met me in her private office in Parliament and listened intently to my story, the examples I shared from the harrowing letters I'd received from mothers and the huge public response to my recent debate. I handed her the list of requests from my speech and she took the time to go through each one. I could tell that although she was new to our specific asks on birth trauma, she seemed genuinely interested in improving maternity care, in contrast to her predecessor. This was a relief, and I pushed heavily for her to add birth trauma to her updated priorities for the upcoming Women's Health Summit in January. She told me she would see what she could do and I believed her, though I knew how many simultaneous requests she was receiving from every other area of health policy.

Despite my positive feelings about the meeting, there was still no firm commitment from her and so I needed to find a way to keep the pressure up publicly for Vicky to agree to prioritise birth trauma. I set up a Zoom call with Australian MP Emma Hurst, who was chairing the New South Wales Parliament inquiry into birth trauma, and I began to properly formulate the idea for an equivalent in the UK. I also met with Dame Lesley Regan, Women's Health Ambassador, to ask her to simultaneously prioritise birth trauma in the government's women's health strategy.

In late November, I was honoured to attend my first formal dinner at the Royal College of Obstetricians and Gynaecologists in south London, having been invited by their president, Ranee Thakar. I was invited along with the shadow Women's Health Minister Abena Oppong-Asare, who had responded on behalf of Labour in my birth trauma debate. It felt strange to be sat with so many senior clinicians who had spent their entire career working on these issues and were real experts in their field. As a politician, I had always been more of a generalist.

I also received an invitation to *The Spectator*'s annual Parliamentarian of the Year Awards at the Rosewood Hotel. It was unusual for Henry and me to attend a midweek black-tie dinner and I was surprised to be asked as a backbench MP. I spotted many colleagues, including the Home Secretary, Energy Secretary and Chief Whip, as they worked the room with senior journalists and donors. Former Chancellor Sajid Javid was master of ceremonies and introduced the winners, who were all seasoned, high-profile politicians, predominately Cabinet ministers, such as Grant Shapps, Gillian Keegan, Wes Streeting and Harriet Harman.

It was a fun evening, and I was enjoying an unusual night out with delicious food. We had just got to dessert when editor of *The Spectator* Fraser Nelson went on stage and began to read out a description for the next category. I finished speaking to my next-door table guest and began to tune into what he was saying, which was about maternity. I was interested to know who else was campaigning on this issue, as they would be a good recruit for our APPG. I was shocked when Fraser read out my name and announced that I had won Political Speech of the Year for my birth trauma debate. *The Spectator* hadn't told me I had even been nominated, let alone won. My heart pounded and I was incredibly nervous as I made my way up on stage to accept my award and say a few words in front of so many famous guests. Disconcertingly, I could see the most well-known political print and television correspondents from the infamous lobby sat in front of me, including Andrew Neil, Nick Robinson and Emily Maitlis. I was honoured and delighted to have raised the profile of my birth trauma campaign in a room full of so many of the great and good of British politics, which could only be helpful to our cause.

* * *

One day, my colleague Darren Henry came to see me to discuss a case he'd come across in a surgery appointment, which concerned the awful story of his constituent losing their partner during childbirth. I nearly cried hearing the story of a new dad being left with a tiny baby when the mother had sadly died. Darren explained that shared parental leave and pay was not applicable in the unusual scenario of the death of one of the parents and as a result, the father couldn't take the full amount of parental leave that otherwise would have been available even though he was now the sole parent. He wanted to present a ten-minute rule bill, 'Shared Parental Leave and Pay (Bereavement)', to make a small change to the law. The Labour MP Chris Elmore had also presented a private members' bill on the same topic and he asked if I would support them both. I immediately agreed to try to amend the law on shared parental leave for those facing such a life-altering set of circumstances. It didn't seem right that his constituent did not qualify for parental leave after the agonising situation of losing his partner and having to raise their child alone. It was also good to see MPs from different political parties supporting the issue. It was clear to me that to get anything done in Parliament, it was hugely helpful to have cross-party consensus, and I was proud to support the bill and help to make changes on this important issue.

It was this experience that crystallised in my mind the fact that, despite being only backbenchers, we could make small, meaningful changes that could genuinely impact people's lives if we focused on what we tried to do. It was time to do something bigger with our all-party parliamentary group. My idea now fully formed, I floated the idea of running a birth trauma inquiry in the UK to the APPG and proposed to Rosie that she could co-chair it with me. I was delighted when she agreed, but she also flagged the huge amount of work that undertaking an inquiry would mean. So, we also met with Kim to discuss how the Birth Trauma Association could potentially provide support and began to make a list of other birth-related charities and experts to involve early on.

Normally, an inquiry of this size would be run by clerks if it was undertaken by a select committee in Parliament. We had no such resources, so instead we convened a group of stakeholders to be a special advisory group, led by the BTA as our secretariat, and asked them to suggest ideas for evidence sessions, key people to be witnesses and draft terms of reference for the inquiry. These meetings were invaluable in allowing different groups either involved with maternity campaigning or delivering frontline services to have input into the inquiry and ensure it was comprehensive and wide ranging. We wanted to hear from as many people as possible so we decided to launch a public call for evidence in the new year. I hoped that doing this would also put pressure on the new Health Secretary to take our recent meeting seriously and prioritise birth trauma in the women's health strategy.

CHAPTER TWENTY-ONE

DEFYING THE PRIME MINISTER

As I focused on preparations for the Birth Trauma Inquiry, I was also acutely aware of upcoming contentious votes in Parliament. I put in for a slip request to be abroad as part of the International Development Select Committee's visit to see our aid programme in action overseas to ensure value for taxpayers, and I hoped that the Whips' Office would allow me to therefore miss the upcoming vote on the Safety of Rwanda (Asylum and Immigration) Bill. On Friday 8 December, I spoke at the Kenyan Jamhuri Day reception at Lancaster House to celebrate the sixtieth anniversary of Kenya's independence. On my way, I texted the Chief Whip:

> Hi Chief, I voted for the PM in the leadership election and I have always supported him when he's asked me to. I have also never voted against the government ever on a three-line whip. However, I'm afraid I will not be voting for the Rwanda Bill and I understand the consequences of doing so. This bill is not going to pass and I'm ashamed it has been put forward by this government.

He replied and asked me to immediately come to his office, and I replied to say no but that the Prime Minister could call me over the weekend. I headed up to Stafford and attended the annual St Mary's Christmas Tree Festival and went canvassing in Gnosall, pushing Arabella in her pram across the rural town that would join the Stafford constituency once boundary changes had been implemented. The deputy Chief Whip called me when I got home to ask me to support the Rwanda bill. I also politely told him no, as I believed that we were breaking international law. My view was that we were losing our moral compass as both a government and a party. The controversial legislation condemned itself on its front page, where the Home Secretary James Cleverly had written, 'I am unable to make a statement that, in my view, the provisions of the Safety of Rwanda (Asylum and Immigration) Bill are compatible with the Convention rights, but the Government nevertheless wishes the House to proceed with the Bill.' I reminded the deputy that I had my bags packed to fly out on my international trip the following day, which meant I could still the miss the vote, scheduled for while I was away, if they gave me permission to go.

A few hours later, the new Foreign Secretary also rang me. David opened by telling me that he had heard coverage of my birth trauma debate while listening to Radio 4. He listened to my legitimate concerns, then asked me to change my mind and support the government. He asked me not to resign as PPS to the Treasury or defy the three-line whip, reminded me how the PM was doing a difficult job in an impossible time and asked me not to risk destabilising him when Suella Braverman and others were already doing so. I hugely admired and rated David, but I told him that I couldn't give my support to the legislation. I requested again that the Prime Minister call or meet me to hear my concerns, given it was his flagship legislation.

Telephone calls from the Whips' Office intensified, and the whips became increasingly angry with me as I refused to budge. They seemed to be keeping Rishi in an ivory tower to prevent him from hearing from disgruntled colleagues. I'd previously had disagreements with Boris as leader, but he took the time to have the difficult conversations on votes and would pick up the telephone to call me on a tricky vote or invite concerned colleagues into his office to discuss controversial issues, such as HS2. I was told my permission slip had not been granted and therefore my attendance on the overseas trip was now cancelled. Multiple MPs on the committee began to hear the same news from their whips, as the government began to realise how tight the Rwanda vote was becoming. One by one, we began to drop out of the international visit. With one day's notice, our committee's week-long visit was postponed, even though it had already been organised by our embassy and important meetings set up with senior international government ministers and field visits hosted by local NGOs. Instead of heading to Heathrow that Sunday, I went to the Stafford Conservatives' Christmas lunch and weighed up my options. I was increasingly annoyed with the government's approach, and I began to seriously consider resigning my position after only one month at the Treasury.

On Monday, I headed back to London and attended the One Nation caucus meeting with our chair Damian Green. I was shocked at how the right of the party had hijacked media coverage of the bill to try to bounce colleagues into supporting it. I spoke in the meeting about my frustration and anger at the government and I was surprised, given how many of my centrist colleagues felt the same, that they were not prepared to speak out – with the exception of former Justice Secretary Sir Robert Buckland, who was outraged and tried to persuade our group to collectively oppose the bill.

The next day, I had a pre-planned coffee with Sajid Javid for some advice on being a PPS in the Treasury. I had known the former Chancellor for nearly a decade, since my first campaign as a new candidate in the safe Labour seat of Bristol East where he'd come to door-knock for me. He'd also hosted my general election campaign launch with my supporters back in 2017. I'd asked him if he wanted to cancel given that I might not be in the position only a few hours later, but he said no. We sat and had tea in his parliamentary office and talked through my options, and I found his advice helpful and clear. I had to do what was right for me and my conscience, as I would have to live with my voting record and stand by it, but he pointed out the consequences of not supporting the government on their flagship issue. I began to realise the impact that defying the Prime Minister might have on my lobbying for local issues in Stafford and ahead of the launch of the Birth Trauma Inquiry. I said I was still waiting to see the PM and speak to him before the vote that evening before making a final decision but that I couldn't currently see myself supporting the bill.

It was now teatime on Tuesday 12 December and the vote on the second reading of the Safety of Rwanda Bill was in a few hours' time at 7 p.m. I had requested the Whips' Office multiple times now to be slipped or paired and therefore miss the vote, but I'd heard nothing back. Then the Chancellor Jeremy Hunt texted and asked to speak to me. I had always rated Jeremy as a minister and found him a kind, affable and capable colleague who I was happy to work for in the Treasury. So, I regret now that I replied to say that I would speak only to the PM, which offended him deeply given he was my boss. Jeremy was not aware that I'd received numerous threatening telephone calls that alluded to the fact that I might lose the Conservative whip and be expelled from the party and that I'd been asking for five days to speak to Rishi. I had written my resignation letter and kept it with me at all times in case the PM asked to see me.

By now, I was angry at how our leader seemed to refuse to engage on challenging issues where colleagues might oppose him. Finally, at around 5 p.m., I received a message asking me to come to the Prime Minister's office in Parliament behind the Chamber. I was very nervous about going to see him in person to tell him to his face that I couldn't support him, but I wanted to give him the opportunity to change my mind if he could and felt that I owed him that, at least, before I likely ended my political career. I had learnt during my brief time as an MP that success in politics was more about loyalty than competence and it didn't matter how much work I had done to support my constituents, deliver for the government as trade envoy, contribute in the Chamber or on select committees if ultimately I did not support the government in all votes. Now that I seriously planned to break a three-line whip on government business, I was taking a huge risk.

I went into the PM's wooden-panelled office decorated with silk wallpaper, portraits of old men who looked down on us, a large mahogany dining room table and green leather chairs embossed with the Portcullis logo. I sat down on the sofa opposite him where I could see some of his advisers in the corner, including Will Tanner and his parliamentary private secretary Craig Williams, his main gatekeeper, who I'd privately nicknamed Falstaff as he reminded me of Shakespeare's character in Henry V.

The Prime Minister got straight to the point and told me that remaining a member of his government was not compatible with not supporting him on Rwanda. Rishi looked extremely agitated and tired, and his remarks sounded rehearsed as he had clearly had the same conversation multiple times. As a backbencher, I was likely one of the last to have had a meeting with him and it was clear he was reaching the end of his patience. I pointed out to him that I was one of the few Conservative MPs who'd been to Rwanda multiple times and I didn't believe it was a safe country. I also repeated my belief that we were breaking international law. I reminded him that I had voted for him in the leadership contest and that I had never ever voted against the government. I asked him how he could ask me to vote for the bill when the Supreme Court had just ruled the previous month that the policy was unlawful. I thought he was going through with the bill to appease the right of the party and to bring back voters considering supporting Reform UK. Robert Jenrick had only the week before quit as Immigration Minister for opposing reasons to me, as he wanted the bill to go further in setting aside human rights law.

I put my resignation letter on the table so Rishi could see that the envelope was addressed to him. The bill did not represent the values of the Conservative Party I believed in and had spent over a decade and a half supporting and the Prime Minister's answers did not convince me. I looked him in the eye and thought that he did not sound or look like he believed in his own legislation. With a heavy heart, I told him that I could not support the bill and would be voting against the government. He urged me to reconsider, but my mind was made up and I clenched my fists to remain calm as I fought back tears. He asked me not to resign publicly to avoid causing damage to the party, so in good faith I took my letter with me on the way out. I felt it was safer not to be on the estate when the division bell rang, in case colleagues tried to frogmarch me to the lobby as had occurred during the fracking debacle.

I was furious with the government for putting me in this position in the first place, especially given the Rwanda policy was never in our manifesto and it was clear from legal challenges that the supposed flights to remove asylum seekers to a small country in east Africa would never take off. I believed it was only a marketing ploy to show that we were tackling immigration and attempting to 'stop the boats' when we couldn't actually deliver on the reduction in numbers the public wanted, and I wanted no part of the flawed, illegal policy. I was hugely disappointed and I realised then that Rishi was more suited to senior management than the political leadership required to hold our fractious party together. We no longer seemed to have a clear vision of what the Conservative Party stood for anymore and how we were going to improve people's lives. I was deeply depressed as I rang my husband to tell him what had happened.

I had already left Westminster when, out of the blue and less than an hour before the vote, I received a text from the Whips' Office to tell me, 'Please note you are paired for the duration of today. Please do not vote under any circumstances during this time.' I was confused but thankful that I had unexpectedly been excused at the last minute. It seemed the government had finally realised that I was serious and not bluffing. It was a huge relief that I would no longer have to resign for doing the right thing, and perhaps I could keep my job after all. I went home to do bath and bedtime with Arabella, which was an infrequent occasion on a Tuesday evening. I heard nothing more from the Whips' Office and the vote passed, with the number of rebels disappointingly low. Our working majority was fifty-six, so if only twenty-nine of us had voted against the bill then it would have failed.

The next day, I saw the Chancellor in the tearoom after Prime Minister's Questions and I went up to him and apologised for my rude behaviour. I was embarrassed to have to do so but knew it was the right thing to do. Jeremy still looked annoyed with me, but I think he appreciated my apology. Given I had been paired for the previous night's vote and I'd heard nothing to the contrary, I attended my usual Treasury meetings, sat in the Chamber to cover the minister for the second reading of the Finance Bill and headed over to Downing Street for our Christmas drinks reception for Conservative MPs. A few colleagues asked me what had happened about the vote, given my concerns, and I told them I'd been paired. They were happy to hear that the issue had been resolved.

However, the next morning the Chief Whip Simon Hart left me a voicemail asking me to come to see him. I dropped everything and went straight to his study in a narrow corridor near the Chamber. He did not bother with niceties and got straight to the point: I was to be fired by the Prime Minister for failing to support the government on a three-line whipped vote. Furthermore, he told me that the Chancellor no longer had confidence in me, given that I was parliamentary private secretary at the Treasury and had refused to vote for the government's flagship immigration bill. I was outraged and pointed out that I had been paired by the Whips' Office before the vote, showing him the text message on my phone. He was nonplussed and refused to budge.

I could see straight away how he had outmanoeuvred me. He had no plans to slip me for the vote but only wanted to prevent me resigning ahead of it and therefore publishing my resignation letter publicly, given it would likely have made the news. He told me that the Prime Minister had made up his mind. There were consequences to my behaviour and I was considered a member of the payroll, even though I was unpaid, and therefore by default it was essential that I upheld collective responsibility, even though I was not a government minister. He had snookered me and I saw then that I should have resigned on the day since I had been fired by the PM regardless.

However, I still had one card left to play. I threatened to share on social media that I had been fired for refusing to vote for the Rwanda Bill and to publish my resignation letter, dated ahead of the vote, which I had taken to my meeting with Rishi. Simon looked at me and recalculated his position, not expecting me to fight back so hard. I asked to move to a different department, given the Chancellor's personal views about my behaviour towards him and my failure to support government policy, but he said no. I countered with retaining my role as trade envoy to Kenya. He was surprised, but I could see him consider this middle option to try to resolve our impasse. I pushed him, pointing out how I had done the role for three years under two Prime Ministers and reminding him that I had built a large number of relationships for the government and we were midway through organising the UK-Africa Investment Summit in March, which the Kenyan President had agreed to attend. He was visibly annoyed with me but also recognised that I still had skin in the game and it was worth considering. The Chief Whip said he would go back to the Prime Minister and ask on my behalf.

I could barely breathe when I leave his office as I was so pumped with adrenalin from fighting my corner. He texted me an hour later to agree that I could keep my trade envoy role now that I had stepped down as PPS and said that seemed as good a place as any for us to leave it and check in again in the new year. It was only when I left Parliament to head to my daughter's first nativity play, feeling miserable, that I realised the ramifications for launching the Birth Trauma Inquiry in the new year. The Prime Minister was not going to help me after I had defied him. Had I risked my entire maternity campaign by refusing to support the government on a difficult issue?

I sat watching the show at the nursery, which was complete chaos with children running on and off stage dressed as snowmen. Arabella, now aged fourteen months, shook a small tambourine to a song about snowflakes, which cheered me up a little. But mostly I felt run down, ready for Christmas recess and in need of a break from the toxic world of politics.

CHAPTER TWENTY-TWO

THE BIRTH TRAUMA INQUIRY

I spent a quiet Christmas with my family, where I tried not to read the news too much and focused on spending quality time with my husband and daughter. Arabella would fall into hysterics when I was unable to control my wind and point at me on the toilet each time I farted. It was funny and made me smile, but it was also a painful reminder that my body had not fully recovered after the birth.

I felt bruised but more refreshed when I returned to Parliament in January. The first thing we did was to launch the call for evidence for the Birth Trauma Inquiry, as the APPG wanted to hear directly from the public with their stories of birth trauma. I did another media round of radio, television and print and was surprised to find within minutes that my inbox began to receive messages from mothers sharing their experiences. I knew that as backbench MPs we could get the government's attention only if we heard from as many families as possible and used their first-hand testimony as evidence in order to influence future maternity policy, especially now that I'd annoyed the PM – which I couldn't even tell anyone about.

The Women's Health Summit was the following week, so I popped into new year drinks at the Health Secretary's office and reminded her about the launch of the inquiry, keeping the pressure up. I was also meant to catch up with the whips, but the Chief Whip kept postponing our meeting, which didn't bode well. On 17 January, I headed to the Royal College of Obstetrics and Gynaecology to hear from Vicky Atkins what her new priorities were. This was the first big moment for our campaign since the birth trauma debate. Had the noise we had generated publicly made any difference? I felt the pressure of all the mothers who had written in to try to effect positive change.

Hundreds of campaigners, politicians and organisations crammed in to hear Vicky speak in south London. She began by sharing some of her personal experiences as a pregnant mum using NHS services. I kept my fingers crossed and I listened intently as the Health Secretary said, 'The birth of a child should be among the happiest moments of our lives. And for the overwhelming majority of families, of course – it is. We want this for every woman and every family. But this commitment also requires a laser-like focus on birth trauma.'

I inwardly cheered when she mentioned birth trauma. It was a huge first step to hear this from the Health Secretary. She continued:

> Some mums endure simply unacceptable care and live with the consequences of that trauma for the rest of their lives. Some have told their stories to the media – harrowing experiences of tears, prolapses, operations and agony. They've done this because they want to shine a light on the impact of such experiences. Some of those amazing mums are here today in the audience. You deserve our thanks, our admiration and our applause.
>
> And the importance of women speaking up for other women is

demonstrated through the work of my colleague Theo Clarke, the MP for Stafford. Theo suffered a horribly traumatic birth. And when she regained her strength, and returned to work, she called a debate in the House of Commons on birth trauma. This was the first debate on birth trauma in the centuries that we have had a Parliament, and this shows some of the journey we still have to travel.

I was stunned and delighted to hear her reference the inquiry, which showed that Vicky had listened and that she was going to take some action to improve maternity care. She announced the expansion of women's health hubs and a Maternity Safety Support Programme to help underperforming NHS trusts.

However, as I listened to her describe how NHS England would set out a large programme of work through its maternity and neonatal services plan, I realised how much work we would have to do with the upcoming inquiry. While it was good news that both the Prime Minister and Health Secretary had finally acknowledged birth trauma, they were not yet committed to taking all of the necessary policy steps to reduce and prevent it. Our report would need to be comprehensive, hard-hitting and have a series of concrete recommendations for the government to enact. We had to make our voices so loud that No. 10 could not ignore us. I left the summit filled with energy and determined to make the inquiry a success. We could not let mothers down.

The Birth Trauma Inquiry preparations now took up a huge proportion of my time and I worried that I had little room left in my diary for other important work. I stayed late after votes to focus on writing my speech for my upcoming HS2 compensation debate, which I'd secured in the main Chamber. Back in October, the Prime

Minister had cancelled the second leg of the proposed high-speed rail route from Birmingham to Manchester to save money, which frustrated residents who'd had their homes compulsorily purchased, demolished, dug up or their farms cut in half. I was shocked at how the railway company had behaved to my constituents in Stafford and how underhand they had been. I had decided enough was enough and that I needed to call out the company for their bad behaviour publicly.

I was conscious that anything I said in the House of Commons could be reported, so I called for the government to pay all outstanding HS2 compensation claims and decided to put on the record how I'd discovered in surgery appointments that HS2 had intimidated my constituents. In one appointment with me, a resident had shared that they'd been told that 'it would not be good for you to get your MP involved as that would be bad for your case'. Several neighbouring MPs in Staffordshire came to support the debate, including Sir Gavin Williamson, which ensured that the BBC picked up the story. We were all relieved when the Rail Minister was forced to commit to look at any evidence of intimidation at the despatch box.

I also continued with my work in international development and my interest in strengthening democracies around the world. The Commonwealth Parliamentary Association flew me, Lord Foster and the Labour MP Kate Osamor to Sierra Leone in west Africa to run a workshop for new African MPs on the legislative process and being a new MP. I worried about leaving Arabella behind for nearly a week on a trip overseas. We had shared parenting responsibilities since the birth and I was confident that Henry could look after her and follow her routine, but I was still nervous about leaving her behind. In the airport, I constantly found myself looking behind me to check on her even though she was safely at home. But once

I boarded the flight, I became aware how exhausted I was from the previous year with such long work hours, constant stress and near-constant travel with a toddler back and forth from my constituency every week. I was tired from attempting to keep up with the pace of Parliament while being a new mum at the same time. I felt like I was doing both badly and that my energy was depleted. It seemed like a real luxury to be able to sit on the flight for hours and do small things like have a hot cup of tea, read a newspaper and even watch a film for the first time in months without interruption. I also finally got a few nights to properly catch up on sleep, as I never slept well at home. In the back of my mind, I felt constantly on duty and ready to leap up in case she woke up distressed or hungry in the middle of the night.

I had been to Sierra Leone twice before as a volunteer with the charity Street Child, both before and after the Ebola outbreak. I'd briefly taught in a local school in Makeni, where I'd seen first-hand the lack of health infrastructure and basic facilities that many of us took for granted back at home, such as clean running water and electricity. However, I didn't know much about the maternity provision in the country, so during our trip I asked as a favour for the British High Commission to facilitate a visit to a local hospital in Freetown to meet their maternity team.

We were shown around the rudimentary facility in the sticky heat by a doctor and midwife and saw the two basic beds, which constituted their delivery room. The adjacent ward was full of women recovering from birth, lying on narrow mattresses with their babies in stiflingly high temperatures. The mothers were too tired to wave the flies or mosquitos away and the medical team told me they had no pain relief to offer the women apart from paracetamol and only those pills until supplies ran out. If anyone suffered from birth complications, families would be sent out to buy their own surgical sutures for donation to the hospital, which then allowed for any wounds of the mother to be stitched. There was no formula if women couldn't breastfeed and many of them also suffered from malaria and other tropical diseases, which meant it was very difficult for them to feed their babies. I was horrified to hear how basic their treatment was. I also heard some terrible stories of women who'd been beaten in their villages while heavily pregnant. The doctor told me that sometimes women would walk for days in rural areas to access a medical facility for help, only to discover that their baby had already died in the womb. It was distressing to hear such appalling stories. So far, my birth trauma campaign had only been focused on domestic change, but I decided that in future, I would also look in more detail at the UK's aid budget and funding on maternal health as it was clearly a global issue that required more resources.

On my return to Parliament, Rosie and I prepared to take evidence for the first oral session of the Birth Trauma Inquiry. We invited in witnesses including parents with lived experience of birth trauma; experts from organisations such as the Royal College of Midwives, the Royal College of Obstetricians and Gynaecologists and the Birth Trauma Association; and leading academic Professor Susan Ayers to tell us more about the issue. The Birth Trauma Inquiry met in one of the historic panelled committee rooms upstairs in the House of Commons. We sat in a horseshoe shape as I chaired the meeting with Rosie, flanked by the other MPs, and we questioned and listened for two hours to the testimony of mothers and experts. I was grateful to so many politicians from different political parties coming to support us, as our final recommendations would be effective only if we were seen as truly non-partisan.

Despite being fired by the Prime Minister, I was grateful to have left the Treasury's team when I saw the order paper in Parliament that same afternoon was the remaining stages of the Finance Bill, which would have dragged me back to the Chamber to sit on the bench behind the Minister as PPS, instead of listening to the important first day of evidence to our inquiry. I realised then that if I'd been helping the Chancellor and his team with preparations for the Budget, I would never have had sufficient time to do both.

Over the next two months, the Birth Trauma Inquiry met every week and heard evidence on topics including birth injuries, maternal mental health, baby loss, support for fathers and health inequalities. We listened to the experiences of other countries around the world, including evidence from the chair of the New South Wales birth trauma select committee in Australia. A pattern began to emerge of poor care, which showed us that the current maternity system was not fit for purpose. There was (and is) no formal definition of birth trauma according to the World Health Organization, but we heard research that showed that 4–5 per cent of women every year will experience PTSD after birth – about 25,000–30,000 women in the UK. Many more experienced trauma symptoms, such as intense anxiety or flashbacks, and we listened to evidence of women being treated as an inconvenience and poor care being tolerated as normal.

The inquiry received more than 1,300 submissions from people who had experienced traumatic birth, as well as nearly 100 submissions from maternity professionals. We did not expect such a volume of submissions and had to extend the call for evidence for an additional fortnight. Rosie and I discussed what to do once we realised we could not read so many individual stories ourselves and decided to ask for help. As we were not an official select committee, Parliament did not provide us with any extra resources, including clerks. But it was clear from the outset that every submission needed to be reviewed, so we recruited a panel of extra readers via our special advisory group to help us to review all of the stories and tag each of them in our master spreadsheet to keep track of recurring themes.

If I'm honest, I did not feel mentally prepared to read and hear so many harrowing stories. They ranged from accounts of stillbirths, premature births, babies born with cerebral palsy caused by oxygen deprivation and life-changing injuries to women through severe tears. All of us were shocked to hear of errors being covered up by hospitals and parents' efforts to find answers being frustrated. I related strongly to women who shared stories of ringing the bell for help but no one coming, being left in blood-stained sheets, not being listened to, being denied pain relief and a general lack of postnatal care. We heard that there were both short- and long-term impacts of birth trauma, including difficulties with bonding with the baby, stress on the relationship with their partner and wider family and often an inability to return to work.

Some of the most devasting testimonies we listened to were from women who experienced birth injuries and still endured pain and bowel incontinence as a result. One mother, Geeta, told us of the injuries she'd sustained during the birth of her first child Maya, which still affected her every single day. She'd had an extremely long and traumatic delivery where she was repeatedly ignored and belittled. I was shocked to hear that her daughter was born with lacerations to her face and that Geeta had suffered a third-degree tear, which left her with permanent incontinence.

Other mothers wrote movingly about having to provide round-the-clock care for children left severely disabled as a result of injuries from birth. I was dismayed to hear examples of racism experienced by women from marginalised groups and the difficulty that many women had trying to access maternal mental health services, being told they didn't meet the criteria for help or facing long waiting lists. I was surprised to also hear from fathers and partners who talked about their psychological distress after witnessing a traumatic birth but who'd been completely ignored during the birth and afterwards. It was clear that understaffing within the NHS was a problem and that the maternity system was under considerable strain. I asked every witness the same final question: what would they like to see the UK government do to improve maternity care? Their answers were so numerous and varied that it felt like we were uncovering only the tip of the iceberg. Donna Ockenden, the chair of the inquiry into maternity care failings in Nottingham, told us about the lack of effective coordination between bodies and how maternity oversight needed to be streamlined and made more effective.

As the chair, I felt conscious about my lack of specialist knowledge on birth trauma and healthcare policy, so I read numerous briefings and learnt that some studies showed nearly a third of women described their birth as traumatic, but data on birth trauma was still scarce and under-researched in comparison to men's health. I was struck by how fragmented policy on maternity care was, and when I tried to find and read the government's overarching maternity policy there did not appear to be a single strategy document that outlined their view on the issue. Instead, there were a myriad of different documents that the public and clinicians had to refer to for relevant guidance on maternity care.

Alongside the inquiry, I continued to attend other important meetings where I lobbied the Chancellor for priorities for Stafford ahead of the spring Budget, met the Publishers Association to plan my literacy campaign in Stafford for World Book Day and persuaded HarperCollins to donate free books to every primary school in Stafford. However, in the back of my mind, I constantly thought about the key themes coming through from the inquiry. A pattern had emerged across the evidence we received. There was a failure to listen to women when something was wrong, often there was a lack of informed consent, poor communication appeared common, a lack of pain relief and kindness was too frequent, poor postnatal care was becoming normalised and there were increasing cases of medical negligence. It was time to approach No. 10 and open negotiations on our recommendations and lessons from the inquiry to try to push them to make an announcement.

CHAPTER TWENTY-THREE

NEGOTIATIONS WITH 10 DOWNING STREET

From my previous campaigning, I knew how important it was to start behind-the-scenes discussions with the government before the Birth Trauma Inquiry report was published to try to force a response. I called the Prime Minister's director of strategy Jamie Njoku-Goodwin, who I knew from his time as a special adviser on health during the pandemic and who'd reached out to me when I first shared my story. He came to see me in Parliament and I briefed him on the inquiry so far. He was supportive and interested, but it was obvious that we needed to have both the public on side and extensive media coverage to get any traction. Jamie offered a reception at Downing Street in June for affected mothers and promised to invite the Prime Minister's wife, Akshata. Over the Easter recess, I headed back to the constituency and began to make a list of all the key people we needed to influence to change health policy.

In March, we collected the final evidence for the inquiry and I met with a number of families who'd given evidence to the inquiry into maternity care failings in Nottingham to hear first-hand some of their shocking stories, where babies had died or been injured, and listen to the affected parents' views on how to improve maternity care. Rosie, Bell Ribeiro-Addy and I also went to St George's hospital in Tooting, south London, to visit their maternity ward and met with doctors and midwives to hear what improvements they would like to see. Afterwards, we met privately with the other MPs on the Birth Trauma Inquiry committee to consider the policy recommendations we'd heard over the previous few months and agree what our headline ask to the Prime Minister would be.

I was so busy trying to finish the report for the inquiry that I didn't pay much attention to other government business, so I was surprised when the deputy Chief Whip rang me out of the blue and asked me to rejoin the government as parliamentary private secretary at the Department of Education. It seemed that I was finally back in favour with the PM, which was good timing ahead of our report being published so I agreed to take the position. I was happy to be working for Education Secretary Gillian Keegan, who was a friend, and I was also interested to see up close how her policy of increasing childcare provision to children under two and work to improve school standards was going to be rolled out. Unexpectedly, I also had some time freed up when the long-planned Africa-UK Investment Summit, scheduled for April, was cancelled at short notice, much to my frustration and the annoyance of others in the Department for Business and Trade after all the work we had put into promoting it in Kenya to their government and key business stakeholders. I felt it was a diplomatic disaster after the Kenyan Prime Minister and other African heads of state had committed to coming, and they felt that we had let them down. No public answer was given as to why it was cancelled, which reinforced the impression that the government just wasn't prioritising the continent.

I made a list of everyone I knew in the government so I could lobby ahead of the Birth Trauma Inquiry being published. I also tried to meet as many influential stakeholders as I could, including the Women's Health Minister, the head of the No. 10 Policy Unit and the Health Secretary's special adviser. I unexpectedly saw the shadow Health Secretary Wes Streeting when we both won categories at the Pagefield Parliamentarian of the Year Awards, which was an opportunity to introduce myself and ask him for a meeting to discuss our report in detail, just in case Labour won the forthcoming general election.

I wanted to ensure that our cross-party inquiry recommendations carried over to any new government, so I briefed the shadow Women's Health Minister Abena Oppong-Asare, who had summed up on behalf of the opposition in my original birth trauma debate and seemed sympathetic to the cause. I also had another virtual call with the Australian MP Emma Hurst, who had chaired the New South Wales Birth Trauma Inquiry, to update her on our findings. We had a good chance that our inquiry report would get picked up in the news as long as nothing major broke on the same day. So I pitched to the BBC, ITV, Sky, GB News and others, asking them to cover our recommendations, and I offered *The Times* an exclusive preview of our report.

Wes Streeting finally agreed to meet with me, and on our respective constituency Fridays we had a call to go through the Birth Trauma Inquiry report's findings in detail. He was charming, listened intently and asked me several specific questions about our recommendations. I could see why he was such a senior politician in his own party, as he was one of the most articulate MPs I'd ever met. Wes promised that if he was the next Health Secretary, he would prioritise maternity care and our report.

Halfway through the meeting, he casually mentioned that I

seemed like a sensible, moderate Tory and was I sure that I was in the right political party? There was an awkward pause as I nervously laughed. I suddenly realised the context of our meeting, as in the past few weeks two Conservative colleagues, Natalie Elphicke and Dan Poulter, had defected to Labour. I suddenly wondered if the only reason he had agreed to speak with me directly – and, I belatedly realised, without my Labour co-chair Rosie – was to try to persuade me to move parties ahead of the election. I politely declined and tried to steer the conversation back to what his party would do to support our recommendations.

The final week before the report was published was spent in frantic negotiations behind the scenes trying to get No. 10 and NHS England to agree to do something in response to our findings. Our committee decided to publish twelve headline recommendations on improving maternity care, which led with the overarching ask of a national maternity improvement strategy led by a new Maternity Commissioner. I ducked out early from lunch after the annual mayor-making ceremony with Stafford Borough Council to negotiate further with No. 10. I'd sent the government a full, embargoed copy of the report several days in advance of publication to give them time to respond, as I knew that the only way to get them to act was by putting on the greatest public pressure. So, when I found out it was now planned that a junior health minister would do a broadcast round on the following Monday to try to fill Downing Street's quiet news grid by making another announcement on a small, unrelated and not time-sensitive issue, I was furious.

I rang No. 10 immediately and they admitted to me the minister was only doing it as no one else was available or keen to defend the government and do media that day. I insisted they pulled their announcement and instead officially respond to the Birth Trauma

Inquiry and our recommendations. They reluctantly agreed, but it was evident they did not believe that maternity care would be that day's biggest national news story, as the PM was also set to make a headline speech on foreign policy. And while the government agreed in advance to some of our smaller recommendations, they would not commit to the APPG's headline asks.

At the last minute, I had an idea to get the government's attention. The Prime Minister had invited me to his office for a quick photograph with the winning illustrated bookmark drawn by local school children for my constituency's World Book Day competition. I decided to ambush Rishi when I was shown into his Parliamentary office for my allotted one minute. It was the first time I had been back in his office since our showdown over Rwanda, but he seemed jovial and in a good mood with me. Without asking his aides, including Falstaff, I handed him a preview copy of the Birth Trauma Inquiry report and pitched our policy recommendations to him directly. He looked startled, but I had learnt enough in the past four and a half years as an MP to take any moment I could to influence the Prime Minister. He committed to look at the report.

On Monday 13 May, we published the Birth Trauma Inquiry report and I began a long day of broadcast interviews, more similar to a minister's media round than that of a backbencher with little experience. I got up at dawn and missed getting Arabella up and dressed for nursery to head to the television studios for hair and make-up ahead of being interviewed. It was daunting to speak to some of the biggest journalists in the UK, such as Nick Robinson on the UK's flagship radio programme, and to undertake my first appearance on the breakfast sofa in a live studio. I felt unprepared as a new MP with minimal exposure or practice doing national press, but I hoped that my lived experience and the huge volume of evidence we'd collected for the inquiry would be enough to get me through and give me plenty to talk about. My schedule that day was:

- 07.09 a.m. Today programme, BBC Radio 4
- 08.20 a.m. – Good Morning Britain, ITV breakfast sofa (while Rosie simultaneously did BBC Breakfast)
- 9 a.m. – Tweet report
- 10.15 a.m. – Times Radio
- 10.45 a.m. – Sky News
- 12 p.m. – ITN
- 12.20 p.m. – GB News
- 1 p.m. – Interview with *The Sun*
- 2 p.m. – BBC 3
- 2.30 p.m. – LBC
- 2.50 p.m. – BBC World Service
- 3.30 p.m. – BBC *Newscast*
- 4 p.m. – BBC News
- 4.20 p.m. – 5 News
- 4.40 p.m. – GB News
- 6 p.m. – Birth Trauma Inquiry reception

It was incredible to see that the Birth Trauma Inquiry led the news all day and was the front-cover story on *The Times*, the most-read story on the BBC website, led the lunchtime news and even wiped the Prime Minister's foreign policy speech off from the coveted top spot. Every outlet reported our findings and put pressure on the government to respond to failings in maternity care. My social media followers went up and up and I was gobsmacked to see that even the author J. K. Rowling had seen my tweet and shared our report with her millions of followers.

By early evening, I was completely exhausted, but I still had to attend our official launch of the report in the House of Commons where the Health Secretary would formally respond. I hoped that the huge press coverage we had generated was enough to get her to publicly commit to our recommendations. I headed to the room overlooking the River Thames, where we'd invited hundreds of mothers, campaigners and experts to listen to her as Kim Thomas from the Birth Trauma Association gave a speech where she summarised our twelve core recommendations, which aimed to improve and standardise maternity services across the UK. This was followed by a moving talk from affected mother Gill Castle, who shared her story and called on the government to take action.

I was nervous as I looked out at the expectant faces and introduced Health Secretary Vicky Atkins, as ultimately what she said was the government's official response and until that moment, I still did not know what she would formally commit to. I was overwhelmed when she announced a new comprehensive national maternity strategy and said that the government had introduced standalone GP appointments six to eight weeks after giving birth to ask crucial questions about the mother's mental and physical health. She set out that NHS England would co-produce new decision-making tools for new mothers to guide them through choices on how they gave birth, to discuss what interventions could happen and what pain relief they should be offered. She referenced the inequalities we'd highlighted in our report and said these tools would be available in a range of languages and formats to make sure they could be tailored to different settings and to different local populations. I inwardly cheered when she said how perinatal pelvic health services would be rolled out, including guidance to better support women who had experienced serious tears, such as myself.

She announced that the National Institute for Health and Care Research would commission new research into the economic impact of birth trauma, including how this affected woman returning to work. And finally, Health Minister Maria Caulfield would chair the next session of the Men's Health Task and Finish Group in June to focus on dads' mental health and trauma and help them better understand how to support their partners.

We had done it. The government had listened. I was so shocked that I almost felt numb. I was emotionally exhausted but relieved that our inquiry had made a difference, despite all the challenges stacked against us. That night, I was stopped on the Tube by members of the public who thanked me for our campaign to help mothers like them. It was the first time as an MP that I felt I had made a positive difference to improve policy.

The next day, I went to find the Speaker in the tearoom and asked him if he would call me at Prime Minister's Questions. I did not have to persuade him very hard as he had seen the wall-to-wall coverage of the inquiry and agreed to help to try to get the government on the record publicly. I was conscious of the many affected women and their families who'd courageously written to me over the past year to share their experiences as I stood up in the Chamber of the House of Commons and live on television asked the Prime Minister to back our report and implement the recommendations from the Birth Trauma Inquiry to improve maternity care and reduce birth trauma. It was a huge moment when Rishi, as Prime Minister, replied and acknowledged that birth trauma even existed:

> I thank my hon. Friend for her incredible campaigning on this issue. When we met and discussed this issue, she presented me personally with a copy of this important report. I am hugely

grateful for her and the APPG on birth trauma for carefully considering the issue, and to all the brave women who have come forward to share their stories. I am delighted that the Secretary of State for Health and Social Care and the chief executive officer of the NHS both support the overarching recommendation for a comprehensive national strategy to improve maternity services. We will update the House on next steps in due course, but we are fully committed to improving the quality and consistency of care for women throughout pregnancy, birth and the critical months that follow.

We had done enough to make a difference. The government had now committed to our headline recommendation to improve maternity care. It was a historic day and the voices of women had finally been listened to. I was hugely proud of everyone and in awe of the incredible work that had been done both by our voluntary special advisory group and the readers who had reviewed submissions. Party politics had not got in the way and we'd managed to genuinely build cross-party consensus through the inquiry to address such an important issue. Our relentless pursuit of change had resulted in the government committing to reduce birth trauma.

Throughout the rest of the week, the report spiralled out across the country and the world and seemed to generate a life of its own, with the story covered in more than 200 news outlets and millions of the public viewing our report. It was incredible to see how simply sharing my story had culminated in a national campaign that had made improvements to women's health.

I was delighted and relieved, but as the inquiry concluded, I realised how the past few months had taken its toll, given the volume of work I'd undertaken on top of my regular constituency and parliamentary duties. I began to look ahead to a much-needed summer holiday, booked flights to a friend's wedding in Italy a few weeks later and planned another visit to Kenya to discuss extending our current trade deal to potentially include services with their government. The following week, I invited Kim from the BTA, who had quietly chaired the secretariat and drafted the lengthy 82-page inquiry report, for lunch in Parliament to say thank you and celebrate the campaign's success.

It was just a normal Wednesday until afterwards, sat at my desk, I watched the Chamber in the background on the television screen and noticed that this week's PMQs seemed to have the entire Cabinet in attendance, which was rare. I'd seen reports that the Foreign Secretary had been flown back from an overseas trip and I began to have a dreadful feeling that something was about to happen. The BBC began to report an unscheduled Cabinet meeting at 4 p.m., which could mean only one thing.

CHAPTER TWENTY-FOUR

GENERAL ELECTION

It was mid-May, but it began to rain. As the heavens opened, the Prime Minister came out of the black door of No. 10, stood in front of an unbranded lectern, without an umbrella, and called an immediate general election. I was stunned. He had called it six months earlier than I had expected, and I knew we were going to face annihilation after nearly a decade and a half in government, with the public ready for change. I had never been so tired since the birth of my daughter, from the exhaustion of setting up and chairing the inquiry. I'd been looking forward to a rest and I didn't know how I was going to summon up any more strength to lead a campaign for six weeks to retain my seat in Parliament. That evening, I dialled into my first call with the new party chairman to be briefed on our election strategy, priorities and the policies to raise on the doorstep, and I could see on the call how miserable my fellow colleagues felt, with their voices flat and faces despondent. My planned birth trauma event for mothers at Downing Street was postponed as it now fell within the election campaign.

I felt extremely depressed. I cried in the car park at Stafford train station the first time that Henry took Arabella, now a toddler, back down on the train to London so she could go to nursery and he could go back to work. He could not afford to take six weeks off with no notice and we had no other available childcare, so I saw them only on the weekends. I became dispirited as I spent the next few weeks without my family, pounding the pavements across rural villages and throughout Stafford with only my small but faithful campaign team to keep me company, led by my long-suffering agent and local councillor Carolyn Trowbridge. She came out with me rain or shine and did a good job of attempting to keep my spirits up, but within a month I knew my odds were very slim. Stafford became a target seat for the opposition.

During the election campaign, the Prime Minister left D-Day eightieth anniversary commemorations early and understandably caused a public uproar, which landed very badly in our military town. Reform UK also held a huge rally for their supporters in our local agricultural showground and heavily targeted my farming community, while the Labour Party pumped the seat full of leaflets and sent multiple visits of their campaign battle bus, including their leader and numerous shadow Cabinet ministers, to try to oust me. I struggled to make it through each day and I felt my energy run down to rock bottom, depleted by the exhaustion of canvassing for hours and responding daily to angry constituents criticising the government on the doorstep.

I counted down the days until Thursday 4 July, which was polling day. When I finally attended my general election count at Stafford Leisure Centre, it was around 1 a.m. and my husband held my arm for support as we walked in and tried to keep a brave face for the cameras. I could immediately see from the size of the piles of ballots, laid out for each party by ward on the tables, that I had lost and that there seemed to be a significantly higher number of votes for smaller parties and an increased vote share for Labour. Reform, spearheaded by Nigel Farage, had dominated our traditionally Conservative rural areas and I had lost most of the villages that had traditionally supported Sir Bill Cash as their previous MP under the old constituency boundaries.

The high sheriff and the chief executive of Stafford Borough Council called the room to attention to announce the results of the ballot, and I made my way to the podium. Just four and a half years before, it had been the honour of my life to be elected as the Member of Parliament for Stafford and now, I was about hear that I had lost my job. She read out the results and announced that I had been beaten by around four and a half thousand votes by the Labour candidate. Stafford was a red marginal seat once again.

I focused on my breathing and tried to keep my voice steady as I conceded defeat, thanked my husband, my steadfast team and everyone who had supported me. I had just run the biggest and most successful campaign of my career leading the Birth Trauma Inquiry, but I had been taken out with the political tide that had swept the country and taken the Conservatives out of government. It was the end of my political career and I was completely gutted after how hard I'd worked and the sacrifices my family had made to support me. Politics had been a way of life for me for so long and so much more than a job. Nevertheless, I believed in democracy, especially after having visited so many other countries around the world where they lived in a dictatorship or without basic freedoms, and so I accepted that the people had spoken. I was surprised to hear my opponent, the new Labour MP Leigh Ingham, give a kind, graceful acceptance speech in which she thanked me for my cross-party campaign and mentioned how many times birth trauma had come up on the doorstep for her too. I was touched at her generosity after the bitterness of the national election campaign.

* * *

Now that I am no longer a Member of Parliament and two years on from my experience of birth trauma, I can see that I have changed. While I am proud of the time I spent as an elected representative, I realise that after having spent more than half of my career attempting to become a politician, my priorities have shifted now I've had my daughter. I enjoy being a mother in ways that I never anticipated. So, while it feels strange to have left behind the cut and thrust of politics and the relentless energy and excitement of Westminster, I want to focus more on my family than work. I no longer obsessively follow the order paper for what's on today in Parliament or constantly check my phone for breaking news updates. My days are now more on my own terms. The day after I lost my seat, I resigned from the Conservative Party's official list of parliamentary candidates and told them I would not stand again for elected office, which felt both terrifying and liberating at the same time.

I do not know what my future holds but I have made one important decision with Henry, which is not to have another baby. I feel grief to know that my daughter will never have a sibling to play and grow up with, but I also know that I couldn't face the stress of pregnancy and childbirth ever again after the traumatic experience I endured the first time. The physical and mental scars will remain with me for life and will take years to heal, but I am hopeful that I will recover. I am learning to accept that my body has changed, and that it will never go back to how it was before I had a baby and that is OK. Today, I realise that my career filled the void before I had a family and so I am finally less restless and more content. My ambition now is to be a better mother and more present partner. I want to be able to spend more time my daughter during those important early years of her life, which can never be replaced.

My experience sadly demonstrates that the House of Commons is not a modern workplace that is compatible with raising a young family. I find it shocking that Parliament makes the laws on maternity policy, and expects others to follow them, but doesn't follow those laws itself. As politicians, we have championed and introduced flexible working laws that are not applicable to us in our own place of work.

Women make up 51 per cent of the population but are still hugely under-represented in Parliament. We have a long way to go before 50 per cent of our Parliamentarians are women, and while we often talk about the significant barriers to women standing for public office, such as the high cost of being a candidate or the threats and harassment that women often receive, to date we have not talked enough about how the workings of Parliament need to be updated to reflect the realities of being a new mother while an elected representative. I fail to understand how we could make such swift changes during the pandemic to allow MPs to participate remotely in the House of Commons – changes that would make a huge difference to mothers with newborns, such as the introduction of online voting or the ability to ask questions in the Chamber via a television screen – but subsequently scrapped these more inclusive processes, despite the precedent having been set.

There are fundamental repercussions for our democracy if these concerns are not urgently addressed. The lack of gender parity in Parliament continues to be a root cause of why women's health issues, such as birth trauma, have traditionally been ignored in government policy. I believe that Parliament must modernise if we want to attract more young women of childbearing age to stand to be MPs and thus be a more representative democracy.

I have learnt through my recent experience to be more resilient. I no longer feel so threatened by vulnerability and understand that being exposed has its own raw strength, as sharing my story showed me. While the recent general election marked the end of my elected journey, I realise now that it was only the start of my life as a campaigner. I will never stop fighting for mothers to have the care they need and deserve and for governments to improve maternity services.

It is time we had a global #MeToo movement for birth trauma to push for change. This is why I have decided to expand my campaign to go international and, since leaving Parliament, I have established the new Global Birth Trauma Alliance to advocate for improving maternity care around the world. We bring together affected women, their families, healthcare professionals and parliamentarians in every country to work together to address this issue. We aim to better educate policy makers and ensure that birth trauma is discussed at the highest levels of all governments, including within the United Nations.

It is time to demand action and for mothers to finally be listened to. No one should feel shame or face stigma due to suffering from physical or mental challenges as a result of childbirth. This discussion is long overdue. Join me and together, let's break this taboo.

PART III

PERSONAL STORIES

The following pages contain graphic descriptions of traumatic birth, the experience of post-partum psychosis, mistreatment by medical professionals and the experience of baby loss, which some may find distressing.

CHAPTER TWENTY-FIVE

BIRTH INJURIES

SARAH

I fell pregnant in April 2012, when I was thirty-six years old. This was my first baby. Early in the pregnancy, I started to bleed and was given a scan. I was told my baby had implanted in the wrong place and the heartbeat was very faint. They said I was going to miscarry and offered me an abortion, which I declined. A scan three days later showed that the baby was fine and the hospital apologised.

When it was time to give birth, I requested a water birth, but the birth bath was in use. I asked for an epidural for the pain of being in labour, but I was told I was too far along to have it. I gave birth to a healthy baby boy on 4 December 2012.

I had a retained placenta, which the midwife tried to manually remove twice, but it was not detaching. I signed a form consenting to have the placenta surgically removed. I waited forty-five minutes, then a junior doctor came in and the midwife explained that I was going to have my placenta surgically removed and that she had tried twice with no success. The junior doctor said, 'I will remove it.' The midwife disagreed and said, 'The cord will snap – she is due to go down to theatre.' The junior doctor undermined the midwife and told her his role was superior to hers.

My cervix was no longer dilated and I had had no pain relief, but the junior doctor took it upon himself to try to manually remove the placenta by hand. I was screaming in pain – it was worse pain than actually giving birth. He snapped the cord and I began to bleed. He then left the room. I was left for another thirty minutes, bleeding on the bed. I was taken down for surgery and a student midwife came with me. I was awake through the whole procedure. I was given an epidural and they manually removed the placenta but could not stop the bleeding, because when the junior doctor pulled the placenta he had torn me inside. They massaged inside me to try to stop the bleeding. I felt like they were inside my abdomen – they kept removing clots of blood.

I watched the whole thing in the silver light they used for the surgery. I kept myself calm because I knew that if I panicked, my heart rate would go up and I would lose more blood. I heard the staff member working on me say to another one, 'I can't stop the bleeding.' The anaesthetist said to the doctor, 'Do you want me to knock her out?' He replied, 'No, we need her to tell us how she's feeling.'

I started to feel weak, so I asked the student midwife if she would tell my partner to call my mum and dad and ask them to come straight to the hospital. I thought I was going to die and I wanted them there with my partner and my baby. It kept going through my mind that I had finally had a baby and I was never going to see him.

I was in surgery for four and a half hours. Afterwards, I was told I was going to the high-dependency unit. I was taken to a room on my own, which looked like a storage room because it had computers and beds stacked at the side of the room. My partner was there with my baby boy. I asked whether he had been fed and he said, 'No.' I asked the nurse to feed my baby. I originally wanted to breastfeed, but I was too ill. If you use a bottle at first, there is a risk that the baby won't learn to latch onto the breast, so the nurse tried to cup feed him – unsuccessfully – until I was ready to feed. My partner was told to leave and let me rest.

There was a nurse on duty and I said, 'I'm really uncomfortable down below – can you please check my pad?' She replied, 'I'm not surprised you feel uncomfortable – you look like you've been kicked by a donkey.' Then she walked out of the room abruptly. I was horrified and used my mobile phone to take a picture to see what she meant. I saw what could not be described as genitalia and I burst out crying, thinking, 'I'm never going to be normal again.'

I asked another nurse to pass me my baby to hold, which she did, then left. Five minutes later, the nurse who had made the horrendous comment came to do my observations, and said, 'You need to put the baby in the cot so I can do your obs.' She took him out of my arms, put him in the cot and did my observations. Then, as she was leaving, she pushed the cot out of arm's reach and left the room. I was in total dismay. I could not get out of the bed or move due to the pain, but I managed to lean over and pull the cot towards me. I got all four corners of the sheet and picked my baby up as if in a sling to bring him to me to cuddle. I cried from how I was treated and because I nearly never got to see my baby.

The unprofessional nurse finished her shift and a lovely nurse came on shift. She showed outstanding compassion and care for me and my baby. I felt like she was an angel. She said, 'You look tired, do you want me to change and feed the baby while you have a sleep?' I replied, 'Yes.' When I woke up, she was still sitting there holding my baby.

I was not allowed any visitors because I was in a high-dependency unit. After a couple of days, I was put on a ward. While I was there, a staff member said, 'I've come to bath your baby.' I said, 'I would like to give him his first bath.' She was very rude to me and commented, 'You don't know how to bath him, do you?' I replied, 'I have bathed babies before and I am quite capable of bathing him myself.' She said, 'Fine' and threw the towel on the bed and walked away.

My niece was there when this happened. She too was taken aback by this attitude. I bathed my baby and got him dressed. I was told that if he took a full feed and I felt better, I could go home tomorrow. A nurse came in and put the baby on my chest and was squeezing my breast to the baby's mouth to try get him to feed. I said, 'I will do it,' and she responded, 'No, you need to do this.' I felt really uncomfortable being touched in this way and my baby refused to latch. I told her to stop. She said, 'Well, if he doesn't feed, you can't go home.'

I had packed a small bottle and ready-made baby milk for an emergency, so I fed him this and he drank it all. He was four days old by this time and he must have been starving. I told the nurse I had been to the toilet and felt fine so they would discharge me. I wasn't fine, I was feeling ill and lightheaded, but I wanted to get out of the hospital as I felt horrified and terrified about how I had been treated.

I had no post-delivery follow-up from the hospital. The midwife came to my home and said that my notes said I'd had a post-partum haemorrhage. I told her what happened and she said, 'No, it says you had a post-partum haemorrhage.' I felt I had no voice.

I ended up with a prolapsed bowel, bladder and womb. I was told they would not repair it until I passed childbearing age. I was thirty-seven years old at this time. I had lost 5 pints of blood due to the doctor tearing out my placenta and received a transfusion of 3 pints of blood. I was ill for over twelve months, but I just felt glad to be alive.

In September 2013, I fell pregnant again. I had panic attacks and anxiety, crying, 'I'm going to die.' I had a planned C-section and afterwards they stitched me back up. As they lifted me from the trolley to a bed, I gushed blood. The staff panicked and shouted at the surgeon to come back in. They gave me an injection to stop the bleeding. I lost 3 pints of blood in all. The bleed was caused by severe scarring from my first birth.

My prolapse got worse over time, which affected my relationship. My partner told me I didn't love him because I wouldn't have sex with him any more. I tried to explain it was too painful, but he wouldn't listen. He ended up having an affair, which ended our relationship in 2015. I went for a prolapse repair in 2018 but relapsed in 2019. This ruined any chance of me being in a relationship. My health declined and my thyroid stopped working. I put on weight and struggled with anxiety. Now, due to my weight, they will not repair my prolapse.

The whole experience ruined my life. Although I have two beautiful children, I have been a single mum since my daughter was eight months old. She is now ten. Since the birth of my son in 2012, I struggle with severe abdominal pain. On occasion, I have a haemorrhage if I do too much or lift anything heavy. After an experience at the hospital where a staff member told me my haemorrhage was a period, I now just remain in bed when I have a bleed until it subsides. I have not had a period since my surgery in 2018. I am on a lot of medication for pain and it limits my quality of life with my children. I have lost all trust in the NHS. I don't understand why some people work in the medical field if they have no compassion. I want to share my experience in the hope this will never happen to anyone else.

JAIME

During the birth of my daughter, Ava, in 2010 at Prince Charles Hospital in Merthyr Tydfil, I sustained life-changing injuries. My birth injuries were so bad that I had to have an ileostomy (where the end of the small bowel is connected to a stoma on my abdomen), as the whole of my large intestine was removed in 2021. My life was turned upside down and I am still struggling with normal everyday life. My case was covered up by the hospital, and I fight every day to get some sort of justice for what I have been through and am still going through.

Back in 2010, on the night I gave birth to my daughter, the consultant was more concerned about going home at 9 p.m. than taking me to theatre for a Caesarean. All she kept saying was, 'Ava will be here by 9 p.m.' However, when the next consultant clocked on at 9 p.m., she informed us that Ava was stuck and I should never have been left to give birth naturally. She also stated that Ava was now too low in my birth canal as a result of being left too long, which meant I could no longer have a Caesarean. I was then rushed to theatre, where an episiotomy was performed to aid with the birth. This is where over a decade of my troubles began. If the correct decisions had been made that night, my health would be as it was back in 2009, when I was running marathons for breast cancer charities.

The so-called 'professionals' conducting under-the-carpet reviews of my case have never had the decency to meet up with me or even contact me to see the life-changing injuries I suffered the night my daughter was born.

Since Ava's birth, I have had sixteen procedures, including a colostomy, bladder and womb prolapse repair, Botox in my vagina to help with the nerve pain, parastomal hernia repairs, a reversal of the colostomy and a realignment of my rectum. The reversal of my colostomy was not successful, as consultants finally admitted the damage caused to my nerves during the birth meant my brain could no longer send a signal to my rectum to release the faeces. In March 2019, I had my colostomy put back and my parastomal hernia was repaired with organic mesh. A month later, the trauma of the operation caused a large abscess to form and I had the onset of sepsis, so back into hospital I went to have the abscess drained. Over a period of twenty-four hours, I had over thirty bags of antibiotics intravenously.

My colostomy prolapsed significantly over the course of 2021, meaning my colostomy bag could only be put over my stoma if I was lying flat on the bed. This was a complete nightmare, as my stomach muscles have ceased to exist, so once I was lying flat, getting back upright was not possible without help. My mental health in 2021 was terrible and I often wondered why I was here. I still wonder this today as my quality of life is so hard and exhausting.

I had three emergency operations in March, May and December 2021, due to my colostomy constantly prolapsing. Before my operation in December, my skin around the stoma was starting to split because of the size and awkwardness of my prolapse. This operation unfortunately resulted in the complete removal of my large intestine along with my appendix. This was the only option, as the intestinal tissue was too badly damaged to be saved. Due to this, an ileostomy had to be carried out, which makes my condition significantly worse and harder to live with. My stools are now much more uncontrollable due to the higher frequency of changes required daily and the liquid consistency, which leaks more frequently than it ever has previously. My stools are also very acidic, which causes my skin to burn when they escape from the stoma bag. I find myself constantly touching my stoma bag as I am concerned about it leaking, causing embarrassment and burning my surrounding skin.

Due to the acid-type output from my ileostomy, I now experience burning and irritation daily around the stoma area. I am on medication to help with this and have tried numerous barrier creams, but at the moment I haven't mastered being able to put it on the burnt area without my bag falling off. The cream affects how my bag adheres to my skin. I empty my bag up to ten times daily and three to four times through the night, which is exhausting. I sleep sitting up as I am afraid of lying in a position that could result in leakage. Therefore, I set my alarm to go off every hour, so I can check the output of my stoma. I am mentally and physically worn out by this whole situation.

My consultant has warned me that there will be more operations and hospital stays due to some of the problems caused by having an ileostomy. My stomach is now permanently swollen and painful and feels as though it is dragging on the floor due to the lack of pelvic floor muscles from years of operations. I am also waiting to see my urology consultant, as I have needed a catheter to urinate since March 2020.

I went in to have a baby and came out with life-changing injuries, meaning I will never be the same again. I have been fighting a long legal case against the hospital that is still unresolved, because the hospital are putting barriers up and stopping me from getting justice.

In October 2018, the Welsh government commissioned a review of Cwm Taf Morgannwg University health board, which includes the Prince Charles Hospital, by the RCOG and Royal College of Midwives (RCM). The review highlighted serious concerns about the failings in maternity care, which led to the Welsh government putting Cwm Taf in special measures.

In 2019, the Welsh government mandated the Independent Maternity Services Oversight Panel to carry out a fuller investigation, looking at a number of cases including mine. Unfortunately, instead of being reviewed independently, my case was reviewed by an NHS solicitor and an NHS consultant (not the one involved in my care). They accessed my GP records and, finding that I had gone to my GP with constipation in 2008, concluded that my subsequent problems were related to this single instance of constipation and were nothing to do with what happened to me during birth. My case was dropped from the investigation. My letters to Eluned Morgan (Health Minister at the time) were left unanswered.

In January 2019, I received a letter of apology from Cwm Taf chief executive Allison Williams, acknowledging that I had had an 'extremely distressing experience made all the more difficult by failures in communication and poor attitude of some of the staff who were caring for you'. A few weeks after this, she left her post.

The last thirteen years have been a nightmare and there is no sign of it ending. I will never give up fighting this case.

Over the years, I have had health professionals stating that what I suffered during childbirth was 'one of those things'. This comment would be hilarious if the situation was not so serious. How many other women do you know who have been admitted to hospital to give birth and let out with debilitating injuries that will affect them for the rest of their lives?

Back in 2012, when I first decided to open the case, I wasn't mentally prepared or capable to fight as I had just received a colostomy and had a toddler to care for. Back then, I didn't know the years of suffering that lay ahead of me and the multiple operations I was to endure because of what happened during the birth. Before Ava's birth in 2010, I was a fit, healthy and happy individual with a prosperous career ahead of me. I cannot believe fourteen years has gone by and I am still fighting for the truth. I will carry on with everything I have until the day I die, as what happened during the birth could and should have been prevented.

The only positive to come from this is my beautiful little girl. Unlike so many other parents who heartbreakingly lost their babies, Ava-May was fine and I suffered all the injuries.

CHAPTER TWENTY-SIX

MATERNAL MENTAL HEALTH

MAISY

I live in Barrow-in-Furness. I'm twenty-six and my son was born at South Lakes Birth Centre on 28 June 2023. The first incident happened in February 2023, when I came down with Covid while pregnant. I called the antenatal unit and was incorrectly prescribed double the dose of the blood thinner Clexane, which led to me injecting myself with a double dosage for a week. It was only when I called and asked for more information about the injections that the error was noticed.

I went into labour and laboured until I was 9 centimetres dilated. The midwives thought I would be ready to push soon, but then a doctor checked me and found that my child was back-to-back with me and that I had what they called a 'firm layer' over my cervix. I was told that I could wait an hour to see if anything changed or have a C-section right then. But they also said that the baby was in distress. When I asked when the C-section would happen, they replied that it would be immediate as it was an emergency. So I agreed to a C-section and within ten minutes was in surgery.

Once the surgery started, I had to continually say that I needed more pain relief as I had a slight feeling of the surgery. They were struggling to remove my son from my abdomen, which I was later told was because I had laboured so long that he was too low down. Once they were able to remove my baby, the room was instantly thrown into panic and, as my partner describes it, chaos. It was utterly terrifying. As they began shouting at each other, more employees entered the room. I had absolutely no idea what was going on. They placed my son onto my face for skin-to-skin contact and then quickly transferred him over for his checks. Following his checks, I looked over to my partner who was staring at me as if he had seen a ghost. He and my son were then escorted out of theatre as he was told it was 'not a great idea to be in here now as it is quite traumatic'. I looked to my right to see my family gone. I was not told that they had left or why.

I had no idea what was happening to me. I was just being pumped and pumped with more medication. When I asked multiple times what was happening, I was brushed away and told 'it shouldn't be too long' and that they were 'just closing up my scar'. After three and a half hours in theatre, mainly lying there in pain asking for more and more pain relief and staring into the ceiling not knowing what was happening to me, I was told that I was 'done and can be transferred to the recovery room'. The only thing I replied to this, with extreme emotion, was to ask where my family had been taken. It turned out they had been taken to the recovery room as my partner seemed to be very emotional – which he was, as from his point of view he had just had a child and now his child's mother looked like she was dying.

Once in the recovery room, I felt extremely unwell and had to ask for more pain relief. Shortly afterwards, I was taken back to my room and left to my own devices. I don't believe I was given any extra care and my partner was told to go home and sleep and that I could be left alone. I couldn't even get out of bed to lift my child out of his cot, never mind being able to do anything else. I had to plead for them to allow me to swap birth partners and have my mum come to sit with me while my partner went to rest.

My partner, mother and I all noticed my newborn baby was extremely uncomfortable and quite distressed. This continued for the whole hospital stay. He was unable to lie down flat without screaming in pain and was continually being sick and arching his body in discomfort. I asked numerous times for help and for this to be looked into and they told us multiple times that this was 'normal'. There was even a moment where he began to choke and I couldn't physically move from my bed to help him due to the state I was in from the birth. My mother had to rush out into the hallway with my son to get assistance.

My mother and I repeatedly asked what had happened to me and didn't receive an answer. The following day, the manager of the maternity ward came to my room and produced a letter, told me there was an investigation being opened into what had happened to me and that they were taking full responsibility. At this point, I was so medicated due to a drop in my iron levels and my internal infection rate skyrocketing that my mother took over, asking what had happened. The response she received was that when they were trying to remove my son from my abdomen, his shoulders were quite wide and he was in a difficult position – however, they also said that I had a bleed and that this still should never have happened. When I looked at my baby, his shoulders did not seem wide and many midwives said that he didn't look wide.

This was the only information we knew at this point. The following day, the surgeon and many doctors began visiting my room and I finally received an answer to what had happened and why I was in so much pain and discomfort. The surgeon explained to me that she had torn me internally during surgery and that it was completely their error. I had then gone on to lose 2 litres of blood because of haemorrhaging and had received a blood transfusion. I was left absolutely, utterly devastated and extremely upset, as I had no idea my body was going through so much.

I don't believe I received any extra care due to my emergency. I was left with a drain above my scar, which has caused me nothing but discomfort and pain since. After a seven-day hospital stay, I was so beside myself from the trauma and so upset, I really just wanted to go home. However because of my iron levels, pulse and blood pressure being so low and my infection level being so high (they had started treating me for sepsis without my knowledge), they were reluctant to let me leave. I had to plead to go home. At four weeks post-partum, I had had different midwives come to see me every time. The area where they had my drain and my scar were causing me quite some pain. I was placed on antibiotics and told to just keep cleaning the area.

Within a week of being home, I believed that the discomfort I was in was not normal and spoke to a midwife with some queries. She sent me back up to the birth centre to undergo swabs and tests for infection, as the area was very hot, very red and inflamed. I was sent away with yet another set of antibiotics. When I had my final midwife visit, I expressed my concern because I was still feeling pain in that area, but I was told that it looked fine and that they would discharge me. I was also told that I would lose feeling in the area and that it would probably 'never be the same'.

Because my son was unwell, over a number of months he received different types of milk and different medications, prescribed by the doctor. It was later discovered that he suffered from a cow's milk protein allergy and silent reflux. I also had to get his tongue tie cut privately as the hospital did not pick this up on his checks and it was making his illness worse. To this day (he is now seventeen months old), he still suffers terribly with wind that we have been told he will 'grow out of'. Not only do I feel I was failed, but I also feel like they failed my quite clearly distressed newborn.

I feel so let down by the NHS and truly cannot think about this experience without feeling completely beside myself and extremely anxious and traumatised. Not once has anybody spoken to me to advise me about any help with my mental health or any type of aftercare I could undergo to help me deal with my trauma. It was such a horrible experience and I cannot even fathom how I am supposed to trust them if I am to ever fall pregnant again.

I feel as if I was left completely in the dark as to what was happening to my body. I lay there on the operating table, not knowing what to think or feel, just staring at a white ceiling hoping I was going to be OK. Since leaving the hospital I have had no information about what will be happening with the investigation they have raised, nor have had I any information about whether the internal tear they caused will bring about any further repercussions – apart from what it has done to me mentally.

EILIDH

I live in rural Scotland and my first child was born during the height of Covid at Glasgow Queen Elizabeth University Hospital, on

23 January 2021. The birth was highly traumatic and led me to spiral into such bad mental health that, three months post-partum, I was hospitalised for seven weeks with psychosis.

To prepare for my first baby, my partner R and I took an NCT antenatal class. Looking back, the biases towards natural births, exclusive breastfeeding and attachment parenting in the classes profoundly shaped my outlook. I wrote a one-page birth plan that said things like 'Do not offer me an epidural' and 'No episiotomy – I want to tear naturally'. Naively, I packed it in a bag my partner was to bring to the labour suite for my induction at thirty-eight weeks (my baby was measuring small) along with a TENS machine, battery-operated tea lights and mini-speaker. We had the birth plan and a Spotify playlist. We were ready.

As it was during lockdown, partners weren't allowed on any hospital wards outside of visiting hours. So after dropping me off, R waited in the car and I was examined and given my first pessary. I was told in twelve hours, if not before, I'd be examined and that my baby and my contractions would be monitored every few hours. The details are fuzzy but that was early evening. I heard someone give birth on the ward and the sound of the baby brought tears of happiness to my eyes. I didn't think it was a bad sign at the time.

Initially, I was fine and went and ate a sandwich in the car with my partner. I was contracting but not too painfully. I went back to hospital and he went home. Later that night, the contractions got stronger and stronger. I wasn't coping well with the pain and I was alone. I was given codeine and later diamorphine, but they quickly wore off. I remember speaking to R on the phone in the bath and him talking me through my breathing. At 3 a.m., I was examined by a doctor who wasn't happy with how baby was handling the induction and had me lie on my side while they removed the pessary. This all really worried me, but the baby started to perk up and as I hadn't dilated much, I was told to wait and rest until morning.

In the morning, another pessary was inserted. The same thing happened again. The pain was incredible and I was alone. Diamorphine helped a little until it didn't. The contractions were bad, but unlike what I'd learnt in NCT, there was no break between them. Between the stabs it felt like someone was ramming a red-hot shopping trolley into my lower back. I wanted to die. I was glad the windows on the ward didn't open.

I lost my mucus plug in the toilet. I remember screaming and swearing and the midwife coming and holding my hand for a bit. I begged for an epidural. They were finding me a place on the labour ward, she said, but as I wasn't dilated, I wasn't a priority. She removed the pessary as I was contracting too much and when she did, a gush of liquid shot out. She didn't believe that it was my waters, though I swore that I hadn't peed myself, and took it away to be tested and tend to her other patients.

The other woman on the ward, separated from me by a screen, was so kind to me. I apologised for the swearing in between contractions and she said not to worry, it was her second baby so she understood. She coached me to breathe through them. I started feeling like I needed to poo and shuffled to the toilet, straining, but nothing came. I told the woman behind the screen and she said I needed to call the midwives urgently.

I pressed that bell and about ten minutes later I was taken down to the labour suite in a wheelchair. I was 8 centimetres dilated, having got there without my birthing partner or a dedicated midwife, with no gas and air or pain relief for hours. And my baby was in distress again. By this point, I was dissociating from the pain and I thought we were both going to die.

On the labour suite, the midwife hooked me up to the monitors and taught me how to use the gas and air, but it was too late for it. My partner joined me from the car just in time. The midwife told me that my baby had to be born quickly. His heart rate was going too low and not recovering quickly enough. He was back-to-back with me, which is why I'd had the back pain along with my contractions. My partner recalls seeing him bob in and out of me, and I know now this is a sign of shoulder dystocia, which is when the baby's shoulder has become stuck behind the mother's pubic bone, preventing the baby from being born.

The room had been slowly filling up with people, but the exact sequence of events is a blur. The same doctor who'd examined me at 3 a.m. was there. He told me he was going to cut me and try to remove my baby with suction. If that didn't work, it would be an emergency Caesarean. I remember saying I didn't care, please knock me out, whatever, make it end and make my baby safe. He said I'd have to push as hard as I could when he asked me to. 'Team baby?' he asked. Yes, team baby.

It worked, but I don't remember my son being born. Apparently, I held him, he latched and I went for a shower. I am so thankful that he was born healthy. I realised that what I had learnt at NCT was rubbish. I felt like a failure for having interventions, but what was the alternative? Doctors don't do interventions for any perverse reason, they do it to get the best outcomes for mum and baby. My partner was shellshocked. We felt like we'd been lied to.

On the baby ward, the same doctor came and spoke to me. He said he had thought about taking me to the labour suite there and then at 3 a.m. and getting me prepared for a Caesarean. I'd have had a dedicated midwife while I laboured, the support of my partner and been looked after by doctors. I wonder how different things would have been?

I went home a day later. I was being seen by the perinatal mental health team, but when I told them that every time I closed my eyes I felt a doctor's hands in my body trying to flip the baby the right way round and couldn't sleep, they told me it was normal. I didn't sleep (even when the baby slept) for weeks. My bed reminded me too much of a hospital bed. I was too worried for my baby. I was hypervigilant and all sorts of scenarios played through my mind. When I told my perinatal mental health nurse my birth story, she said I should feel proud and strong. I couldn't feel further from that. When I asked about birth trauma, she shut me down. Maybe it was normal after all?

My stitches were incredibly painful and I thought they were infected. I was told to take baths, not showers, but every time I did, my stitches fell out into the water. I couldn't sit down and even lying down hurt. I had to stand up to feed my baby. I was prescribed antibiotics and lidocaine liquid to put on the wound. I applied this according to the instructions, but I believe that I overdosed. I felt panicked and breathless and my heart was racing. I was slurring my words, and jittery. At the hospital, I was told it sounded like an overdose. The next day I felt better and threw the lidocaine in the bin.

The second round of antibiotics did the job, but my mind was still not right. About a week and a half post-partum, I was holding my son as he fell asleep after a feed and his body started jerking. He was already being closely monitored as he was born small and jaundiced. I told my mum what I thought I saw and after putting down the phone I called NHS24, who sent an ambulance. We spent a week in hospital. He had an IV placed and they tried everywhere to place it, even shaving a patch on his tiny head and trying there. It was horrible. Blood tests, MRI, lumbar puncture. No answers. I was climbing the walls. In his little hospital room, I felt hot all the time and irritable. There was an itching under my skin and I felt guilty. So guilty. My blood pressure climbed through the roof.

When we returned home, my partner soon went back to work. Two months post-partum, I started feeling bad again. I'd become increasingly overprotective of my son and worried about hygiene, hand washing, infections and people dropping him. I'd started to not like anyone holding him except R. I was also finding it hard to love him. I think in some way I couldn't let myself believe he was alive or going to stay alive.

I remember a call with my mental health nurse that I had to take while on a walk, as it felt like the dust in the corners of the house was threatening me and I couldn't cope. She told me it was normal and not to worry about the housework. I told her this couldn't be normal. If it was normal to not sleep for two weeks after giving birth, to experience flashbacks, to feel so terrible and anxious all the time, then normal just wasn't good enough. When I read back my notes from the perinatal mental health team at this time, they said that I was becoming 'increasingly aggressive with staff'. I still hadn't had a face-to-face appointment.

Things got worse and I started hallucinating all sorts of things. People groping me in the night. Ambulances and police outside. Snipers waiting for me to appear at the window to shoot me down. People beating up my partner every time he left to get supplies, which I was trusting him less and less to do. People poisoning or replacing our food with rotten stuff when my back was turned. Switching the baby's formula tin with one gone sour. Killing my baby when I was in the shower or asleep. Breastfeeding was a divine connection between me and my son. Every trip out was a test, as everyone in the shop or the street was someone I knew and if I spoke to them I would have failed. The CCTV and the aeroplanes and the birds were watching. Someone had switched my baby with a dolly. I couldn't watch TV or listen to the radio as everything felt like it was sending me a message.

I had gone off the deep end and ended up having a seven-week stay in the mother and baby unit. I believe that I had (preventable) birth trauma due to how my birth was handled. My experience was minimised by my mental health team and this directly led to my psychotic breakdown. I'm lucky to have made a full recovery. At one point, in the thick fuzz of shame and heavy antipsychotics, I thought I'd never live normally again, be alone or go back to work. I did eventually go back to work. I had another child and stayed healthy. Her birth was handled well, I remember everything and I felt we were safe and in control.

The experience tarnished the first year of my son's life. No one had a normal time with Covid, but waking up from psychosis and all the embarrassing, uncomfortable and deranged things I did and said to the people I love was like waking up with the worst hangover shame you can imagine. I suppose it would be nice if one outcome of all this is that it could be part of an effort to improve things in the future. Women's health is so neglected across the board, and when I think about it, I feel so, so angry.

CHAPTER TWENTY-SEVEN

MEDICAL EMERGENCIES

ALEX

I often fantasised about being pregnant – what it would feel like, mostly. I assumed I'd continue to look like myself, albeit with a perfect bump, which I'd have fun dressing each morning. I blame this ideation of mine on images and stories of effortless pregnancies and holistic, celebrity-endorsed birthing techniques fed to me morning and night. TV births have a lot to answer for. Many women are simply not prepared for the reality of what can happen if they are fortunate enough to become pregnant. And it's this mindset of shying away from the often hard-to-digest truth that permeates society, allowing the grim reality of what is really happening on our maternity wards to skulk away unnoticed.

Here's what happened to me.

Having spent over a decade living in London chasing the glittering career I promised myself as a student, all the while daydreaming of the 2.4 children scenario that tormented my ovaries, I eventually met John, the love of my life and the person who would soon become my husband and father to our gorgeous little boy, Moses.

By the time I gave birth, I was the wrong side of thirty-five. Not exactly part of my life plan – and geriatric by medical standards. But despite the statistics – and not mentioning the morning sickness, which lasted all day – I was frequently told that things were on track. And so, we proceeded with our dream and left the bright lights of London for a quiet life in the country.

As my pregnancy progressed, the bigger I became and the harder it was to function. While other pregnant women glowed, I could no longer wear regular shoes and stringing a sentence together left me breathless. I must admit that deep down I was concerned and alarm bells were ringing. But never having been pregnant before, I didn't know what was and wasn't normal. I was relieved that, despite my elevated blood pressure and the protein in my urine, pre-eclampsia was repeatedly ruled out.

Then one day, while I was attending an appointment in Hastings to discuss my worsening sleep apnoea, the consultant took one look at me and told me I had pre-eclampsia. Referring to my notes, she said it was obvious I'd been suffering from the condition for many months and I was quickly ushered onto a ward. Confused and alone, and surrounded by chaos, the consultant wanted to deliver my baby there and then. I was petrified. I was nearing the end of my third trimester and had been assured two days before, in Pembury, that everything was fine. We were all set for a 'natural' birth. A few hours later, I was discharged, with strict instructions for the receiving team at Pembury. But the midwife I spoke to there was adamant that I did not have pre-eclampsia and seemed overly keen to get me off the phone. She told me that if I was concerned, we should go to Crowborough Birthing Centre for a blood pressure check. We did as we were told, and I was given the OK before heading home to the safety of my bed. Sheer relief flooded my body.

A few days had passed when I felt a tingling sensation in my spine. I immediately put it down to Braxton Hicks contractions. I had weeks to go and, as with most first babies, I'd assumed he'd arrive late. That's what everyone says, right? But when the pain ramped up it was debilitating and there was no doubt in my mind that Moses was on his way. We needed to get to hospital and fast.

John phoned multiple times and each time we were told to wait until my contractions were five minutes apart. This was quite unexpected considering I was high risk – my notes clearly stated that I carried a virus known as Group B streptococcus, a life-threatening infection if passed on to newborns. Now I'm no medical professional, but a quick google will tell you that women with Group B strep require intravenous antibiotics from the start of labour every four hours until delivery and so it is critical that labour is slow and controlled. Google will also inform you that pre-eclampsia can cause a woman to labour very quickly. Thus, Group B strep and pre-eclampsia are two forces working against each other, one requiring a slow labour and the other accelerating it.

Confused, I tried to remain calm, taking deep breaths as advised. But then my waters broke and my survival instinct kicked in. Somehow, I heaved myself into the car. Somehow, we made it to the hospital – and somehow, I made it on to the labour ward. From then on, it all becomes a blur.

I had been on the labour ward for less than two hours when the crash team were called. Noise and chaos ensued and bright lights whizzed overhead as they sped me down the corridor into theatre – a surreal feeling. I felt a detachment as the surgeon shouted my name repeatedly, asking me to sign a form – otherwise, I'd die, she said. But I'd lost all ability to open my mouth and speak, to raise my hand and hold the pen. I guess it was the combination of the shocking realisation of what was going on around me and the pain, which was so intense it was paralysing. I remember very vividly John looking particularly handsome in scrubs – beautiful, in fact – a familiar face of belonging, which provided reassurance and comfort. Then a peculiar feeling of calm washed over me as he was forced out of theatre and I was at peace, resigned to the fact that these might be my last moments. I closed my eyes and prayed. It was out of my control, my and Moses's lives were quite literally in the hands of God and the surgeon that stood before me.

I awoke to a large and empty, unfamiliar room. My voice was small and hoarse as I shouted out. Dazed and high on morphine, I don't remember much that followed. Although I do remember meeting Moses for the first time, I still can't quite fathom if this 'memory' is real or something I've devised from studying the photographs over and over, willing myself to remember, to feel.

After nearly a week in hospital, I lost all concept of time. I was exhausted and sleep-deprived. Not because of Moses's continuous crying, but because I dared not allow myself to fall asleep. I was too scared. I'd lost all trust in the professionals who surrounded me. I didn't know who I could believe.

With her hands on my shoulders, looking deep into my eyes and insisting I get some sleep, a matronly midwife told me I should be grateful. Not everyone was as lucky as me. When I got upset and asked questions or complained of chronic pain, I was made to feel like a hypochondriac – an ungrateful inconvenience at best. Sleep, it seemed, was their answer to everything. It was the same midwife who made me sign an account of what had happened, an account she had written and one I was forced to agree to, saying I was happy with the birth and my care. If I didn't, I would be trapped in hospital for another three days at least, and I needed to get out for my sanity, if nothing else.

As the days and weeks rolled by, John and I struggled – we got worse before we got better. We were supposed to be making happy memories, fit for a photo album, which Moses would pore over in years to come. But our experience didn't allow such scenes of elation, as a state of heightened anxiety overshadowed everything. Having missed the birth of my own child, I was left with raw feelings of anger and grief. The sound of a passing siren would leave me shaking and in tears. Being on constant high alert was mentally and physically exhausting. Crippling.

I needed answers, and as I proceeded to push for an investigation into what had happened, I was met with resistance at every turn. Eventually, it was my psychologist who managed to retrieve my notes. They were taken from me at some point during the labour. It took six months and multiple letters to get them back. Flicking through them, it's evident that crucial information was omitted and written in retrospect. There is mention of labetalol being prescribed to stabilise my blood pressure. Yet I never received it.

Two and a half years have now passed, and as I look back on my first year of motherhood, my stomach churns. Post-traumatic stress disorder doesn't just disappear, it takes time. It may never go away. It has impacted every aspect of my life, from work to relationships with family and with friends. My relationship with John. My relationship with Moses. My relationship with myself. Remembering my lifelong daydream of 2.4 children, I'd love to provide Moses with a sibling. He'd make the most wonderful, caring older brother. But I dare not even contemplate it. What if I left him motherless? The idea of becoming pregnant again scares the hell out of me.

I may not be able to go back in time, but I will campaign for change – and this is why I've shared my story. Medieval attitudes towards women and birth-related trauma pervade our society and institutions, and this has to end. As the UK birth rate continues to decline and more and more people are choosing to put having children 'on ice' due to financial pressures, surely we should be encouraging families to have children if they want to. My experience, together with the lack of provision for maternal mental health within UK law, means that my decision has been made for me. My choice as to whether I have another baby has been taken away from me. And no woman should ever have a choice as monumental as this taken from them.

RACHAEL

Conceiving my twins was a case of throwing the kitchen sink at IVF. After seven years of multiple failed attempts and surgeries, one semi-detached house remortgaged and countless credit cards maxed, getting two for the price of one small country left me so elated I didn't dare believe that the effort had paid off.

At thirty-six weeks pregnant, on a Monday, I suffered crippling pains that were nothing short of terrifying in their intensity. I told Liam, my husband, it was time and started to gather myself to get into the car. Suddenly, the pains eased as quickly as they'd arrived, so I called my midwife on her mobile to ask her advice. She answered the phone, but when I identified myself, she immediately cut me short with, 'Rachael, I'm on leave, I'm not back at work till Wednesday.' I was mortified to have disturbed her while she was on holiday, particularly as the pains had now gone, so I gave a brief explanation of what I'd experienced and said, 'But I'm feeling OK now…'

The midwife told me that I sounded fine, this was all to be expected and that she'd see me on Wednesday when her holiday was over. Again, I was reassured and thought little more of it – after all, everyone complained that they felt simply dreadful towards the end of a pregnancy.

At around 9 p.m. the next day, I drew back the covers and clambered into bed. As I lay down, I felt a popping sensation and warmth between my thighs. I looked down and realised I was haemorrhaging.

I snatched the phone and called 999. Within six minutes, I was being loaded into an ambulance – lights, sirens, the full works. The horror of this journey is etched into my memory for ever. En route, I contemplated the depth of cruelty that we had pushed ourselves to financial ruin paying for IVF, the physical and emotional toll had been indescribable and now we'd come within a hair's breadth of happiness, only for this to happen. That just seemed like the hardest thing to bear. As we neared the hospital, I began to try to resolve the fact that we would inevitably be returning home as a couple, not as parents to the twins we had fought so hard for.

I recall just snippets of the next hour, the hour that I became a mother at last. I remember hearing things I couldn't respond to – like my blood pressure being just eighty over forty, the surgeon saying she was 'in grave danger of slipping' in my blood, the anaesthetist saying, 'She's not been stable for three minutes', and wanting to tell them that my arm hurt but not being heard. It was my husband who finally alerted them as I passed out.

It turns out a cannula had been misplaced. They'd had a compression pump fast filling my arm with over a litre of life-giving Hartmann's solution. Instead of going into my vein, though, it was merely pooling under the skin.

Liam says he was sent reeling as the anaesthetists flew across to my other arm to start injecting me with ephedrine and attaching tubes to the back-up cannula that was in my wrist. More medication and fluid was given through this site. I came round in time to hear, 'OK, that's baby number two' and a shrill cry. They brought this baby round to me, wrapped in a towel, and said, 'You have a son…'

While trying to conceive over the years, I had endured miscarriages and I had been through multiple failed IVF cycles. I had dreamed so many times of hearing the words 'You have a….' Yet when they came, I felt nothing. No desire to see the baby, no joy, no interest. Instead, bizarrely, I found my attention focused on the fact that the midwife was covered from head to toe in my blood. I wondered why she hadn't worn longer surgical gloves. My daughter was still being resuscitated; I didn't even ask about her.

I went back to the labour unit and spent the next three days being cared for there. Rather than the rush of maternal love I'd been told to expect, I was hit with a rush of diagnoses. I'd lost 3 litres of blood during the C-section. My blood loss was caused by an abruption of my daughter's placenta. I also had pre-eclampsia, acute renal failure and blood pooling round my liver.

Sadly, I didn't produce any breastmilk. Without consulting either myself or my husband, the hospital staff stopped providing donor milk and started my children on formula. Instantly, I felt like I'd failed as a mother by not being able to feed my children.

When I was deemed well enough to be moved to the maternity ward, I encountered a cavalier attitude from almost all the staff that I realised was cultural within the hospital. From the insistence by a midwife that I be 'left to fly solo' to feed the twins overnight, despite having an untreated dehiscence to my Caesarean scar, to being left lying in a pool of my own blood for hours while the afternoon shift neglected to hand my case over to the evening shift.

There was the fifteen-year-old work experience girl who would stand in my room giving me a monologue on how bored she was, gossiping about her friends at school and telling me that my daughter was by far the sickest baby on the neonatal ward – she had a bilirubin level of 379. In my head, this was because of my failure to breastfeed her. There was the student midwife who, under the supervision of the same midwife who insisted I 'fly solo' while neglecting my ruptured scar, somehow managed to leave a stitch from my C-section in my abdomen. This wasn't removed until months after the birth.

I've reached a point where the only word I can find to coherently describe the culture and behaviour of the treatment I received is 'bullying'.

Whenever I asked questions about diagnoses or solutions and whenever I asked the staff for help, I was met with:

- Sarcasm. 'Don't think you're anything special, we've had bigger abruptions than yours,' a midwife said when I questioned the incessant stream of medical students who were being sent to see me as a case study.
- Hostility. When I started crying at the fact that I was in so much pain with a dehisced scar and feeling so ill, I was told that the midwives couldn't take responsibility for my babies and if I was so desperate to sleep then my husband needed to stay at the hospital.
- Defensiveness. 'Well, we're short-staffed.'
- Neglect. After my scar burst at 8 p.m., I was left lying in a pool of

blood until 2 a.m. despite repeated pleas for help. Doctors then ignored the dehiscence, leading to my developing a severe infection that required an urgent readmittance to hospital for further IV antibiotic treatment.

The dehiscence of my scar led to my needing months of daily treatment. The smell from my infected abdomen was utterly repugnant. My children would consequently scream if I picked them up but could be passed to a complete stranger (who didn't smell!) and settle immediately.

My physical and emotional state, coupled with the horrors of what we had endured, led me to view the children with a degree of at best apathy and at worst contempt. Tissue viability and district nurses became my mainstays. When other new mums were out showing off their babies and undertaking buggy fit classes, I was at home waiting for my dressings to be changed, too embarrassed to socialise due to the foul smell from my abdomen that nothing could mask. This went on for months. It was tearing at my self-esteem and gradually making me even more reclusive and isolated, when what I needed most was connection and support. God knows how my husband managed to stand it, but I'm so grateful he did.

After four and a half months of treatment and self-imposed isolation, my GP referred me back to the tissue specialist nurses, who fitted a vacuum in my scar. Twenty-two weeks after giving birth, my C-section wound finally closed. At last, I felt as though I might be able to 'begin' motherhood. It was only around this time that the babies and I 'clicked'. I promptly switched from ambivalence to obsession about my babies' activities.

Sadly, I have continued to be plagued with issues with my scar. I should have had further surgery to have the entire thing resected, but this experience left me – like so many other people who experience birth trauma – with a deep mistrust of healthcare professionals and therefore unable to access healthcare effectively. This is just one of the emotional scars I have from my birth experience.

I'm not the woman I used to be. Of course, parenthood changes us all. But I used to be a woman who'd move mountains to achieve a goal – I finally got pregnant, for example.

The mental health provision for PTSD is abysmal. After flying under the radar for over a year, it was the Birth Trauma Association who helped me when I had nowhere else to turn. My GP simply prescribed medication and put me on a long list for cognitive behavioural therapy. A decade on, I am still classed as having PTSD.

It has also impacted my relationship with my children. For years, every time the twins did something I found frustrating, I wondered if I felt that way because of what happened. I was plagued with guilt that I took so long to bond with my children because of this experience. The slightest thing that's wrong with them I see as my fault – ever since Millie's anaemia was attributed to my failure to breastfeed in the first week of her life, it's become a structural thing in my thinking. Michael is on the autistic spectrum and has some motor issues and a learning difficulty. I will always wonder if the traumatic birth is to blame for at least some of the challenges he faces.

My husband was broken too. He received absolutely no care or consideration, despite everything he'd been witness to. Our marriage has survived, thankfully, but we are not the people we used to be.

On a practical level, my traumatic birth has longer-term implications for my health. I have gained 50 kg in weight since the birth of my twins. Think of the future ramifications. I know logically I need to deal with this, but logic doesn't always equate to action.

Due to the mental and physical health issues I was left with, I couldn't return to my former employment in the media. For the first time in my life, I was forced to claim benefits and I spent five years on disability living allowance. I was so grateful to the BTA for the life-changing help they had provided to me that I wanted to pay it forwards and started volunteering with them. I now work for the BTA, earning a fraction of my former wage but at least feeling like I'm with people who understand, in a role with a charity that means the world to me and hopefully utilises my experience to improve outcomes for other people.

My official complaint about my birth to Countess of Chester Hospital was handled so excruciatingly badly that I decided to consult a solicitor. They agreed that medical negligence was obvious, and six years later I received a large out-of-court settlement. I would give anything to not have needed to pursue legal action and no amount of money could ever make up for what I went through, and continue to go through, as a direct result of the neglect and poor care that I was subjected to.

What should have been a moment when all my dreams of finally becoming a parent came true turned into a living nightmare, the impact of which I will face for the rest of my life.

CHAPTER TWENTY-EIGHT

FATHERS AND PARTNERS

HENRY

After days of waiting and false starts, we were finally called to the hospital for induction. I was full of excitement and apprehension. I came to the Royal Stoke fully equipped with a camping mat, pillow, suitcase full of clothes, my laptop and sweets. A friend whose wife had recently experienced a traumatic birth had warned me that birth was no plain sailing.

We were shown into our bay in a shared room of the maternity ward, next to other mothers in different stages of the induction process. I observed my wife's interactions with a strong, matriarchal nurse, who was helping Theo as best she could. The ward felt like a production line, with competent nurses who were clearly overworked and overstretched. They didn't have time to speak to us properly and I was wary of making too many requests for fear of being reprimanded. As a dad-to-be, I was very aware that my role was a supporting one only. I felt that we were in good hands, but as time went on the experience became more and more stressful.

I went for walks in the park next to the hospital, with occasional visits to a fast-food outlet, in the periods between Theo's dilation checks when nothing was happening. When Theo tried to rest that first night, I distracted myself by watching a Netflix film about the Thai football team getting trapped in a cave – perhaps not the best choice of film given that I have claustrophobia. My biggest role was to try to calm Theo, who was getting increasingly agitated. I wasn't allowed to be present at Theo's first vaginal examination and she returned incredibly distressed. I accompanied her later for multiple inspections in these cold and neon-lit rooms, which reminded me of a prison cell, and stood by my wife as she was administered laughing gas and screamed in pain while she underwent yet another examination. The whole process seemed like a scene from the 1500s. It was horrendous the first time around and had become unbearable by the time she'd had multiple checks.

After at least six examinations and nearly forty-eight hours of induction, I thought that the birth was never going to happen. They told Theo that they would break her waters, and after that we were moved into our own room with a lovely midwife who wore a nurse's watch attached to her uniform with a Disney *Beauty and the Beast* clasp. I felt some relief that we'd got our own room, which felt safer. After getting very little sleep in the shared ward and feeling battle-weary, I managed to drift off to sleep.

I woke up several hours later to Theo pacing around the room. She told me that her contractions had started. I felt extremely groggy and the whole experience felt very surreal. I thought that the baby would be here any minute and I tried to battle my tiredness and force myself to get back in the zone. In among the fog, I recall the moment she was informed that she needed a cannula in her hand, which was something that, knowing Theo's phobia of needles and blood, I had been dreading. I tried to reassure her with positive affirmations to calm her down and distract her from the needle being put in. I insisted that the senior anaesthetist carry out the procedure and told them that they only had one shot at it. They did a very good job despite Theo's shock and visible distress and it went in perfectly first time. I wrapped a pashmina around her hand so that she couldn't see the tube or entry point. This might seem like a routine procedure for most people, but I knew that for Theo it was something that could tip her over the edge.

When she was offered an epidural, I felt anxious about having another huge needle go into her body, this time into the bottom of her spine. Luckily, there were no complications. Throughout the whole process, my chief job was to reassure Theo, who cried in distress and was overwhelmed, but she held it together and was incredibly brave.

I had almost lost hope in the induction process and didn't believe she would be able to give birth naturally. Theo and I finally fell into a deep sleep from exhaustion and I was proved wrong when a midwife woke me and told me that Theo was now 10 centimetres dilated and we needed to get ready for the baby's arrival. With my heart pounding, I immediately jumped to Theo's side to hold her hand. I felt dazed and confused, as it had all happened so quickly. How could it be that a few hours before nothing was happening and now my wife was delivering our baby? I felt a mixture of excitement, pain and fear for Theo, who was in extreme physical distress. At one point I told her to breathe to push through an intense pain, which I believe now to be the moment her tear happened. I told her, 'If you don't do this, darling, you will have to go down the Caesarean route.' The midwife gave me a ticking off for being too pushy, but I knew how much Theo didn't want to end up in theatre. I was very involved and saw the full exit of our daughter, which was incredible but in hindsight possibly too much for my brain to take in. It was raw and reminded me of watching a David Attenborough wildlife documentary on the plains of Africa. They cleaned off the blood and wrapped Arabella up, as per Theo's instructions, before handing her back to her.

I was delighted that Arabella had arrived and I remember these dark brown eyes looking up at me like a wild animal, with no tears in them. I was so full of adrenaline and so concerned about Theo that I didn't feel that I had the bonding moment that some people do. However, I did feel immediate love for her and will never forget her calm demeanour as she looked all around the room. I was relieved to see that Arabella was all right, but there was something in me that felt everything was not quite right. Theo was absolutely broken and down to her last 5 per cent of energy, and when the placenta was expelled, I realised that something was wrong as she was still bleeding.

The midwife began to panic and solicited a second opinion from a doctor, who said that Theo had lost a lot of blood and would need to go to theatre to repair a tear. The room filled up with people and a sense of urgency set in. Arabella was put in a hospital cot while Theo was taken off to theatre. Nitish, a doctor who'd checked in on Theo earlier in the day, held her hand down the passageway to the operating table and reassured me that it would be OK and he would look after her, for which I'm incredibly grateful. I was left in the room with Arabella for what seemed like a long time, with her eyes looking up at me. I remember thinking, 'Shit, this is not how I envisaged being a dad.' I genuinely feared that I might end up a single parent. Knowing Theo's vulnerabilities about surgery, I was concerned that her heart would not hold out, given that she was already so weak and traumatised.

Half an hour later, someone fetched me to go into theatre. I knew that, despite my tiredness, I just had to get through the next few hours. I felt utterly on the edge of what I was capable of mentally as I scrubbed up and donned the plastic theatre gown. I don't recall who took Arabella, but I was later told that she'd been in the staffroom being looked after by the midwives. I sat next to Theo in theatre for the next two hours and talked to her, which was the biggest test of endurance I've ever had. I could see that Theo was not in a good way and I could also see the look of fear on the faces of the nurses. Two of them looked at each other and grimaced. Nitish was sitting next to her holding her hand and talking to her about politics to keep her distracted.

I remember the surgeon threading the needle in and out of her vagina – her hands like those of a puppet master, with the needle and threads going up and down and wads of bloody cotton wool being used to stem the bleeding. I could tell from the look on her face that she was having a difficult time and sure enough, after about an hour, she handed over to Nitish as the senior consultant. He spent the next hour contending with a very jagged wound. I wonder now what could have happened to Theo if he'd not been at the hospital that day. My biggest concern was that she would have a heart attack, given that she was conscious the whole time during the surgery. This was the worst-case scenario that we'd tried so hard to prevent. They certainly didn't mention this happening in NCT class! Having seen a documentary about the Shrewsbury and Telford maternity scandal, I also knew the perils of a fourth-degree tear and the fact that she could be incontinent for the rest of her life. Given the serious nature of her tear, she was only millimetres away from that happening.

At the end of the operation, we went to the next room for recovery. I was told that Theo might have an infection as her temperature had spiked in theatre and they were worried that both she and

Arabella could develop sepsis. I felt like I was going to implode. A nurse came and took some bloods from Theo. Thank God she was only semi-conscious because she would never have allowed them to take six vials normally. We slept for a bit and Arabella was finally brought through to us. I held her and we had some lovely bonding time.

I remember a sense of absolute celebration when we were given the all clear to go through to our room. I wheeled Theo and Arabella in her hospital trolley bed through the corridors to a private side room, where we were finally able to be a family. I went for a walk for some fresh air and rang my mother-in-law to let her know the news and that her daughter was fine but that there had been complications. She instinctively knew something major must have gone wrong and she drove to the hospital to help.

Although we were in our own room, there was a sense of anxiety that something could go wrong with Theo's stitches at any minute. I had to take on the role of mum for those first few days while she came out of the shock of intensive surgery. I had to shower her, carry her to the toilet, feed her and look after the baby as well. When Theo struggled to breastfeed or produce colostrum, I went to buy formula in the supermarket nearby. My mother-in-law did a shift pattern with me over the next few days in the hospital, sharing duties such as feeding Arabella, changing her nappies, doing skin-to-skin contact and rocking her to sleep.

My experience of the birth was far more intense and stressful than I could ever have imagined. Being able to talk about it to Theo while writing this story has been incredibly cathartic, as I hadn't realised quite how much of an impact the experience had on me. I will never forget how stressed both Theo and I were and I feel that all fathers should have access to mental health support in situations like these. I'm incredibly grateful to everyone involved in ensuring that Arabella and Theo were safe and I'm proud of my wife for the amazing work she does to raise awareness for birth trauma, but I will never forget those few days for as long as I live. Thankfully, we have the most beautiful daughter, as quite honestly, I'm not sure if I have it in me to go through it all again.

JAMES

My name is James, I live in Bridgend, I'm thirty-eight years old and dad to a four-year-old girl. My wife gave birth in mid-2019 by emergency C-section in the Princess of Wales Hospital, Bridgend. Some of the experiences I went through are foggy in my memory. I believe I'm suffering from PTSD or a similar condition, although what I can recall is accurate, confirmed via medical notes and my wife.

My wife is a type-one diabetic and has been since she was five years old. Her condition is well controlled and was more so during pregnancy, as we paid £160 per month for a continuous glucose monitor that the diabetic clinic refused to pay for as she was not considered high risk – despite being told she was high risk in the same clinic. I attended every meeting and appointment with my wife and so witnessed poor care throughout and ingrained bad practices. This has completely changed my view of hospitals and medical professionals. I have now lost all trust that they will do the right thing.

My first concerns were in diabetic birth meetings, where no one seemed to talk to each other and staff would openly complain about colleagues. It was during the birth planning meeting that the consultant wrote 'epidural' in her notes after being requested to by my wife. This was the one page of the notes they 'lost' when she later submitted her initial complaint. There was no evidence or options presented; she was told what would happen and not given a choice. We asked about a planned Caesarean section due to the risks involved in her giving birth, only to be told, 'There is no need, you will have an induction.' She was not educated or directed to any information on this choice, just told she would be induced.

The second occurrence that stands out is when my wife went in for steroid injections to help develop the baby's lungs, as she was being induced early. After she had been injected with the steroids and put on a sliding scale device to administer insulin, I was shocked to discover they were about to administer the wrong insulin, the one that my wife is allergic to. This was the first worrying sign. Luckily, we stopped them and they changed it.

I was very shocked at the way their system worked, as it seemed antiquated. Normally, my wife plans what she eats, adds up the carbs and injects twenty minutes beforehand to keep her blood sugar level steady. On the sliding scale, she was expected to not administer insulin; they would do a finger-prick test and wait for her blood sugar to go high before altering the insulin given. This was despite her wearing a continuous glucose monitor, which apparently they couldn't trust, despite prescribing them. The food offered was white toast – no low-carb options for diabetics – which obviously skyrocketed her blood sugar.

When we came in for the birth, she was induced and asked to go for a walk. Her waters broke in a doorway. She was then taken into the bed, where her contractions started, but she was not dilated enough for the labour ward. Her pain gradually increased over the next few hours and she begged for an epidural. They gave her pethidine, which did not take the pain away, and a TENS machine.

They repeatedly examined her and said she wasn't dilated enough and by the end, she was writhing in pain and begging them to help – it seemed like torture to me. Hours later, we were taken to the labour ward, where she was told she would get her epidural, but again, we waited hours as they said there was no doctor available. They administered some drug to try to speed things along and my wife started shaking uncontrollably. After some time, she fell asleep as she was exhausted and she moaned and cried in her sleep, the sound of which will stay with me for ever.

The next morning, a doctor came in and everything moved very fast as the heartbeat of baby indicated she was in distress and needed to come out. In the room next door, the patient also needed an emergency C-section so the doctors convened to decide who to operate on first. They came back after deciding my wife would go first and took all the fluids down, including the insulin, which they said she'd have to go without.

In the operating room, I felt like they knew what they were doing. They delivered our daughter into my arms. I feel guilty that at that moment, all I cared about was my wife. She was sliced open, being violently sick and I heard a doctor say they needed to stop the bleeding. When we got back to the labour ward, I noticed my daughter was twitching, which I later found out was due to low blood sugar. She was taken into the special care baby unit (SCBU) hours later. My most vivid memory is that before admitting her, at about 4 a.m., a doctor was trying to shove a feeding tube down my daughter's neck while saying he'd never done this before and was really struggling. My daughter was obviously screaming and crying and this experience has absolutely traumatised me. I work in a public place and whenever I hear a baby crying, despite it being almost five years later, I feel a wave of panic and have to walk away. It affects me for the rest of the day. This is despite attending counselling to try to work through the issues I have from the birth experience.

I was so sleep-deprived at this time, as I was allowed to stay with my wife on the ward, but I wasn't allowed to sleep, something which is just inhumane. For two days, we visited my daughter in the SCBU. It was hard being on a ward where everyone else had their babies with them. Later, we had issues where my wife struggled to breastfeed, even with a pump. She was pressured to do so and she felt like a failure when she couldn't. It's only since then, after researching, that I've discovered how unlikely it was that she would be able to breastfeed at that time, due to all the complicating factors.

I remember the first visit from the local midwife after we got home to check everything was OK, which they said it was. It staggers me when I think back, as my wife was in uncontrollable floods of tears and we were both so evidently scarred by the experience. We were offered no support after the birth and had to pay privately to see a mental health professional.

My wife spent a lot of time writing a thorough account and complaint to the hospital, as she felt she was obligated to raise awareness to stop it happening to others. This was not easy for her to do. The hospital basically discounted her account and seemingly tried to find flaws, even saying that someone suffering with PTSD could not have mentally written the complaint. The eventual outcome was that the hospital admitted failures and settled out of court after stringing her along for over a year, in the hope, I believe, that she would give up. My wife felt guilty for potentially taking them to court as the NHS has no money, but we didn't see any other way. They didn't seem to want to listen or have an appetite for change. If the hospital had admitted failures and explained what they were doing to prevent it happening again, this would have ended the process, which would have done something to help gain our trust back and also would have saved them money.

I still have no trust in hospitals and medical professionals and I suffer from flashbacks. The birth has changed me and affects me every day. I am a manager and one of my team said she was pregnant last week. Instead of saying congratulations, I didn't know what to say as I just felt sorry for her. I am open about the experience even though I still don't feel I've properly processed it – if that is even possible. It astounds me what others tell me when I open up about my experience. I would estimate that eight out of ten people I speak to have suffered trauma and mental distress from preventable causes to do with birth. This *must* change. Most people are ashamed to speak up and the pain experienced by women in birth is almost seen as a badge of honour. The medical profession needs to learn from its mistakes. At some point in the future, my daughter may want children of her own. How will I deal with this when I now know the truth about our maternity services?

CHAPTER TWENTY-NINE

MARGINALISED GROUPS

LILLIAN

I gave birth at St George's Hospital in Tooting in August 2007. I was due to give birth at the end of December but went into labour early. A family friend who was a midwife told me to go to the maternity unit because they would know what to do. I remember seeing another couple who had their suitcase ready for a planned Caesarean. They're all nice and relaxed, no drama. I turn up huffing and puffing, Lamaze breathing, the lot, sweating and saying, 'I really need your help, is there any way that I can see someone?'

The two ladies at the desk, who were black like me, were having a chat. The culture at the maternity unit was that everyone was worried about what shift they were going to do next and that's what they were doing: chatting about shifts. And I stood there waiting. I said, 'Excuse me, I need help,' and they looked up like I was in the wrong place. Eventually, I said, 'I'm having problems. I couldn't go to A&E because I've been told to come here and you'll be able to help me.'

They took a very long time and then in slow motion asked me for my notes. Luckily, I had them and handed them over. I said, 'I can't stand for much longer because I'm out of breath. I'm going to take a seat.' When I sat, they shouted across to me, saying, 'What's your name again?'

I thought, 'I've got a file that gives you everything you could possibly need inside – why are you asking me what my name is? You've got it there.' But I repeated my name and then I told my husband he would have to speak to them because I couldn't move. Ten minutes after he came back, they called over again and said, 'Can you ask your wife to come up to the desk?' I said, 'Tell them I can't move, I'm in so much pain. If they want to know anything, they need to come to me. I can't.' He was upset and he was saying, 'You've got to get up.' So I got up! Like an idiot! I'm so angry with myself now.

They kept asking me nonsensical questions about my husband's age and date of birth because they were interested in our personal information. There was nothing professional about it. I said, 'Can you get some help?' And they were just acting and looking at me like 'How dare you?' Then they told me to have a seat. I was there for maybe thirty minutes. Nobody helped me.

I stood up and said, 'What does anyone have to do to get help here? I thought this was a place that helped people.' Then blood started pouring down my leg. I said, 'Oh my God, they are trying to kill me and my baby!' Then everyone started rushing in. The lady with her husband with her, they were white and they got an elite service: 'Would you like to come with us, Mr and Mrs Smith?' Oh yes, of course. Everyone was on their best behaviour. But they left me.

It was one of the most horrendous moments of my life. They rushed me into this room and told me to lie on the bed. Blood was spouting everywhere because I was lying on the bed. Then this different lady started the same thing: 'Your name, your date of birth, your husband's name, his date of birth.' What's his date of birth got to do with anything? He's not having the baby. I said, 'Shall we just leave, go to A&E, because I don't understand.' She replied, 'No, no.' As soon as I said that, the obstetrician came in. He went into professional mode and started saying, 'Sorry about what's going on; let me check you over first.'

He checked me over, asked me a lot of questions, very thorough, and just said, 'Look, I'm really sad to say that you are in labour now, so the best thing we can do is just to work with you so that we can deliver your baby for you. I know this is not the right time.' He said all the empathic things you need to hear. But I believe that I might have been in a different situation had I not wasted forty-five minutes to an hour with the other people at the front desk. I believe my story would have been different if not for their negligence.

We waited a little bit and then got moved into a birthing theatre. They gowned me up, but by this time I'd lost so much blood it was ridiculous. They said, 'We're going to do something to help speed you up, because you're dilated to 8 or 10 centimetres. It's happening now.' It seemed like a horror movie and I was just thinking, 'This isn't the right time.' Then the obstetrician left and the other guy who did all the medications kept shouting in my face: 'You're going to have this baby, but your baby could be born dead. Do you understand? Your baby could be born dead.'

He said this about five times. I just lay there sobbing, 'What are you saying to me?' He kept tapping my shoulder and saying, 'Do you understand, do you understand?' It was like I was dropped into a war zone and someone was trying to shout in my face that I'm going to lose the baby because I've been shot in the stomach or something. It was so factual and non-compassionate that I couldn't get my head round the madness. My husband tapped him on the shoulder and said, 'We've got it and you've got to stop shouting that now because we've got it, we understand.'

When I gave birth, it was all quite quick. The same nurse gave me this injection and he punched it into my leg like a stab. I'm fairly dark-skinned, but I had a massive bruise for about six months afterwards, from my hip down to my knee.

After that, they said, 'Baby's born, baby's crying.' At twenty-one weeks old, our baby was tiny. They put him into a little incubator. We had already named him: Ethan. He was breathing. We were then transferred to a completely different team and another lady came and gave me instructions: 'Please have a shower, then there's a wheelchair here, go with your husband. We'll be down in the neonatal ward; come straight there so you can see him.'

I had a shower, we went over and we saw Ethan in an incubator. He was in a Tesco freezer bag – that's what you do with premature babies. We had a marvellous team. The doctor introduced himself and said, 'We'll look after your son and take good care of him. He seems to be OK.' On his watch, everything was great. We would go to the neonatal ward throughout the afternoon and the night-time. Then, unfortunately, the doctor had a day off and that's where it went all wrong.

Again, we had a woman who was doing that same chat about shifts. She had to clear the tube for the mucus in the baby's mouth. She's got this little tube and she's poking it into his mouth, but you can see his reflex is like when you jab someone with a needle. That's what my baby was doing – flinching each time she put the tube in his mouth. Why? Because she was looking sideways and talking to a friend about shift change. She wasn't really concentrating on what she was doing. I banged the window and said, 'If you want to talk about your shift, why don't you stop doing that. Get away from my son and talk about shifts as much as you like, but can you just stop doing what you're doing because I really don't want you to do that any more.'

She looked at me like, 'How dare you.' I thought, 'Oh my God, we've got another one of these idiot people.' I don't know how she got the job, but she clearly felt that she was so experienced that she didn't have to look at the child as she's trying to feed them. It was really bothering me. Meanwhile, she kept doing what she was doing.

I went off and told one of the other nurses, 'I do not want her to touch my son any more.' I explained what happened and they said, 'Oh my God.' She then got taken off touching Ethan, but I believe the damage was already done. That night, a few hours later, we had doctors come up to us and they said that unfortunately, when they were doing their checks and observations, Ethan had a brain haemorrhage and he was now on life support. They went on: 'He will be brain dead if we turn this off because he's reliant on the machine.'

I was not digesting any of this. Then the lady said, 'Shall we turn the life support off then?' I replied, 'What are you saying? It's not like you've fried a bag of chips and want to take them out of the fryer. You've just told me an intense piece of information that I've had to digest.' I asked if there was anyone who could pray over him before they switched it off and she said they had a chaplain. I said, 'I'm not making any decisions now. Thank you very much, but I need to be left alone.'

I was put into a little room. Upon entering, I was surrounded by people holding their babies, babies crying, people cooing at their babies. My child was in an incubator and I'd just been told that he wasn't going to survive. Being placed with people who were holding their own children was just mind-blowingly insensitive. And my room was right opposite the busiest desk in the world. You could hear the door slam, you could hear the phone ringing. It was just like a paper wall with a door in front of it. There was a vibrant, very stressed-out receptionist, who was quite curt and rude at first, and I said, 'I don't think you understand what's just happened to me, can you read my notes?' She came into my room and said, 'I'm so sorry.'

The hospital support was absolutely null and void. My friend who was a midwife eventually came and got me moved. From then, I had a bit of peace and tranquillity.

The doctor who came when it was time to say goodbye was brilliant. I held Ethan in my arms and they took away the monitor and took him off the respirator. I just held him, feeling him slowly getting colder and colder. The doctor gave me another thirty minutes to hold him. Then he had to say, 'The time of death is this,' and then the neonatal nurse providing the aftercare had this lovely little jumpsuit for him and she said, 'Look, I'm not going to do the top button up because we don't want it to pinch him.'

It will just stay with me for ever.

I couldn't understand. It's like being in a horror movie. How did I get here? You turn left down a wrong alley and all of a sudden you're just here. How? I went to a place that was supposed to be safe, supposed to be professional, and they treated me so badly that I couldn't protect my little boy.

They classed it as a miscarriage, but it wasn't, because I gave birth to a child that cried. They wanted to do some tests and they were more interested in doing an autopsy and being able to use his organs. I said no: 'I can't endorse that. I think you've done enough to him, just leave us be.'

I've had to dig deep and try to rebuild myself in order to be able to have other children at the Chelsea and Westminster Hospital.

I have two children now, a son and a daughter. I'm so blessed to have them.

MONICA

I'm forty-three years old, I live in Bedford and I have two daughters aged eleven and nine. Both my births were traumatic and have left me with lasting mental and physical effects. My first daughter was late, but I hadn't been referred earlier for a cervical sweep. I was fourteen days over my due date when I was told to go to Bedford Hospital for a scan and check. They decided I should come back for an induction.

Induction proceeded slowly, with concerns over my baby's heartbeat slowing. Every vaginal inspection was painful as I suffered from vaginismus at the time. When it came to breaking my waters, the obstetrician forcefully shoved his finger into my vagina, causing immense pain. He begrudgingly handed over to a midwife and made me feel ashamed, dismissing my reaction.

On 13 January 2013, the team decided to deliver by emergency Caesarean, which was actually a relief for me. When my daughter was born, they immediately took her for tests and didn't bring her back to me for what felt like hours. I struggled to bond with her, having missed skin-to-skin contact. It turned out there had been nothing wrong with her, but they didn't bring her straight back to me after testing. I struggled with depression and feeling on high alert for a long time afterwards. I received no mental health support but was added to a waiting list.

I developed gestational diabetes during my second pregnancy. This was highly medicalised and stressful. I spent each day testing my blood sugar levels and trying to keep them down. I was working at a university at the time and I found if I wore my work badge to obstetric appointments at Bedford Hospital, I was treated more respectfully (I am Indian British and have a northern English accent). For a stressful meeting deciding how I would give birth, I took my white, privately educated husband with me. Again, I was treated better than when I was on my own. Despite this, the meeting ended badly. After spending the appointment patronising me, the obstetrician slammed down his pen and said, 'You WILL have a C-section when I say!'

I transferred to Addenbrooke's Hospital in Cambridge after that incident. I was brought in for induction, which progressed slowly. After nearly three days in labour, my baby got stuck behind my pelvis. They tried to manually move her, but she moved back immediately. She had no signs of distress and the midwife didn't seem worried.

Just before the registrar obstetrician and registrar gynaecologist's shift ended, the gynaecologist (a man) decided they needed to use forceps to deliver my daughter. The obstetrician (a woman) was not keen and I heard her explaining her concerns to her colleague. The gynaecologist was adamant – he wanted my daughter out. I didn't want a forceps delivery and began to cry. I didn't think it was necessary and wanted to try other techniques first. The midwife seemed reluctant too. The delivery went ahead regardless, and I was given an episiotomy.

On 21 September 2014, my baby was born healthy. As she was having her first feed, I saw the obstetrician at my feet picking up blood from the table. She asked out loud, 'Where is all this tissue coming from? This is why I don't like forceps.' Then, everyone sprang into action.

The consultant obstetrician appeared. She explained what had

had happened. As my baby had been pulled out, she had sheared the inside of my vagina away. Essentially, my vagina was like a sleeve, my baby an arm. The arm coming out had torn and disintegrated the sleeve. My urethra had no support and was floating.

They called their specialist gynaecological surgeon in to reconstruct me. The room flooded with medical staff, including student doctors, because no one had ever seen anything like this. I had made obstetric history and would be featured in textbooks.

I had cannulas up both arms and I was losing blood fast. In total, I lost 2.5 litres of blood and had seven blood transfusions. My husband was whisked away, holding the baby. Surgery took seven hours, during which the surgeon asked the registrar gynaecologist (who hadn't been able to finish his shift on time after all) why he'd chosen forceps without trying suction first. I don't remember his answer, but I remember it impressed no one. Everyone knew a mistake had been made.

Staff offered me a general anaesthetic, but I refused because I wanted to feed my baby. This decision saved my life. Partway through surgery, I became extremely hot and alerted the anaesthetist. Another doctor checked my temperature and I saw the colour drain from everyone's faces. It turned out I had gone into perioperative hypothermia.

Afterwards, I was moved to intensive care. My baby developed jaundice because of the forceps birth, which had injured her slightly. I couldn't walk and had to learn to do so again. I was in agony from both injuries and from wearing a catheter.

After a week, I was sent home with paracetamol, a week's worth of co-codamol and three urine collection bags. I couldn't sit. I couldn't stand very well. I could barely walk. It was my health visitor who suggested I phone my GP for extra pain relief. My husband and

I had to search the NCT contacts for a ring cushion so I could sit more easily. I had to chase for extra urine bags – I wore the catheter for three months.

I was on a waiting list for NHS mental health support. Until I got it, I displayed all the symptoms of severe PTSD. Constant flashbacks, trouble sleeping. It felt like the smallest thing was difficult to cope with. I would self-harm. I had frequent suicide ideation and used to go to bed hoping I wouldn't wake up in the morning.

I eventually got psychological treatment but through my husband's work insurance plan. They assessed my symptoms, found a therapist and arranged sixteen weeks of treatment. My therapist said my symptoms were so severe, she was surprised I hadn't been sectioned. I had EMDR, which helped immensely and saved my life. My therapist explained I probably needed more treatment to help with trauma from my first birth, but the insurance couldn't offer more.

Things improved to a degree. While coping with the remaining trauma, I developed an eating disorder. I now know this is common in anyone diagnosed with diabetes, including gestational diabetes, and PTSD. The anorexia and orthorexia allowed me to avoid thinking about my experiences, but they also numbed me and slowed down my physical healing because I wasn't ingesting sufficient calories. Some days I couldn't walk. It hurt every time I urinated and defecated. I stopped having my period and my hair started to fall out. After one year, a cystoscopy showed my urethra was still inflamed, which surprised the doctors.

I began eating disorder recovery without any help in 2020 – nearly six years after my second birth. Today, I eat well and very rarely think about suicide. Going to the toilet is pain-free. But I still suffer from anxiety. I get stressed easily. And I still feel guilty.

Shortly after my second birth, my husband and I asked for my notes and a meeting with a midwife at Addenbrooke's. I was told I should probably meet with consultant doctors, given my case, but they couldn't find my file. I was so traumatised and so focused on just surviving, I decided not to pursue it.

Where would I improve maternity care?

1. Tackle unconscious bias in the NHS. Racism and classism are endemic. Even among South Asian staff, I've experienced internalised racism. There is little socioeconomic diversity among doctors. And it shows in how patients like me are treated. If I'd been white, I suspect suction might have been used. If I'd been black, I've no doubt I would be dead.
2. Sexism is endemic too. Compare how mothers giving birth are treated with equally serious symptoms, procedures or surgeries that men experience. In my case, even the female obstetrician's correct instincts were bulldozed by a male colleague.
3. There must be joined-up postnatal care. Community midwives, health visitors, GPs and hospital outpatient care all need to work together, with one taking the lead. I was supposed to be under the care of many departments, but each one thought someone else would take care of little things such as pain relief, urine bags and cushions. No traumatised person should have to chase these things.
4. Mental health support should be offered automatically and immediately. We need more funding. We need to bring more things in-house, so funding goes further. We're spending so much money on external staff and public-private partnerships and not enough on NHS staff. We're losing staff in droves, and stretching the remaining ones too far. It breaks my heart to think there are traumatised parents out there who are suffering and dying because they can't afford mental health treatment.

CHAPTER THIRTY

BABY LOSS

SARAH AND JACK

I was in labour for six days under the care of Nottingham University Hospitals (NUH) maternity services. I made multiple phone calls and was seen three times before the final admission. We had to provide our phone records after their original, inadequate internal investigation to prove to them we had made contact so often.

On the night of 12 April 2016, I began having painful contractions every six to nine minutes. The next day, I had a show so I phoned Queen's Medical Centre, Nottingham. The midwife said the show and the contractions were normal. They said to buy a TENS machine, keep moving and take baths. I was told my contractions were not long enough or regular enough to warrant admission and that I should keep the community midwife appointment that same day.

At the appointment, the midwife carried out an internal assessment. I was 2 to 3 centimetres dilated. A sweep was performed. She took the foetal heartbeat before and after the sweep. The heartbeat was 150 bpm – normal. I told the midwife I was worried that I would not be admitted. She said that the unit normally waited until someone had phoned three times and after that they would admit me.

Painful contractions continued, some as frequent as three minutes apart. At 7.45 p.m., I called the labour suite and was advised to come in. I was given 60 mg of codeine. A foetal Doppler was normal. I was told there had been a change in the foetal position to back-to-back with me, which made labour more painful. I was given a leaflet on latent labour. When I told the midwife that I had had three contractions in ten minutes while she was out of the room, she said that it didn't matter.

My sleep was bad with painful contractions. The following day (14 April), I phoned the labour suite at midday. I told them that I was still having contractions, many three minutes apart, but was told they were not regular enough and that I could continue with baths and sleep. They asked if I could feel foetal movements. I told them I wasn't sure, as the contractions were so painful. They were not concerned.

On 15 April, the contractions were increasing in intensity so I phoned the labour suite at 3.27 p.m. Again, I was told that the contractions were not regular enough and I should continue taking baths and so on. I was sick of being told by them to take a bath.

Just after midnight on 16 April, I called the labour suite and was advised to come in. I was examined and found to be 3 centimetres dilated. My options for pain relief were limited, as I needed to be 4 centimetres dilated. I was offered a water bath and declined. I asked about an epidural and was told diamorphine was the better option. My contractions continued through the night.

In the morning, I asked for additional pain relief and was given paracetamol. The midwife told me that she thought my labour would progress better at home and that she thought I would give birth in the next twenty-four hours. I agreed to go home with the proviso that I could come back immediately without having to be reassessed by phone. I was told this wouldn't be a problem and to just give my name. No further examination was carried out.

I called the labour suite around 1.50 p.m., gave my name and mentioned the conversation I'd had with the midwife about re-admission. I was told, 'It doesn't work like that' and had to go through it all again. Apparently, my contractions weren't regular enough so I should have a bath and call back in an hour. Exhausted, I said I'd had a bath and felt they weren't working. She asked if I could feel foetal movements. I said it was hard to know because of the pain from the contractions, but they were not concerned.

Around 2 a.m. on 17 April, I called the QMC labour suite. They said it sounded as if I needed to come in, but because QMC was closed to admissions, I needed to contact City Hospital. My phone call was transferred to City. The midwife said my contractions weren't regular enough, as I'd only had one contraction in the (too) short time I was talking to her. I told her they were every minute when I lay down and that they eased when I walked around. She said this was the opposite to what every other woman says and added that she was 'confident' I was not in established labour.

My contractions continued. At 3.30 a.m., the water sac became visible. Jack, my husband, called the QMC labour ward on my behalf. The midwife recognised our story and told us to phone City. She expressed shock that we were not already in hospital.

Jack phoned City. The midwife wanted to talk to me, but Jack told her I was in too much pain. She did not seem concerned about the fact there was something hanging out of me but told us we should come in. We left immediately, arriving at 4 a.m. They timed our arrival as being at 4.45 a.m., which is untrue.

I staggered in. The four members of staff stayed sitting at the desk. Midwife A, who had received the phone calls, shouted, 'Is it still hanging out of you?' while we were in the corridor. She took my maternity notes and said, 'We were having bets your husband was a doctor by his manner on the phone' in an unnerving and derogatory way.

We were taken to a bed in the 'birth sanctuary'. Midwife B discussed my birthing plan, which was to use whatever was needed for a safe labour for me and the baby. The midwife asked if I wanted her to break my waters. I said I did not mind (how would I know?) and to do what she thought was best.

She did an internal examination. I was 9–10 centimetres dilated and fully effaced. She said, 'I can see the baby's head. The baby's about to come, but you're too late for an epidural as it takes time to work and you're very close to giving birth. Opiates will make the baby drowsy so that is out too. We will use the water bath and gas and air.' We were so excited.

The midwife then performed a foetal Doppler but struggled to find a heartbeat. Jack was taking my pulse while the digital monitor was facing us and when the midwife found a heartbeat of 88–92 bpm, Jack knew: 'That's Sarah's heartbeat.' Midwife B broke my waters, calling them the 'hind waters'. She noted they were clear in colour. My medical records have recorded three foetal heartbeats of 135 bpm.

Two midwives struggled to set up the water bath. Jack helped. Midwife B then had to go next door to help someone else deliver, which was strange as I was about to deliver too. Attention was focused on the slow-running bath. A new midwife, Midwife C, performed a Doppler but couldn't find the heartbeat. Two other staff members failed to find the heartbeat. The doctor was called.

Midwife A asked Jack about what had happened to the waters.

Jack said, 'Midwife B broke the hind waters earlier.' Midwife A replied, patronisingly, 'It can't have been the hind waters; they are behind baby, hence the name. You mean the fore waters.' Jack said he was just repeating what he was told.

The doctor came and scanned me, but my bladder was full. The midwife asked her why I didn't tell her on the phone that I was passing small amounts of urine, as I was a physiotherapist. A catheter was inserted and nearly 2 litres of urine drained. The doctor performed an ultrasound scan. There was no foetal heartbeat. 'I'm sorry, your baby's dead.' He walked out without saying any more, leaving us to the midwives.

We were moved next door, out of 'birth sanctuary' to an identical room now called 'labour ward'. I attempted to deliver Harriet but was unable to do so. The anaesthetist performed an epidural.

Midwife C, a senior midwife, said that I would have a maximum of two hours trying to deliver unassisted now our baby was dead as I was tired. After two hours, she went to get medical help. She said that they had not responded to her request for help. Jack, increasingly worried for my health, kept insisting a doctor come. A hospital doctor himself, he said that if this was happening on his ward there was no way he would not be there. Midwife C said, 'It doesn't work like that.' Five minutes later the consultant anaesthetist arrived, clearly irritated.

The obstetric registrar came in and unsuccessfully tried to get the baby in a better position using her hands. By now, I had been pushing for well over twelve hours. I was eventually taken to theatre, where I tried to deliver without an episiotomy, but one was needed. Our baby girl, 6 lb 12 oz and completely perfect, was delivered. The consultant said, 'Clear liquor, no problems with the cord, no problems with the baby or placenta.'

The consultant said she could not see any reason why Harriet died – there were no obvious cord or placental problems.

My bladder was stretched so I was sent home with a catheter and told to return the next day. The next day, no one knew the protocol for removing the catheter and checking bladder function. They made the protocol up incorrectly. We went home, following an apology, and were told to come back in again the following day. The next day, we were told by the obstetrician that as there was a bladder stretch injury, we would receive a urology appointment. We did not.

My episiotomy scar became infected. Jack phoned maternity services. He was dismissed and told to ring the community service. They were closing, so he was told to phone 111 and organise a GP appointment at 5.30 p.m. on Friday. We managed to do this, reliving the trauma of what had happened to 111. Our appointment was at the out-of-hours GP team on a cold night in a building next to Nottingham train station.

The unexpected, avoidable death of a baby is unfathomable in the twenty-first century. After enduring the worst thing to happen to us in life – our healthy, full-term baby's death by negligent care – we had to embark on the unimaginable. We had to fight powerful multi-million-pound organisations with media relations teams for our grave concerns around culture and safety to be acknowledged. There were three reviews into Harriet's death, but only the third was actually independent. NUH finally accepted negligence. We had to keep Harriet's body in the mortuary for nearly two years so we could prove her innocence, so wrongly stolen from her after she died.

As both grieving parents and senior clinicians at the hospital at the time of Harriet's death, the fight and the trauma has resulted in irreparable damage. We were blamed, hidden, pushed away. We should have been heard, nurtured and cherished. We were perceived as a threat instead of an opportunity. They could have learnt from us to make maternity services safe. We knew we could not be alone; if they treated us, clinicians with over thirty-five years' experience between us, like that, what were they doing to others?

Utterly broken, we started to search for other bereaved and harmed families. It took years. Eventually, we succeeded. Families started making contact. It snowballed. We knew that NUH was failing to keep our community safe. We successfully campaigned for an external review, which now has evidence from over 2,000 families who have suffered potentially avoidable harm or death at the hands of NUH over a ten-year period. Harriet's death was very far from the tragic, isolated incident so many insisted we believe.

Our hearts break. Harriet, eight-and-a-half years old, should be here. Every minute of every day, we wonder what she would be like – alongside all of the children and families in Nottinghamshire who should be here. A whole school full of missing children.

MOLLY

It was the morning of 18 February 2019. When I walked into the Chelsea and Westminster Hospital, I believed I was ten weeks pregnant with my second child. I had been having some pain in my right side so I was there as a precaution. In the Early Pregnancy Unit (EPU), I lay on my back for the scan in total ignorance and with no anticipation of the words that followed: 'I'm so sorry, there's no heartbeat.' This was my first 'missed miscarriage', which is when the baby dies but there are no symptoms of miscarriage; there is no bleeding and no pain.

Following the scan, I was in total shock. I wanted to tell my family what had happened and I could not stand the idea that anyone thought I was pregnant when I was not. We did not know this at the time, but that morning would mark the start of what would be years of loss and grief for our angel babies that would never be born. I was advised to have an ERPC, which stands for 'evacuation of retained products of conception'. My dead baby would be surgically removed while I was under general anaesthetic.

Over the following months, my body slowly returned to normal. I spent hours researching the statistics on the chances of having a second miscarriage and was reassured: a woman is more likely to have one miscarriage than to not have a miscarriage and having a second consecutive miscarriage is very unlikely.

Despite knowing this, every day of my third pregnancy I lived in dread of losing another baby. Although I developed mild 'spotting' (very light bleeding) when I was eight weeks pregnant, a scan showed that my baby had a strong heartbeat. Reassured, we went away to France on holiday. However, midway through the week the spotting came back again. The holiday became a nightmare. I felt that my baby was like Schrödinger's cat – neither alive nor dead and with no way of knowing until I had another scan.

We returned to England and when I was just over nine weeks pregnant, we went to the EPU for a scan. I lay on my back for what felt like an eternity, staring at the ceiling, waiting far too long for the inevitable words that followed: 'I'm sorry, there's no heartbeat.' It was another 'missed miscarriage' and I had another ERPC. We had the pregnancy tissue tested and it confirmed that we had lost a chromosomally normal baby girl.

Ten days after the ERPC, I spiked a temperature and experienced continued bleeding. I was told to come back to the EPU. A scan showed that I still had pregnancy tissue left inside me and I had a temperature because that tissue was infected. I was admitted to hospital for IV antibiotics. My husband was only allowed to visit in hospital visiting hours, so I was alone with part of my dead baby girl still inside of me.

I was advised to manage the remaining tissue 'conservatively' and to see if my body would expel it naturally. I was sent home to wait. I did not want to see anyone and I did not want to be comforted by anyone apart from by my little boy, who wrapped his tiny arms around my neck when I cried, his large blue eyes peering at me with concern. I mourned my baby and I was overwhelmed by the feeling of crushing guilt that I had done this, that I had 'miscarried' my baby.

By the end of October, having sat on the sofa for almost three months waiting for the bleeding to start and for life to move on, I could not stand it any longer. I wanted answers as to why I had lost my baby and the only way I could get answers was if my body was able to return to normal for tests to be carried out. I went for a second opinion and we agreed that the remaining pregnancy tissue should be removed. I underwent a 'hysteroscopic resection of the retained products of conception'. This is basically an ERPC with a camera; I wanted certainty that there was nothing left inside of me.

Following the surgery, my body began to readjust, but mentally I was struggling. I found a recurrent miscarriage consultant who ran blood tests. The tests confirmed a minor clotting issue and he recommended that in my next pregnancy, I could treat this with enoxaparin (an anticoagulant). I finally felt that, after almost five months, we had some answers. He gave us the 'all clear' to start trying to conceive again. I truly believed that everything was going to be different now.

My fourth pregnancy was challenging from the start. I was just under five weeks pregnant when bright red bleeding started. We went to the EPU for a scan to confirm the loss, but to our surprise and delight, we were told that there was a heartbeat. However, I had a subchorionic haematoma (where blood collects between the baby's amniotic sac and the uterine wall), which was causing the bleeding. I was told that many women develop subchorionic haematomas in early pregnancy and go on to have successful pregnancies.

I was just over eight weeks pregnant when another missed miscarriage was confirmed. I asked whether there was an alternative to having an ERPC given my previous experience. Dr C said she could do an MVA, a 'manual vacuum aspiration'. The benefit to this was more certainty, as I could be scanned afterwards, and I would not need a general anaesthetic. With hindsight, having an MVA was a mistake. I can still hear the noise of the vacuum as my baby was sucked out of me. A test of the pregnancy tissue confirmed that, once again, we had lost a chromosomally normal baby girl.

In those eight months since my second miscarriage, I had changed as a person. I felt I was drowning and so far away from the person I used to be. I wanted to understand why this was happening to me and what I was doing wrong. I desperately wanted answers. I began to count down the days to my appointment at the recurrent miscarriage clinic, which was in early April 2020. But then something beyond anyone's control put a stop to this; it was March 2020 and I would not be getting any answers for a very long time.

The only advantage of Covid was that we were able to hide away from reality. I was in no place to see anyone. My feelings of loss and guilt permeated everything I did. I mourned my babies. I could not come to terms with what I perceived as my failure to carry a child. And I was angry. I was angry with my friends; I was angry with my family. I was angry with people who I was once close to but who no longer knew what to say to me. I felt a million miles apart from the friends who told me how tired they were from looking after their two children in lockdown. I would have swapped anything for the privilege of that tiredness.

In July 2020, I returned to work. With the country opening back up again, we were able to start further tests. A saline scan showed that I had mild uterine adhesions, a common side effect of the surgeries. In October 2020, I had surgery to remove the adhesions, carried out by my recurrent miscarriage consultant. After the surgery, he came and sat by my bed and explained that my lining was so thin (3 mm) that he was concerned that I would not be able to carry another child. He recommended that we look into surrogacy if we wanted to expand our family.

The turning point for us came in November 2020. We went for a second opinion and then a third opinion with two recurrent miscarriage consultants, both of whom believed in wider treatment for recurrent miscarriages. We ended up putting our faith in a quiet and softly spoken recurrent miscarriage consultant who I trusted.

In July 2021, I became pregnant for the fifth time. My beta hCG (this refers to the hormone human chorionic gonadotropin in the blood, which provides an indication of the age of a foetus) was rising as it should and my uterine lining looked good. I went for my first scan when I was six weeks pregnant, feeling confident that all was on course. However, my consultant could not find the pregnancy sac. Later that day, he called me and told me that, given how high my beta hCG was, I needed to go straight to the EPU as I could have a 'pregnancy of unknown location'. This is a pregnancy that is not located in the uterus.

At the EPU, Dr Y scanned me. This scan took a long time and

eventually he said that he thought the pregnancy was in my cervix. He explained that this was called a cervical ectopic pregnancy and could be dangerous. What stuck in my head was that he said the worst-case scenario was that I would need a hysterectomy. I was sent home to see if my body would get rid of the pregnancy naturally.

The next morning, I started bleeding. I assumed that the massive blood clots falling out of me were what most people had to go through with a 'normal' miscarriage. By midday, I was feeling light-headed, but the EPU was too full to see me and advised me to go to A&E. I had not anticipated the amount of blood that would pour out of me as I waited for six hours in A&E, sitting in blood-soaked pants and trousers. I was admitted to be monitored, but by the next morning I had lost too much blood and any further loss would require a blood transfusion. I was quickly rushed through to the EPU and without so much as having the chance to call my husband to tell him what was happening, I was given gas and air and I was told that the pregnancy was going to be scraped out of me. There was no time for a local anaesthetic. I blacked out from the pain.

My fifth pregnancy had the biggest impact on me physically because I had lost so much blood. However, because the pregnancy had been non-viable from the start, I found it easier to process mentally. I also felt that the recurrent miscarriage protocol that I had been put on would still work. I just needed the baby to be in the right part of my uterus.

I found out I was pregnant for the sixth time on 31 December 2021. Even now, being thirty-one weeks pregnant with my third child, I have no idea how I managed to get through each day of that pregnancy. I was suffering from PTSD and I was absolutely terrified. We found out early on that I was pregnant with twins. However, when I was eight weeks pregnant, one of the twins died and I felt the death of my second baby was now an inevitability. I spent so much time researching what a miscarriage at each stage of the pregnancy would be like in order to properly prepare myself.

The antenatal clinic, somewhere that I had fought so hard to get back to, became a place of horror as I struggled to be around other pregnant women. I believed I was not one of them. I was not able to connect with my baby as I wanted to protect myself; I felt that this would make the anticipated loss easier to bear. However, the loss never came and slowly, the days stretched into weeks and the weeks stretched into months. On 19 August 2022, our miracle baby, our rainbow baby, was born.

CHAPTER THIRTY-ONE

THE WIDER IMPACT OF BIRTH TRAUMA

SAIRA

The day my child was born began with a mix of anticipation and nerves. Little did I know it would be a journey filled with unexpected turns, profound emotions and moments of awe that I will never forget. I encountered numerous instances of medical negligence. These included misdiagnoses, such as health professionals failing to realise I was in active labour, a retained placenta and a general lack of proper care and attention from healthcare providers. This experience left me feeling traumatised, extremely anxious and overwhelmed, and it also had a negative impact on my baby's health.

My daughter, Natasha, was born at a hospital in London in 1989. A week before Natasha was born, my husband rushed me to the maternity unit at the hospital due to regular, strong and painful contractions. The midwife, who I believe was a junior nurse, attended to me that evening. Despite instructions from the senior nurse, she conducted some tests – blood pressure, pulse etc. – but neglected to perform a urine test, which I believe would have indicated that I was in active labour. Even though my contractions were five to ten minutes apart, the nurse assured me that everything was fine and sent me home.

My pain intensified over the course of the week, making it impossible to sleep. I was utterly exhausted and beginning to feel overwhelmed. Fortunately, I had a routine antenatal appointment scheduled with the obstetrician later that week. During the appointment, the obstetrician expressed concern about my blood pressure. I explained that I had been experiencing pain for a week and had previously visited the hospital but was sent home. The obstetrician conducted an examination and informed me that I was already in labour, with 6 centimetres dilation and only 3 centimetres left to go. He remarked, 'You did most of the work yourself at home!'

Upon further examination, he noted that my hind waters had broken and advised that labour would need to be induced to prevent infection. He also asked for the name of the midwife who had been in charge during my earlier visit to the maternity unit.

The obstetrician performed an amniotomy induction around 11 a.m. to accelerate labour. Within hours of the induction, the contractions intensified. I was presented with the choice of receiving either an epidural or gas and air for pain relief. Opting for gas and air, however, meant that I was restricted to the hospital bed until I gave birth at 11.05 p.m. that night.

In the evening, there was a shift change among the midwives. The new midwives informed me that the baby was showing signs of distress because she was in a challenging position, facing the opposite direction with her back against mine. Consequently, they advised that a forceps delivery would be necessary. They promptly arranged for an obstetrician and made preparations for the procedure. Once my feet were in the stirrups, I felt a natural urge to push immediately. Despite the midwives advising me against pushing due to the risk of a perineal tear, one of them proceeded to make a cut in the perineum. At 11.05 p.m., I gave birth to my beautiful baby girl. She was born face up, which was the reason for my intense back pain.

Shortly after Natasha's birth, the cuts were stitched while my feet were still in the stirrups. Being in that position for prolonged periods, combined with the pressure exerted by the baby, resulted in a fractured tailbone and subsequent chronic back pain that I still suffer from.

From the beginning of labour, I sensed the midwives were rushing to hasten my departure from the delivery room, which ultimately led to them missing a partially retained placenta. I later discovered (from a health professional) that the midwives were supposed to weigh the placenta, which should have weighed the same as the baby. I don't recall the midwives weighing the placenta, and I believe they neglected to do so.

I was transferred to a ward late that night. Since I had gone to the hospital for a routine check-up earlier that day, I wasn't expecting to be admitted, which meant I didn't have an overnight bag with me. The nurse wrapped me in a bed sheet (due to a shortage of gowns) since I didn't have a change of clothes and then tucked me into bed. As I settled into bed, my husband was preparing to head home and asked the nurse if he could drop off my stuff, but she told him he wouldn't be allowed back into the hospital because the hospital doors would be locked. She advised him to return the following afternoon, during 'visiting' hours.

After my husband left, the nurse whisked the newborn away. I struggled to sleep that night, as every movement caused pain and I was bleeding heavily. During the night, I pressed the call button to ask for help because I was in excruciating pain and lying on blood-soaked sheets, but unfortunately the button wasn't working. So, I got out of bed, but I couldn't walk because it hurt so much and blood was dripping onto the floor. The patient in the bed opposite, who had been asleep, quickly got up and told me to get back in bed, saying she would get the nurse for me. As she went to get a nurse, she accidentally stepped in my blood (she didn't have any slippers on) and then had to shower.

The nurse came over and reprimanded me for getting out of bed, while another nurse cleaned up the blood on the floor. She said, 'You're bleeding; you shouldn't have gotten out of bed.' I explained that the call button wasn't working and that I had been in excruciating pain and needed some help.

The next morning, the same nurse helped me to the bathroom with a sheet still wrapped around me and asked if I had complained about her to another nurse. I told her that I hadn't spoken to anyone. Her comments made me feel very uncomfortable and I felt it was incredibly unprofessional of her.

A few hours later, during visiting hours, when fathers were allowed to visit their partners, I was lying in bed with just a sheet wrapped around me while I waited for my husband to arrive with my essentials. I felt my dignity had been completely stripped away and I felt exposed and vulnerable in front of everyone.

I spent five days in the hospital. A few days before my discharge from hospital, I noticed something that resembled an organ in the bidet. I showed it to the nurse, who said, 'If you see anything bigger than that, let me know.' A few weeks later, I realised that the membrane in the bidet was a piece of placenta, which the nurse failed to identify, and that the retained placenta was the reason for the excessive bleeding!

I was having an incredibly difficult time. Sitting was extremely painful due to the stitches, and nursing the baby was also painful because I felt an urge to push every time I nursed my baby. This made me very anxious and scared and as a result, my baby was not feeding properly. I mentioned this to the nurse, who responded that she had never heard of such a sensation during breastfeeding before.

At home, I continued to bleed heavily. Sitting was still painful and nursing the baby remained difficult and very painful. Over the following weeks, a health visitor visited my home to check on both me and the baby but failed to recognise that something was amiss.

For sixteen days after my baby's birth, the placenta was still in my womb. This explained the excessive haemorrhaging, the soft tissue in the bidet and the urge to push every single time I nursed my baby. In the early hours of Saturday 10 June, I was fast asleep when I began experiencing painful contractions. I woke up to find the bed soaked in blood. When I went to the bathroom, blood was everywhere – my bathroom looked like a crime scene. Before I reached the toilet, parts of the placenta had already fallen onto the floor. I was so scared because I was haemorrhaging heavily.

My husband called an ambulance, which arrived in less than twenty minutes. The paramedics carefully picked up the placenta from the floor, placed it in a plastic bag, and took it to the hospital. They rushed me to the hospital, with my traumatised husband and our baby coming with us.

Upon arriving at the hospital I was examined by a doctor, who inspected what was given to him by the paramedics and confirmed it was indeed the placenta. I was then transferred to another hospital in London, where a surgeon performed a D&C to remove the remaining placenta. When I regained consciousness after the operation, the surgeon informed me that a significant portion of the placenta had been retained. He explained that the midwives had tugged on the placenta, causing it to tear in half. He also mentioned that small pieces of placenta might still be left behind and would likely come out during my periods.

He suggested that it would be beneficial for me to spend a couple of days in the hospital for rest and observation. However, Natasha was very distressed and unable to settle, and I was advised not to nurse her due to the heavy loss of blood. Despite the hospital providing her with a bottle of milk, she refused to drink it. Consequently, I was discharged and left the hospital that morning.

My baby and I endured significant hardships due to several mistakes made by the health professionals. These errors not only caused immediate physical and emotional distress but also left a lasting scar on both of us. The mismanagement of my post-partum care led to severe anxiety, making me tense, nervous and unable to relax. This, in turn, affected my baby, who was subsequently diagnosed with failure to thrive. The experience of watching her undergo numerous tests, including a lumbar puncture, only to find out that her condition was linked to my own untreated trauma was devastating. The realisation that health professionals' mistakes had such profound consequences on our well-being has left an indelible mark on our lives. Afterwards, I was offered therapy to help cope with my severe anxiety and its impact on both me and my baby. The harrowing experience was so traumatic that it deterred me from having any more children.

During that period, my husband worked long hours, leaving me to handle the baby alone on a daily basis. Traumatised and overwhelmed with caring for my newborn, coupled with feeling generally unwell and lacking energy, I chose not to pursue legal action against the health practitioners for their negligence and breach of duty of care. I simply wanted to block out the entire experience from my mind, but thirty-five years later, I still find myself haunted by its lingering impact.

AMY

On 3 February 2021, I delivered my daughter in a hospital in Belfast. I was considered a high-risk patient due to having epilepsy and lupus. I came off two epilepsy medications before pregnancy and was advised not to have a C-section, as the recovery would prove more stressful for my body than a vaginal delivery.

My daughter was measuring large and I was advised to have an induction and deliver her early. Despite my concerns and preference for a C-section, I followed this advice. For the induction I was given the drug Pitocin, which my body did not respond well to. Very early into the administration of the drug, the contractions were coming back-to-back with no break. I was shaking and the pain was unbearable. I requested an epidural, but there was a significant wait for an anaesthetist.

When the anaesthetist arrived, he flew into the room without acknowledging me or my husband and then left to get the consent form. I was in so much pain after waiting nearly two hours that I couldn't read it but said I had done my research. He asked me what I knew about epidurals and I responded, 'I know if they go wrong they can cause paralysis.' The doctor laughed and said, 'I am much more likely to give you a really bad headache.'

You need to be still for an epidural, but I was struggling because of the Pitocin and the contractions. The anaesthetist had zero patience and was rushing me. He had the midwife try to restrain me by holding me from the front. On the first pass he hit the bone and on the second pass he placed the epidural.

I was very fortunate to have a team of midwives and other doctors who helped deliver my daughter safely, which I will be eternally grateful for. What we did not know was that the anaesthetist had punctured my dura. My husband and I now look back and blame ourselves for not spotting the clear red flags around the conduct of the anaesthetist – his agitation, how he spoke to me, his lack of regard for me or his lack of patience. But in the moment we were grateful for the pain relief and did not want to create a fuss.

A few hours after delivery, I noticed the onset of a headache, which we assumed was due to a long and difficult labour, but we notified staff. I spent the first night on the ward with my daughter and due to Covid restrictions, I was unable to have anyone there with me. The following morning, I woke up surprised to find I could not lift my head without excruciating pain. The noise of machinery was grinding in my ears and I could not bear to look near lights. Strangely, I felt normal when I lay down.

I would lift my head an inch to eat a bite of toast and lower it again. Hours went past and I lay down to try to feed my daughter, looking at her in the bedside crib rather than lifting her. Eventually, I told a ward nurse about my headache and a few hours later an anaesthetist came to visit me. He mentioned the possibility of dural puncture but said I could go home and someone would phone me the next day.

I can't remember how I did it, but in the worst pain of my life I walked out of the hospital with my all my things, my daughter and no understanding of what had really happened to me.

Driving home, every bump in the road sent shockwaves through me. I could barely talk to my husband. I lay down straight away and he would place my daughter on my chest to feed and lift her off. I crawled to the bathroom and sat on the shower tray floor to wash. My husband helped me change my catheter. I barely remember interacting with my daughter.

Eventually, I had a call telling me to return to the hospital for a blood patch procedure. In immense pain I waited in the waiting room to be called. Sitting upright made me feel like my head was going to explode.

We were taken back to the ward. I was allowed to lie down and my daughter was put in a crib beside me. All I could do was reach for her tiny hand. It was eventually explained to me that I had suffered from a dural puncture. The anaesthetist had pushed his needle too far and punctured a hole in the dura, and cerebrospinal fluid, which is the fluid our brain floats in, was leaking out. This supposedly happens in approximately one in 100 cases and I had signed the form accepting the risk during labour. This was the 'bad headache' the anaesthetist had referred to.

I was told it could be fixed with a blood patch, which required blood to be drawn from my arm and injected in the area, either sealing the puncture or causing inflammation so the body self-repairs. I was also told the procedure is not always successful on the first go and may need repeating. I was not made aware, however, that the problem could extend beyond two potential blood patches. I was so happy this hell was going to be over and signed another form.

The procedure was uncomfortable, but I felt my brain 'float' and the pressure in my head lessen. All of this was a good sign. I returned to the ward and lay flat for two hours as instructed and then slowly my bed was raised. It was very late at night and I was conscious of trying to balance this new condition with managing my epilepsy. I was told during pregnancy that I was at most risk for a tonic-clonic seizure in the first few days post-birth and I knew I needed a lot of help and a lot of sleep.

Because of Covid restrictions, my husband was not allowed to stay in hospital with me. I had no choice but to go home to try to rest and get some help with my daughter. I carried my 9 lb 3 oz baby out to the car in her heavy car seat.

I later learnt that guidelines in other parts of the UK and the world are to lie flat for a minimum of twenty-four hours post-blood patch, not to lift anything over 5–10 lbs and to not undertake any bending, lifting or twisting for at least six weeks. Unfortunately, Northern Ireland do not issue this aftercare advice.

In the immediate days following the procedure my head improved, but I would still experience pain when moving or turning it. On a brief follow-up call, we discussed this with an anaesthetist and I was told my brain was recalibrating and this was normal.

I tried to live life normally as a new mum. I was doing a lot of lifting and bending – and still experiencing the flurries of head pain. Two weeks post-birth, I had a tonic-clonic seizure while sitting holding my daughter on the sofa. Luckily, I managed to set her safely down to the side, but it was traumatic for my body and mental health.

The headache I had afterwards felt familiar and it resolved when lying flat. I was worried I had blown the blood patch, so we contacted the anaesthetists who refused to see me again. I went to my GP who advised me to attend my nearest A&E to rule out a cerebral venous thrombosis. When this was ruled out, we pleaded again for another blood patch. This was declined and I was told that as I had gone to an A&E in another trust, as advised by my GP, I was essentially their problem now.

I spent the next six months in a fog, going to private appointments and various doctors to try to find the cause of the pain, visual disturbances, tinnitus, dizziness and so on. My GP put the problem down to 'new mum stress'. Meanwhile, my husband was managing all the care of my daughter and his job.

We made one last attempt to request a blood patch and the anaesthetists again declined. They did not even offer to see me in person. Luckily, I had an epilepsy review with my neurologist, who picked up on my newer problems too and agreed my symptoms were consistent with that of an ongoing dural puncture. I am so grateful for that call, as I felt like I was being listened to for the first time. He wrote to the anaesthetics department and requested they consider me for a second patch. They seemingly didn't receive his letters, though I managed to receive my copies.

I sought out private treatment in England. This team was fantastic and their knowledge and empathy was much-needed. Belfast Trust finally offered a second blood patch ten months after the incident but to no effect. I have since learnt that speed in treatment and arranging imaging is crucial in circumstances like mine.

After making a complaint, I found that I should have had an in-person appointment around two weeks post-blood patch, which is standard procedure. This appointment was supposedly made for me and then cancelled on the hospital's computer. I was never aware of this appointment despite all the calls I made to the department. The trust cannot explain this. They have apologised and said that changes will be made.

The location of my epidural is also not consistent with that of my first blood patch, so I now have two potential leak sites or areas of investigation. This is due to confusion over the recording of the epidural site.

Three years on, I am paying for private pain management treatments in London. I have a maximum of a couple of hours upright at a time before needing to lie down to reset. I can't bend over or lower my head as this exacerbates the pain. I struggle to do any significant exercise, which has a huge impact on my physical and mental health. Bright light and sounds are uncomfortable. I experience tinnitus, dizziness, neck pain and pain in between my scapula. My head feels like it is full of bricks and it is being pulled down the back of my neck. If I stay upright too long, the pressure in my eyes is so strong it feels like my eyes may burst. I get nerve-like pain over my head, forehead and ears and my scalp will tingle.

The impact this has had on me and my family cannot be expressed. My husband had to take over all childcare duties due to the management of my pain. I cannot bathe or lift my daughter and he did all night feeds from one month on. She has a much better bond with her father and cries for him when she wants comfort.

I can't push my daughter in a swing. I can't push her pram for more than a minute. We didn't get to go to any mum and baby groups. I can't play with her for too long as I am immensely sound sensitive. I was supposed to be a stay-at-home mother. Instead, we pay for four days of nursery care while I do not bring in a wage.

My husband had to change jobs, as he was working closely with doctors and it was too close for comfort. He was also under so much stress that his health was impacted and he was ill for a period during 2022. We have had to delay having a second child and, three years on, we do not know when or if that will be possible. Our finances have been severely impacted from paying for treatments, travel and childcare that had not been anticipated.

What is most likely next for me is explorative surgery to try to repair the leak, which involves removing bone in my spine. This is major surgery that will have a significant recovery time.

THE WIDER IMPACT OF BIRTH TRAUMA

I have immense concerns about the number of women and their families in the same position as us. While I suffered the birth trauma, the true trauma is suffered by not only me but by my entire family.

CHAPTER THIRTY-TWO

COVID AND LOCKDOWN BABIES

NEYA

I was thirty-three weeks pregnant when lockdown hit the UK in March 2020. Looking back, I'm glad I didn't know then what a profoundly negative impact this would have on my birth and postnatal experience. My husband and I were looking forward to the arrival of our first baby and the news about maternity unit visiting restrictions didn't alarm me too much.

At thirty-nine weeks pregnant, my waters broke but I didn't go into labour, so I was admitted to the antenatal ward at Croydon University Hospital to be induced. My husband wasn't allowed in with me. The consultant mentioned that they typically like to deliver babies within twenty-four hours of your waters breaking, as the risk of infection rises after that. By this point it had already been around forty-eight hours (initially I didn't realise it was my waters breaking, so delayed going into hospital to be checked) and I began to worry. The induction was started and the plan was to move me to the labour ward within the next six hours to start IV oxytocin, where my husband would then be allowed to join me. Six hours turned into over twenty-four hours – there were no beds available on the labour ward and a shortage of midwives. I kept being told I was the highest priority to be taken down, but the hours kept passing and I somehow spent the entire night alone dealing with contractions in a room full of other women. Some of them were crying in excruciating pain without birth partners to support them. I just kept thinking, how is this fair? There were so many times where I felt I couldn't cope much longer on my own, but there was nothing I could do. Eventually a bed became available; it was now seventy-two hours since my waters had broken.

I finally felt relaxed now that my husband was allowed to be with me and was hooked up to IV oxytocin through the night to increase the intensity and frequency of contractions. The drip unfortunately caused hyperstimulation and my baby's heart rate kept dropping with the contractions. After ten hours, I was still only 4 centimetres dilated and was wheeled down to theatre for an emergency C-section. Arjun was delivered at 7 a.m. I felt relieved hearing him cry, but after two nights of no sleep I was exhausted and dozing off on the operating table, unable to hold him for long. We were told that I'd had an obstructed labour, likely due to cephalopelvic disproportion, which prevented Arjun's head from descending. I was taken to recovery and after about an hour my husband was made to leave and I was taken up to the postnatal ward. There was a strict no-visitors rule there too, so I would be alone until I was able to go home. I assumed there would be staff on hand to help.

Still numb from the waist down, I was left in a bay. Arjun started crying in his bedside cot and I couldn't reach over to him. I pressed the buzzer and a lady (a healthcare assistant) came over. I asked her for help with comforting Arjun. She laughed and asked, 'How old are you?', told me I had to figure it out on my own and walked away. I felt so incompetent and helpless. Arjun kept crying and I felt awful being unable to soothe him. At one point he was passed over to me, but even then I was struggling to hold him as one of my hands was attached to a drip. The lady commented that I wasn't holding him 'right' but still didn't offer help. She then ripped out my cannula, splattering blood everywhere, and tutted her teeth at me when she realised Arjun's clothes were covered in blood and had to be changed. I was shattered from two nights of no sleep and was shaking, dizzy and nauseous. I started panicking, as the hostility showed no sign of letting up.

I called both my dad and husband in desperation, asking them to ring the ward to tell them that I really needed help, but the phone rang out. I was hysterical and felt so relieved when a midwife saw me through a gap in the curtain. I said that I wasn't well enough to be alone with Arjun but was still offered no help. She walked away, leaving me crying. Nobody would listen. Soon after, I pressed the buzzer again as I needed water and felt really faint. Another lady (a healthcare assistant) came by and said she would bring some over. I had to press the buzzer another two or three times, begging for water and saying I was literally about to black out. Eventually, the water was brought over and placed on the tray table near the bed. The lady walked away immediately, before I even had the chance to say that I couldn't reach it. I had to press the buzzer again to ask if it could be given to me to hold. I felt like such a burden.

No one helped me with getting out of bed or walking for the first time after the C-section. Then, when I raised concerns about Arjun's milk intake, instead of supporting me with breastfeeding the midwife suggested topping him up with formula. She massively overfed him around 120 millilitres of milk, causing him so much discomfort – he kept gagging and spitting up milk. I was horrified to later find out that babies only require around 10–20 millilitres of milk per feed at one day old. It was awful watching Arjun in that state while being unable to keep getting up from the bed to hold him.

Throughout the night, no one came to check on me. The pain in my stitches was agonising and I was totally alone in a dark room, as the other mums had left. I was in a constant state of intense panic from the fear, desperation and helplessness. I vividly remember messaging my husband saying, 'I'm going to get PTSD.' At that point, I'd never even heard of birth trauma and like most people, I associated PTSD with war veterans. The fear I felt was overwhelming; I was in no fit state to look after myself, let alone a newborn baby. The only thing keeping me going was Arjun. I had to survive somehow for him. Minutes felt like hours and I would keep looking out the window for signs of the sun coming up as it would then be that much closer to going home. It felt like torture. My husband became so concerned he rang the ward again, making them aware how distressed I was.

Luckily, I was discharged the following day, but I was broken. I felt like a shell of the person I used to be. I lost the ability to function; I barely ate and had very little motivation to do anything or even take care of myself. My husband and mum got me through countless difficult days, looking after Arjun and doing everything around the house. Days and nights rolled into one and were spent constantly replaying the aftermath of the birth in my mind. Nights were particularly tough, as the ordeal left me afraid of the dark and being up feeding and settling Arjun through the small hours would trigger flashbacks of the postnatal ward. Reliving the fear, horror and desperation was intensely distressing and it was draining having to explain to people that I couldn't just forget about it and move on. I was so unhappy even though we had our gorgeous baby. I felt angry at the hospital and staff on the ward that day. I felt disconnected from everyone, constantly irritable, struggled to bond with Arjun and found coping with everyday life as a new mum really tough. The resultant relationship strain was so hard to navigate and I felt like my life was falling apart.

In October 2020, when Arjun was five months old, I was diagnosed with PTSD. The hostile behaviour and appalling attitude of the staff on the ward that day robbed me of so much joy in the first precious months of Arjun's life that I'll never get back. I still grieve this, but therapy has helped me to come to a place where I can think about what happened without the intense emotions associated with it. I still struggle in the days around Arjun's birthday every year, as it brings back the trauma and the awful memories. Strangely, I also notice a lot of pain in my C-section scar around this time, which links with the trauma manifesting physically. In February 2022 I fell pregnant with our second child, which caused the traumatic memories to resurface again. I had therapy throughout the pregnancy to help me manage the anxiety about giving birth and coping in the early post-partum days.

I'll always be so grateful to my psychologist Mia Scotland, who helped me through the darkest days of my life. And also to the Birth Trauma Association for all they have done and continue to do to help parents traumatised by birth.

LISA

My waters broke at 5 p.m. on Thursday 23 July 2020 – a difficult time to be pregnant because of the Covid pandemic. I had been self-isolating for months in the run-up to giving birth and my grandmother had passed away six weeks before I went into labour. I was therefore apprehensive, but I understood the rules and I followed them to keep my baby and me safe.

After an examination at the hospital, I was sent home to allow my labour to progress, which I was happy with. I called the hospital in the middle of the night as the contractions had become incredibly painful, and while I wanted to stay at home as long as possible, I felt I had reached the point that I needed to go in. The professional on the phone was somewhat dismissive, almost implying that my pain wasn't as intense as I had explained. She advised me to stay at home for longer. I went along with this, as this was my first experience of pregnancy and labour. I then called back an hour later and had to present myself in a much more assertive way to ensure that I was listened to.

In hospital, I did my best to keep going without pain relief, which was my choice. Because my waters had broken, professionals did not examine me to avoid infection, so they did not know how far along I was into labour. I later asked for an epidural, which was against my birth plan, but I couldn't cope with the pain any longer. They gave me a different form of pain relief in the first instance and it helped, but I then asked again for an epidural. They examined me at this stage and said it was too late for an epidural. I felt frustrated by this because I had asked for an epidural hours earlier. I later found out in my birth debrief (months later) that in fact they did not record my request for an epidural.

At this stage, the birthing pool became free and I used it, which was part of my birthing plan. Entering the pool was a positive experience.

I pushed for some time, but I was eventually asked to leave the pool for an examination. I continued to push for hours. Being new to labour, I wasn't sure if this was standard practice. A professional was introduced as a 'cheerleader' to encourage me. However, instead of finding their words motivating, I felt judged and humiliated. Hearing, 'Come on, you've got more in you than that' made me feel like I was failing. I'm successful in my career. I'm the type of person who would not give up in the gym no matter how tired or in pain I was. As a very determined, committed and hardworking individual, I knew I was giving my all, so this comment was deeply disheartening and still lingers with me.

I then experienced an episiotomy and required a Ventouse (suction device) to support delivery. At this stage, I saw the horror in the eyes of professionals when they shouted, 'Shoulder dystocia!' Suddenly, the room was filled with staff performing emergency manoeuvres to deliver my baby. I thought we were dying. I genuinely felt like I was on the ceiling watching down and my thoughts were, 'I never got to say goodbye to my family.'

Luckily, Alexander was born alive. I had a bruise of a handprint on my arm – I still don't know how I got this. He was born at 3.23 p.m. on Friday 24 July 2020. As soon as he was born, I was rushed off for surgery to repair a severe tear. My husband was left in the delivery room alone with our newborn son. The professionals in PPE and the bright lights made me feel terrified.

I returned from surgery and I felt unwell. It felt like people weren't listening when I said, 'I don't feel well. I feel hot and I can't hold my baby.' The Covid restrictions compounded our distress; my husband was sent home shortly after I returned from surgery, leaving us no time to process what had just happened. I understand the Covid rules were in place to look after everyone, but it felt cruel to send him home without any time for us to even talk for half an hour as a family.

That night, my son began vomiting green fluid and was taken to special care. I asked the hospital staff to let my husband return, but they refused due to Covid rules. I found myself alone on the maternity ward, surrounded by other mothers and their babies. I was grappling with the trauma of the day and the fear for my son's health. Hours later, a midwife thankfully showed compassion, moving me to a private room and allowing my husband to visit. We visited my son together and were informed he would need transferring to a different hospital with a neonatal unit for further assessments. I asked to go with my son in the ambulance and this was refused, again because of Covid rules. My son wasn't even twenty-four hours old. We were separated twice: once when he was born for my surgery and again when he started vomiting. Now we would be separated for a third time. I cried and begged to go with him, but they refused. I had to sign a form to give my permission for this to happen yet I felt like there was no choice in this consent process. Signing the consent form to send him away without me felt devastating, and I still question why I wasn't stronger in challenging this decision. My recent negative Covid test and the fact that he had been part of me just hours earlier made the separation feel senseless and cruel.

I experienced incontinence for a few days after the birth, travelling back and forth to see my son, which was a 45-minute drive away. It didn't stop me being by his side – I couldn't bear the thought of him being alone in there. When my son was discharged – and thankfully, he was OK – I had difficulty at home for months. I was experiencing flashbacks to the birth, nightmares, difficulty sleeping and generally feeling anxious and completely overwhelmed. I explained this to the GP in my postnatal check and again I was dismissed. I was informed that 'this is normal and it's likely to pass'.

There was one fabulous health visitor who was empathic and encouraged me to have a debrief with the hospital. I didn't even know this service existed. To this day, I have not been offered any form of therapy or signposted to any psychologist or therapist for assessment or intervention. As a registered psychologist, I find this shocking and alarming. I was left to work through this alone during the Covid pandemic, which was already an isolating time for everyone but especially for first-time mothers. I most likely demonstrated some symptoms consistent with post-traumatic stress disorder, but this was not acknowledged or discussed.

I remain deeply grateful to the consultant who recognised it was shoulder dystocia and saved us. I will forever be thankful to him. However, I do think this could've been prevented. My baby was measuring on the slightly larger side and I'm petite; earlier intervention could have made a significant difference, in my opinion.

More support is required for families. I am so very passionate about this. The culture in some maternity units needs to be altered through training in trauma-informed care – understanding the importance of the language they use and the lasting impact that actions can have on patients. Mothers and families need to feel listened to and cared for in an empathic way. We are at our most vulnerable at this time, and healthcare professionals need to remember this and act accordingly and provide compassionate care.

This also needs to be applied in postnatal care to ensure that mothers and families are given adequate psychological and emotional support following birth, though I fully understand and appreciate that there are so many professionals out there working tirelessly in this field who are incredibly committed and compassionate in their approach. Empathy and compassion should be central to both maternity and postnatal care. Systemic changes are needed to prevent experiences like mine. To those who showed care and understanding during my journey, I am forever thankful.

CHAPTER THIRTY-THREE

GLOBAL BIRTH TRAUMA

Every day, approximately 800 women die from complications related to pregnancy and childbirth – that's one woman every two minutes. More than half of these deaths (around 500 a day) occur in countries with humanitarian crises and conflicts. In Yemen and Afghanistan, which are among the countries with the highest maternal death rates, a woman dies every two hours during pregnancy, childbirth or its aftermath, from causes that are largely preventable with access to skilled care. In Gaza, a woman's chance of miscarriage or dying in childbirth has trebled. The stories below are from the United Nations Population Fund (UNFPA), the leading organisation providing access to maternal healthcare during crises around the world. Making motherhood safer is a human rights imperative and is at the core of UNFPA's mandate. The following three stories (Hanifa's, Kadiatou's and Halimah's) highlight the plight of women who have given birth in dire circumstances. The final story is from Kenya and is provided by Gill Castle through her charity Chameleon Buddies.

HANIFA, AFGHANISTAN

Early in the morning on 15 October, twenty-year-old Hanifa felt them: the contractions that signalled her baby was on its way. The timing was less than ideal. Just one week prior, a 6.3 magnitude earthquake had rocked Herat Province, Afghanistan, reducing Hanifa's home and thousands of others to rubble. Displaced and sheltering in a canvas tent, Hanifa felt lost and hopeless.

'I thought, "How can a mother bring a child into this chaos?"' she told UNFPA. 'But then Rahna, the midwife, arrived like an angel.'

Childbirth during displacement can be dangerous. Pregnant women who have been forced from their homes are more vulnerable to violence, malnutrition and disease. And they are more likely to give birth without the support of a skilled healthcare worker, raising the risk of life-threatening complications.

Fortunately for Hanifa, Rahna, a UNFPA-supported midwife, was on hand to help guide her through labour and bring her baby safely into the world. 'She held my hand and her words were like a soothing balm for my fears,' Hanifa said. 'I went from panic to comfort in moments.'

In the aftermath of catastrophe, addressing the sexual and reproductive health needs of women and girls often takes a back seat to other urgent humanitarian priorities. Midwives are critical to combating these challenges. According to UNFPA, midwives can cover about 90 per cent of the global need for interventions across sexual, reproductive, maternal, newborn and adolescent health. Yet the world underinvests in their development, putting millions of lives at risk. To fill the gap, UNFPA trains and supports midwives around the globe and, when necessary, dispatches them to emergencies.

Rahna is one of eight midwives that UNFPA sent to Herat as part of a contingent of five mobile health teams, which have been offering medical care, psychosocial support and sexual and reproductive health services to those affected by the earthquake.

Healthcare workers like Rahna provide more than specialised care, though. Hanifa described the midwife as solace personified: 'Hope arrived in the form of Rahna.'

Hanifa's labour lasted six hours and during that time, her blood pressure spiked. High blood pressure is a leading cause of maternal mortality, despite being largely preventable and treatable. Quality healthcare is essential to navigating this danger and, fortunately, Rahna's skilled support enabled both Hanifa and her newborn, Ahmad, to survive.

KADIATOU, GUINEA

'It happened at the hospital. I realised I was leaking urine,' fistula survivor Kadiatou Bah told UNFPA.

Kadiatou first fell pregnant more than four decades ago, when she was seventeen. With few health centres on hand in her mountainous village in Labé, Guinea, she'd had little chance to avail herself of services during her pregnancy; nor had she planned to give birth at a health facility.

But her plans changed after two days of labour. 'When we wanted to go to the health centre, I gave birth on the way,' she said. 'The child was already dead.'

Though she didn't realise it at the time, Kadiatou had suffered an obstetric fistula (a hole in the birth canal), a devastating childbirth injury that carries life-threatening risks for women and their pregnancies. About nine in ten women who develop obstetric fistula suffer stillbirths; meanwhile, research shows obstructed labour – the cause of a fistula – drives 6 per cent of maternal deaths.

The effects of a fistula are also severe for survivors; many encounter incontinence, mental and physical ailments and societal ostracisation. Kadiatou's disability drove a wedge between her and her husband, who offered her little support.

'I could no longer show myself in public,' she said. 'People avoided me; I suffered a lot.'

Half a million women and girls across the Arab states, Asia, Latin America, the Caribbean and sub-Saharan Africa are estimated to be survivors of obstetric fistulas. Many are girls and young women who, like Kadiatou, were married as children and may have become pregnant before their bodies were developmentally ready. According to 2018 data, about 124,000 women in Guinea are affected by obstetric fistulas – more than 4 per cent of women of childbearing age in the country.

Despite its prevalence, survivors of obstetric fistula remain subject to extreme levels of stigma. According to experts, caring for fistula survivors requires addressing their medical, psychosocial and socioeconomic needs. Most fistulas can be repaired via surgery, although this can be difficult to access given a lack in surgeons trained to provide this care. In Guinea, for example, only one hospital in the country's northeast regularly offers fistula repair surgeries. Despite these challenges, more than 500 women were able to obtain free fistula care between 2018 and 2023.

Kadiatou had lived with an obstetric fistula for almost twenty years before her first repair surgery. 'I underwent a first operation, then [a second], but I was still losing urine,' she said. Following a third surgery in 2019, however, she was able to make a full recovery.

With UNFPA's support, the government of Guinea has developed a national strategy to combat obstetric fistulas, creating fistula management units across seven regions of the country. Within these units, teams of surgeons, nurses and anaesthetists are trained to offer fistula repair surgeries to help women like Kadiatou heal.

HALIMAH, YEMEN

'I felt death every kilometre to the hospital,' says Halimah, thirty-five, from a remote village in Al Dahi District.

Halimah, eight months pregnant and severely malnourished, was in intolerable labour pain when her husband used up all his savings to hire a motorcycle – the only quick mode of transport available to take Halimah to a health facility. The closest facility was 43 kilometres away. More than eight years of conflict has impoverished Halimah and her family.

'The roads were very rough. I cannot describe the pain. I was holding on to my husband with all the strength left in me so I could save my child,' adds Halimah.

Four hours later, Halimah reached Ad-Dahi Rural Hospital – a UNFPA-supported health facility with funding from the European Union's Humanitarian Aid department. The health team rushed Halimah for delivery. She safely delivered twin girls.

'Thank you for saving my daughters. If not for this hospital and its staff, I don't know if me or my daughters would be alive today,' Halimah says.

Maternal mortality rates in Yemen remain extremely high – one of the highest in the Middle East and North Africa region. Less than half of births are assisted by skilled medical personnel and only one third of births take place in a health facility. Only one in five of the functioning facilities is able to provide maternal and child health services.

UNFPA supports ninety health facilities across the country to provide reproductive health services, reaching nearly a million women and girls with lifesaving reproductive health services since the beginning of 2023.

ANONYMOUS (A), KENYA

A is fifteen years old and lives in Migori County with her parents and seven siblings. She is a good student at school. A had been in a consensual sexual relationship with her seventeen-year-old boyfriend for one year. They did not think that A could get pregnant unless they had sex when she was on her monthly period; the pregnancy was not planned. After A became pregnant, she split up with her boyfriend and she no longer loves him.

A began her labour at home at the end of her full-term pregnancy, but very quickly was taken to the Migori Referral Hospital by her mother, which is a two-hour drive from their home. A spent two days in serious labour with some pain relief, but not enough to prevent severe pain. She didn't feel scared as she had her mother with her. Near the end of the labour, the doctor and the nurse began simultaneously to press down on and squeeze her abdomen and stretch and pull on her vagina to encourage the baby to come out. This was extremely painful. On the third day of labour, A gave birth to a stillborn baby boy who was large in size.

Afterwards, no nurses or doctors came to check on A and she was left alone on her hospital bed until the following day, when she was discharged into her mother's care.

Four days after she came home, A noticed that she was leaking urine. Initially, she thought that when the doctor had pressed hard down on her abdomen he had ruptured her bladder, but then she remembered a woman in her village had had a urine fistula. She realised that she had a fistula and knew her life was not good because she was not able to leave the house, go to church or be with her friends. She was using rags to soak up the leaking urine and life was a challenge.

A told her mother about her fistula, who arranged for A's father to take her to the Gynocare Women's and Fistula Hospital in Eldoret. All of A's family and friends knew what had happened to her and she was not abandoned by any of them.

A saw Dr Mabeya in the fistula clinic, who said that as her fistula was fresh, she could come back in two weeks for surgery. On 28 October 2024, A had successful fistula repair surgery and is continuing to heal well. Once she has fully healed, she will be able to return to school, where she would like to train to become a nurse.

A felt sad, but has been sleeping well and has not cried. She thinks of the birth and what happened, and thinks that if the baby had been smaller and the doctor and nurse hadn't been squeezing her, she would be holding a live baby in her arms today.

AMY, AUSTRALIA

This year marks nine years since I was diagnosed with a bilateral levator avulsion and subsequent prolapses after the birth of my first daughter.

I'll spare you the gory details of that December day. I ended up with a forceps birth, a third-degree tear and haemorrhage. Although the perineal tear was quickly picked up, the true trauma wouldn't reveal itself until sixteen months later.

My first week post-partum involved lots of liquid: champagne (finally!), urine and blood. I required a catheter for five days and then, when it was finally removed, my mum wheeled me outside in a wheelchair for some sunlight and fresh air.

I didn't know that wasn't normal. I thought I was OK; everyone told me I did well, that I got the birth I wanted. I clearly remember how I felt then: broken, bewildered, shocked, vulnerable and empty.

Leading up to my birth, I'd truly drunk the Kool-Aid. I was very fit when I found out I was pregnant; you hear that birth is like running a marathon, and I could do that. I could lift my body weight easily, I was strong and 'empowered' and after participating in a private birth course, I had expected to breathe my baby out in a meditative way. What I didn't expect to happen was for the birth to steal my identity and replace it with this broken shell of a woman, old before her time.

We made it home a week after we welcomed our baby into the world. I was incontinent (wind, faecal and urinary), bleeding heavily and unable to sit comfortably without rolling up two towels in parallel and ensuring I wasn't sitting on my bum!

My time was spent mostly crying and feeling like a failure. I'd not been good enough to give birth and I wasn't good enough to breastfeed. I now know how common it is to experience breastfeeding difficulties, let alone after experiencing a traumatic birth.

At that time, I had no idea I'd experienced trauma. I had nothing to compare it to. I guess I assumed feeling like I'd gone forty rounds with Rocky Balboa was a normal part of post-partum recovery. I now hear that if you feel like that, it is quite likely you've experienced some physical birth trauma.

At six weeks post-partum, I was advised to see a pelvic health physio; she likened my injuries to that of being in a car crash, but I remained optimistic that life would resume as normal, maybe just with a bit of extra work along the way. I'd soon be the 'fit mum' in the park doing bootcamp while my baby soundly slept.

It was a solid no on all accounts.

At fifteen months post-partum, I did a mindful triathlon: a 5 kilometre run, followed by ninety minutes of yoga and concluding with a fifteen-minute meditation. It was my first and last run post-baby. It was that day that I felt this unfamiliar, heavy, dragging feeling in my vagina. I didn't know what it was, but I knew it wasn't good.

A month later, at an appointment with a women's health physiotherapist, I received my diagnosis of levator avulsion (LA) and pelvic organ prolapse, in which your uterus, bowel or bladder slips down into the vagina.

LA happens when the pelvic floor muscle (levator ani) is torn away from the pubic bone during childbirth, causing permanent damage to the pelvic floor structures. The condition is associated with significant long-term consequences, including pelvic organ prolapse, bladder or faecal incontinence and chronic pelvic pain.

Partial avulsion occurs in between 15 per cent and 30 per cent of vaginal births, while full avulsion, in which the muscle is completely torn away, ranges from 10 per cent to 25 per cent of births. Both are more common during forceps births.

That appointment was a pivotal moment in my life. I was loving my motherhood journey. I didn't have any other symptoms; I had managed to improve my faecal incontinence; I didn't suffer urinary incontinence. I had no idea that my pelvic floor muscle was now hanging on by a thread. Why didn't I know anything about the risks associated with forceps? Why had no one warned me?

The only time I'd heard of pelvic organ prolapse was when I asked the registrar who delivered my baby whether I could weight train like I used to. His response was, 'Just live the life you want; if you prolapse, you can just get surgery when you finish having kids.' Just an FYI – this is not good advice.

When I got home from that appointment, I frantically googled 'physical birth trauma'. Nothing came up. From that moment on, I decided that I was a freak and shame reared its ugly head once again.

At a subsequent appointment, I discovered how common it is to experience physical birth trauma such as prolapse and incontinence. It is still hard to understand why something so common and grim is shrouded in silence. Who are we protecting by not discussing risk with parents?

For a while, I plummeted into a deep well of despair. I was no longer the woman I thought I'd be and my body had limitations that I never thought possible. I was even advised to avoid lifting my toddler, which I dutifully did. At my darkest point, I had thoughts of ending my life. It's a time that I'll never get back.

My pelvic physio became my saving grace; she introduced me to other women with similar interests who were also navigating motherhood and life with birth injuries. I had my professional guidance and trusty pessary (something the registrar had said is 'just for old women who don't have sex'), but I also had a way to connect with a person who 'got it'. There really is power in sharing our experiences with someone who won't try to make them better but will listen, understand and not pass judgement.

In my mothers' group, I expected to make lifelong friendships. The reality was that I felt alienated and broken while everyone seemed to be doing amazingly. I kept wondering, am I the only one who felt like an empty, broken shell with a baby that cries all the time? (It turns out she was hungry.) Now I had some mums that I could really talk to.

I also got comfortable with getting uncomfortable, as silly as it sounds. For the greater good, I would rather a trained but relative stranger use their fingers to determine the integrity of my pelvic floor muscles than risk surgery at this stage. Conservative management doesn't work for everyone, but it's worth giving it a shot.

I didn't realise at the time, at the grand old age of thirty-five, that I would need to learn how to poop correctly or that I would require a splint to hold my organs inside my body. You can't help but revisit that question – why didn't anyone tell me? But you learn to cope and you will be OK.

I learnt to make my vulnerability into my superpower. I started sharing my story. I was compelled to break the stigma attached to birth injuries and I wanted to help others along the way if I could. That's the reason I co-founded Birth Trauma Australia – for the power of peer support, which was so crucial in my own recovery.

Flash forward to another child delivered by elective Caesarean, which led to a lot more stress incontinence. I'm forever a work in progress, especially as I am now perimenopausal. However, I'm happy with where I'm at now. My prolapse doesn't dominate every waking thought. I lift heavy (ish) weights, love exercise and will try anything to see how it feels. I am an active person and the good far outweighs the bad.

You have to find what works for you. Meditation continues to be a huge part of my life and so does my psychologist – after a few failed attempts at finding the right one for me. One of the first things she said to me when I explained why I was so anxious was, 'Yes, you're anxious, but it's completely understandable.' She has been supporting me ever since.

Do I still get angry about it? Yes, especially when, over a decade later, I continue to hear stories that echo my own. But I channel that anger for good. What happened to me has fuelled a sense of resilience I had no idea I possessed.

My dream is for women who have experienced birth injuries to know that they aren't alone and that they don't need to suffer in silence. We have seen the stigma surrounding perinatal mental health improve, but if we don't start talking about common issues that occur from childbirth (especially after interventions), then how will we ever fix our overall quality of life?

If you're reading this and any of it resonates with you, please seek support. This doesn't have to be your new normal.

Amy Dawes is the chief executive of Birth Trauma Australia.

CHAPTER THIRTY-FOUR

HEALING

RACHEL

I have fibromyalgia or fibro, an autoimmune condition that causes chronic pain as well as severe fatigue, known as fibro fog. I don't think many members of the hospital team had heard of the condition, let alone knew how to manage a labouring patient with it.

My waters broke at 5 a.m. on 29 December 2015. We arrived at the hospital soon after but were sent home after a couple of hours and told to return when the 'surges' (as we were told to think of them in hypnobirthing!) were closer or when the hospital called us. I recall feeling quietly excited and terrified. We left and I plonked one of the baby's nappies from my hospital bag into my pants as water was gushing everywhere and whacked on my TENS machine to see through the day back at home, trying to find comfort in watching Michael McIntyre. The TENS machine was amazing at getting me through the pain that night and I felt a bit delirious, being in and out of sleep.

Although the next day the contractions still weren't close enough to go in, we called the hospital in the afternoon and they told us to come in immediately.

We arrived in the maternity ward that evening. When a nurse checked to see how dilated I was, it was utterly excruciating. The initial scan and tests they undertook indicated that the baby had a low heartbeat and that he didn't seem to be moving. They put a peg on his head to monitor him. It's all a bit of a blur, but I recall a panic button being pressed and suddenly a team of about fifteen medical people all in scrubs flooding the room. At that moment, I thought either I or the baby was going to die. It was sheer panic. I remember the trolley with its shiny hard metal sides being pulled up and people racing me along the brightly lit corridor, sprinting at a rate of knots. 'Am I going to die?' I whimpered to my husband, who was running along next to my side holding my hand.

They got me into a room that felt like an operating theatre and after a lot of activity, where I was prodded and tested in various ways, the team comforted themselves that our baby was OK. I, however, was not OK, either physically or mentally.

Then came the epidural, something I had been dreading but desperately wanted. I recall a bright yellow piece of paper being flung in my direction for me to scribble my signature on to provide my consent and outlining the potential risks – small things like permanent paralysis.

I am terrified of needles. I was beyond exhausted and in a state of utter panic, while all the time the contractions – sorry, 'surges' – were coming thick and fast. I was told to curl my upper body over a foam roller. 'STAY STILL, DO NOT MOVE!' they kept shouting at me. I remember thinking, 'What if I don't? Will I be paralysed?' It was intensely distressing.

My memory of the labour becomes hazy from that point on account of the pain, sleep deprivation, drugs and general trauma. I remember various meetings with doctory people and clipboards.

The second night of my ordeal wore on, with midwives checking in to see how dilated I was. I remember feeling terrified. I was in agony and I felt totally out of control. Early in the morning of the third day of being in labour, my son got very stuck. By this point, I was almost totally out of it. I remember very bright lights everywhere as again I was rushed to theatre, where they now planned to deliver the baby via ventouse. I remember being told, 'You have one chance at this, one chance to push when we say or we will have to do a C-section.'

I felt utterly petrified, confused, alone and bewildered – was this pushing like doing a poo? But I can't feel a fricking thing! I remember shouting, 'I can't hear anything anyone is saying; it's all jumbled up!' I looked to my right and saw my husband on his little stool and then my midwife, who had taken over from a million others, and I held her hand. She had the most beautiful turquoise eye liner on with long black eyelashes. 'I will listen to you and only you,' I whispered. She was so kind.

They tried the ventouse first – not a chance! The surgeon had to go in with forceps. Our son was finally born at 3.10 a.m. on New Year's Eve. He was placed on my chest and I felt absolutely nothing.

I stayed in hospital for the next eleven nights with three different care teams on my case: the psychiatric team, the acute pain management team and the 'normal' team. My body had locked down, in large part due to my fibromyalgia. I was asked if I had psychosis. 'What the hell is that?' I remember thinking.

I could not hold my precious baby as my wrists and arms didn't work – I couldn't even twist a bottle for his formula. I was put on morphine to manage the chronic pain from my episiotomy. I had one slightly psychotic episode where I hallucinated – I saw huge black hairy tarantulas climbing up my body and the white sheets and into my mouth (I have severe arachnophobia). No more opioids for me!

I was unable to sit down comfortably for seven weeks after having my son. The first poo after having him was utterly terrible! I was so badly constipated. I was offered suppositories by two midwives who were then vile to me, being both harsh and incredibly unsympathetic as I struggled.

I lay on the bathroom floor with my son next door and it felt like trying to give birth again. I lay in that room straining like a cow, snorting like a pig, counting all the thousand varying degrees of grey-coloured tiny tiles on the floor.

The fibro 'flare' I experienced post-birth made me feel detached from the real world. My pain was acute throughout my whole entire upper body, with my shoulder blades feeling as if jagged bits of wood were being shoved into them, repeatedly being jabbed and stabbed. On top of this, the pain I had from the episiotomy was like nothing else. I desperately wanted to crawl out of my body and die.

Trying to breastfeed was so painful and the anxiety I felt was horrific. My NCT girlfriends seemed to be feeding beautifully, and my own mother had breastfed me and my two sisters without a problem. What the hell was wrong with me?! The little voices in my head got louder and louder as I was lying there: 'You are useless, Rachel, you are a failure, your pain will never leave you.'

I felt terrified every time my little baby stirred. I was thinking, crikey, I've got to feed this helpless, perfect little thing and my wrists don't work, never mind the pain in my nipples, which was excruciating. 'How on earth am I going to reach for him in his crib, let alone try to hold him? I might even drop this precious, much-longed-for bundle onto the hard floor.' Some of the midwives at this point were extremely unsympathetic.

The pressure I felt to breastfeed was enormous. I cannot tell you how many times 'breast is best' was thrown at me ahead of my birth, while in the hospital and when I had left to go home. It was dealt with extremely badly. The message should have been that 'fed is best' – especially if you've had a very long and traumatic birth.

Both of us – actually all three of us, as my husband was heavily involved in my post-partum recovery – were learning to feed for the first time: supply and demand, which side to feed on, pumping, nose to nipple, different feeding positions, on and on goes the list! It was a totally foreign language to us all and I remember feeling utterly bemused as my husband taught me patiently how to make up formula. Eventually, I vaguely got the hang of breastfeeding. But from six weeks I started to combination feed. I remember that because of my weak wrists, my husband would milk me. I felt like Daisy the cow with the breast pump attached to me. As soon as my son was combination feeding, things were so much better for all of us.

I visited Sainsbury's for my first trip out with my mum about ten days after being let out of hospital. It was intensely traumatic; maybe it was the bright lights, the noise, the assault on my senses or perhaps it was down to the pain I was still in and my general fatigue. I ended up collapsing by the checkout queue. I desperately wanted to lay my head down on the shiny metal surface.

At home, I had numerous visits from social services and MIMHS (mother and infant mental health services) as well as lots of telephone calls. When I initially heard that social services were coming, I immediately freaked out – the shame of it, the connotations, the judgement. But they needed to check: could I hold my baby safely? Would I be able to move fast enough with him if there was a fire? How was my husband holding up? Was I OK? Looking back now, I am able to see this in a positive light, but at the time I felt like I was failing.

It was a combination of things that helped my recovery after having my son: therapy, a lot of guided meditation, yoga nidra (focusing on various breathing techniques to calm the entire central nervous system), reflexology, a lot of paracetamol, chatting with friends, walking in the fresh air and maintaining a healthy diet and sleep.

I was put on sertraline by my GP as a precaution as she thought I was suffering from postnatal depression. Maybe I was, but I think it was also deep trauma. I started seeing a therapist who was an incredible help. Sticking to a routine also helped me. I'm a teacher and I found it both calming and reassuring to know, for instance, that when my son was having his lunchtime sleep I could hop into bed or onto my yoga mat. I am still absolutely religious about this daily practice!

One thing that really helped was a long conversation with my younger sister who is a child psychiatrist – she is fiercely intelligent but also calming. We had managed to get hold of the bible of notes from the hospital. Going through the detail of exactly what happened and when during my son's birth and the days afterwards was beyond helpful. I will be forever grateful to her for spending her precious time with me talking, reading and 'humanising' the whole series of events – timings, how he got so stuck, why my pain was so brutal (a fourth-degree tear, no less!). It helped reframe a positive picture of a medical team that just wanted to get me off home safely.

On my son's first birthday, I cried throughout the entire day. It was cathartic. Although it was painful, I also felt unbelievably grateful to have him.

For the birth of my daughter, five and a half years after my son's birth, I had a planned C-section. I had hyperemesis gravidarum (extreme morning sickness) throughout the pregnancy: imagine the worst food poisoning combined with a terrible hangover and you are 10 per cent there. On my regular visits to hospital, I had to be wheeled around the corridors in a wheelchair as I was often so weak I could not stand up. During the birth, it was agony when the epidural needle went in. I collapsed down on my side in utter terror, felt violently sick and gripped the nurse's hand so tight I nearly broke her bones. On the whole, though, my second birth was considerably less traumatic than the first.

I am fortunate to now have two wonderful children and be able to look back and see that the medical teams in both of my births were acting as best they knew to provide the support I needed. I am grateful to so many of the amazing people who helped me on my journey, but my memories are not without both emotional and physical pain, driven, in part, by a feeling that so much could have been managed better.

GILL

I fell pregnant quickly and easily with my first (and only) baby in spring 2011, with a due date of the end of November. My pregnancy progressed without incident, and as a fit and healthy police officer I had no reason to believe that my birth would be anything other than the same. On 20 October 2011, I went into spontaneous labour six weeks early. The premature labour meant I had to remain on the bed attached to various machines, with cannulas in my hands and wires dangling off my body.

I desperately wanted to get off the bed, to walk my pain away, to kneel on the floor, anything to relieve my agony, but I had to remain on the bed. It was the first inkling that I was no longer in control. After a few hours, everything was becoming a blur, and I noticed that more and more people were coming into the room, a professional flurry of activity, monitors beeping and careful hands checking my stomach. There were three attempts to put in the epidural. Then, suddenly, there was a shout and a small, white, scum-covered little body was thrust into my face for a few seconds before being whisked to special care.

It was curiously unsettling to have given birth to a baby but not to have touched, smelled or held him. I kept trying to summon the picture of him in my head, hoping to feel the surge of love you read about in magazines, that huge rush of maternal devotion. I felt oddly numb. Almost disappointed. I had never felt such a lack of emotion before. It was like I was flying high above myself, looking down on the room, at this shattered, bewildered couple sitting alone in their room without a child to gaze upon in awe. I felt as though my brain had collapsed, simply unable to deal with the drama of the day. The quiet of the room matched the quiet of the bedroom I had woken up in that morning, a surreal mirroring of silence that missed out the noise, blood and raw emotion of what had gone on in between.

I had been told that I had suffered a third-degree tear during the delivery, most likely caused by the forceps that had been used to get Sam out. (Initially, the consultant had stitched up what she thought was a second-degree tear, then decided it was a third-degree tear, took the stitches out and redid them.) I was shocked by how much pain I was in. I found it very difficult to sit, even on pillows, and it was slow progress to walk anywhere, let alone get on and off the bed. Fortunately, at 4 lb 7 oz, Sam was very small and light and I was able to hold him easily once I had got myself into a comfier position on the bed. Nevertheless, it was almost unbearable at times – the pain was increasing slowly by the hour. I started to feel almost deranged and I began to feel afraid. I knew something was going wrong, but I couldn't work out what it was. I felt extremely hot, but the temperature checks I insisted on having kept coming back as normal.

A couple of days after the birth, I noticed a brown discharge in my underwear and mentioned it to midwives, who told me that my wound was healing and that the heat and pain I could feel were the tissues knitting back together. I had a shower and could see faeces running down my legs, so I fumbled around trying to find where it was coming from. I was panicking, my mind in overdrive and I felt faint. I burst into tears in pain and fear, shouting for a nurse. When one arrived, I was naked in the shower, crying and trying to explain that I couldn't work out where my anus was. She looked shocked and, rightly, must have thought I was going mad.

No one listened. I mentioned to the attending midwife on her rounds that I was incontinent, that there were faeces in my underwear and I thought I was going mad with the pain. She examined me but said again that the stitches looked like they were healing and the heat was simply the tissue knitting back together. The following morning, I half-heartedly mentioned my incontinence to the midwife on the morning shift and she was surprised – there had been nothing written in my notes about my worries of the previous day. It dawned on me then that I was alone. No one was listening to me. No one was taking me seriously. I was vulnerable, in pain, deeply distressed and frightened.

Later that day, I managed to walk to the toilet, clutching on to the wall as I made my slow, painful way along the corridor until I felt weak. I knelt on the floor, just as a male midwife came past. I burst into tears and said I was in agony and I couldn't cope. He was very calm as I cried and explained that I knew there was something wrong with me. I wasn't getting better; I was getting worse. I will never forget the words that came out of his mouth. He looked me straight in the eyes and said, 'Maybe it's your perception of the pain.' Something in me died, the spark inside me snuffed out. My terror and my pain were simply dismissed as me being unable to hack it, as being not as strong as other women after birth. I felt shattered.

Fortunately, I was later examined under gas and air by a consultant, who diagnosed me with a missed fourth-degree tear, rectovaginal fistula and a perineal abscess. The only option to clear the rampant infection was for me to be fitted with a colostomy.

The damage to my sphincter, due to the botched repair done by the original consultant, was irreparable. My stoma was permanent. It took a year of almost monthly hospital admissions to drain the septic fistula tract before my fistula was eventually repaired. During that time, I battled with my GP surgery for appointments (taking my own swabs of my perineum in the GP toilet), and I was missed off the counselling list and given no emotional support. In the aftermath, I was diagnosed with PTSD, severe anxiety and depression. I was unable to work as a police officer on the front line and was medically pensioned out in April 2013. I suffered a miscarriage in 2014 and was at rock bottom. It was then that I started to turn my life around.

'Will I ever be happy?' I asked my health visitor in summer 2014, as I grappled with deep depression and almost constant anxiety. The reply was, 'You can be happier.' The emphasis on the 'ier' stung me. I didn't want to simply be happier; I wanted to be happy. I realised that no one was going to knock on my door and make me happy. I had to take responsibility and do it for myself. I turned from being an observer in my life to being proactive and determined to prove the health visitor wrong. I've never liked being told what to do and I didn't like being told that being happy was out of my reach. Even this subtle mental difference – happier to happy – was significant, a turning point in my approach to my situation.

I distinctly remember reflecting on everything that I had overcome in the previous three to four years – the trauma, the heartbreak, the physical and mental health battles – and realising that if I could overcome all of that, then I could also be happy. I had accepted my stoma, but acceptance is a benign emotion and doesn't propel you to do anything. Around the same time, I read an article by a triathlete with a stoma, who said that she felt gratitude for her stoma because it had taken away the pain of her debilitating bowel disease (Crohn's) and enabled her to be physically active. It was very hard for me to feel gratitude for my stoma, because as far as I was concerned it had lost me my dream job, my pension and my ability to play any sports. Then I thought back to the five days I had spent in hospital, incontinent and wearing adult nappies, before I was fitted with the stoma, which enabled me to leave the hospital continent. It was like a lightning bolt to the brain. I was in fact lucky to have a stoma!

Gratitude is a very powerful, positive, proactive emotion and it permitted me to embrace living with my stoma – I began to fit the stoma around what I wanted to do, instead of the stoma dictating what I would do with my life. I had spent quite a lot of my life too timid to try things I wanted to, afraid of failure, afraid of things being too hard. I knew that nothing could be as bad as everything I had been through and that life can change in an instant – if you can try something you've always wanted to do, do it now, before it's too late.

I had always wanted to take part in a triathlon but never thought I'd be fit enough. By this point, my physical injuries had healed and although mentally I was still fragile, I resolved to join the local triathlon club and sign up for a triathlon. I remember the first time I took part in an indoor cycling class, when I was able to stand up on the pedals for only one rotation before collapsing back on the seat. I didn't even finish that first class. However, with every little physical improvement I made, I noticed my mental health improving too. Each step is like a brick in a bridge – you keep building steps, building that bridge, until eventually you can cross that bridge into the new, happier, healthy land on the other side.

I completed my first triathlon in 2015, which empowered me to embrace more and bigger physical challenges – all of which require mental resilience too. Over the next few years, I completed further triathlons, including a half-ironman, before a 105-mile endurance race where we kayaked, trail ran and cycled from east to west Scotland. Scuba diving, sky diving and hiking the National Three Peaks Challenge in twenty-four hours all followed. In September 2023, I became the first person in the world to swim the English Channel solo with a stoma, completing the 21-mile crossing in thirteen hours and fifty-three minutes. I raised over £50,000 for my own charity, Chameleon Buddies, which I set up in 2022 to support women in Kenya who are learning to adapt to living with a stoma after a fistula.

Alongside my physical challenges, which helped my mental health due to the natural serotonins that exercise releases, three years after the birth I was allocated some counselling in the hospital's women's health department. I felt like I was going round in circles and not really getting anywhere, so I changed my counselling to one outside a hospital setting to mark the shift into a new life, away from medical problems. I was able to see how strong I had been as I talked freely about my grief at losing my beloved police job. I had been prescribed antidepressants in the year after the birth and after a couple of years' gap in taking them, I decided to start again with a new, low prescription. For me, drugs aren't the sole answer, but eleven years later I still take my daily dose, which I find helps take the edge off any low mood and gives my mind an even setting to approach life's ups and downs.

The physical and mental health impact of my traumatic birth will always be a part of who I am, but I no longer feel defined by what happened on that maternity ward. I feel defined by the way I have managed, with hard work, some luck and a supportive family network, to refocus on making the absolute best of the life I have been given, with my sights always on what lies ahead.

POSTSCRIPT

THE MATERNITY MANIFESTO

1. IMPLEMENT A NATIONAL MATERNITY STRATEGY

The UK government must implement in full the recommendations of the Birth Trauma Inquiry's report 'Listen to Mums: Ending the Postcode Lottery on Perinatal Care'. The most important recommendation was to create a national maternity strategy, hosted on the government website, and appoint a national maternity commissioner to oversee improvements in care.

It became clear during the Birth Trauma Inquiry that individual NHS trusts and boards are able to make their own policies without having to follow national guidelines. The result is a variation in care that means a baby whose life would be saved in one hospital dies in another. The implementation of a national strategy and commissioner would offer much-needed central direction. The strategy would need to be updated regularly to take account of new data and best practice information.

2. MAINTAIN A FULLY STAFFED WORKFORCE

Funding for maternity care should be increased and the UK should train, recruit and retain more midwives, obstetricians and anaesthetists. The RCM estimates that England is currently short of 2,500 midwives and that midwives work 100,000 hours of unpaid overtime every week. So many stories that came into the inquiry involved women being left unattended in labour because midwives were busy caring for women elsewhere.

Retention is particularly important. Too many midwives are leaving, to be replaced by agency staff or not replaced at all. Plans to improve retention could include, as the RCM suggests, flexible working so that rotas are built around times when staff say they are available for work. Employers also need to look after staff, making sure they are able to take breaks and have access to hot food if they are on a night shift.

3. IMPROVE ANTENATAL CARE

Like many women, I didn't have access to an NHS antenatal class when I was pregnant. Instead, I attended an NCT class, which turned out to be useful for making friends but not so good at informing me about the risks of childbirth.

I'd like to see NHS antenatal classes made available to all pregnant women and their partners. Women need to be informed about what labour involves, without any sugar-coating. Their partners, too, need to understand what is happening so that they can support women and advocate for them during labour. Knowing the symptoms of pre-eclampsia, for example, can be lifesaving. Equally, women need to be aware that sometimes babies have to be delivered very quickly because they have become stuck or their heart rate has dropped. So many women find themselves faced with making decisions about forceps or emergency Caesareans without knowing in advance the risks and benefits of the different options.

In antenatal appointments, midwives should discuss a woman's own individual risk factors so that she can make an informed choice about labour and birth. Factors such as age, ethnicity, BMI and previous obstetric history are all important. The process can be made easier through the use of a standardised risk assessment tool, such as UR-CHOICE. Women should be given the option of a planned Caesarean if that is what they prefer.

4. PROVIDE WOMAN-CENTRED CARE IN LABOUR AND BIRTH

All maternity professionals should be trained in the importance of informed consent. No maternity unit should be allowing its staff to carry out procedures such as cervical sweeps or vaginal examinations without the woman's consent.

Women should not have pain relief denied to them during labour and birth. The Birth Trauma Inquiry received an overwhelming number of stories of women being denied epidurals and offered inadequate alternatives such as paracetamol – or no alternative at all. Many women denied pain relief still carry the psychological scars years later.

It's not too much to ask that all maternity staff treat women with compassion, listen to what women tell them and not dismiss their concerns. Some of the worst stories I've heard involved women being told they were 'over-anxious' when in fact there was something seriously wrong. Sometimes the outcome was catastrophic, involving death or injury to the baby.

Research has shown that poor interpersonal care from staff is a major factor in birth trauma. At the minimum, maternity units should ask their staff to behave professionally. Many of the stories sent to the inquiry involved staff shouting or laughing at women, which contributed hugely to their distress and trauma in the weeks, months and sometimes years after giving birth.

5. TACKLE INEQUALITIES

The NHS must tackle disparities in maternal outcomes. Black women are three times as likely and South Asian women are twice as likely as white women to die in the period from the start of pregnancy to six weeks after birth. Babies born to black or South Asian mothers are significantly more likely to be stillborn or die during the neonatal period. Babies born to women in the most socio-economically deprived areas have nearly twice the rate of stillbirth and neonatal death as those in the least deprived areas.

Change can happen only through better collection and analysis of data, so that researchers have information about why particular groups are more at risk of poor outcomes. Once that information is available, the government can develop strategies to address it.

The NHS also needs to think about how to be more responsive to the needs of women in disadvantaged groups. Our Birth Trauma Inquiry heard that some women may have religious reasons for not attending appointments on a Friday, for example, while others cannot afford to take public transport to hospital appointments.

POSTSCRIPT

One good practice example the inquiry heard was of an outreach project in Walsall, which provided care in the communities where women live rather than requiring them to travel.

More than a quarter of babies born in the UK have mothers who were born outside the UK. Some of these women are not fluent in English and sometimes those who are fluent in their own language are not able to read in that language. If a woman can't understand what the health professional is saying or make herself understood, that can create huge problems.

It's important that antenatal information is available not just as leaflets but in apps created in different languages, with audiovisual as well as written information. The NHS should employ specialist maternity interpreters, so that all women for whom English is not a first language have access to good-quality interpreting services antenatally, during labour and birth and postnatally.

6. DELIVER SAFE MATERNITY CARE

Safety should be the number-one priority for maternity units. Nothing can be more important than making sure that mother and baby are alive and healthy. But sometimes hospitals can become fixated on processes rather than outcomes – the 2022 Ockenden report into Shrewsbury and Telford NHS trust showed that the hospital had become so focused on reducing Caesarean rates that some mothers and babies died or were injured as a result.

There are other things the NHS can do to improve safety. One is requiring maternity units to share good practice through conferences, online forums and continued professional development. There has to be a culture shift too. A willingness to learn and to share what has been learnt is at the heart of improving maternity care. So many decisions in maternity are informed by local culture and practices, not by hard evidence.

One particularly devastating outcome of birth is obstetric anal sphincter injury (OASI), experienced by 3.4 per cent of women who give birth vaginally. OASI can lead to long-term pain and incontinence, particularly if it is undiagnosed or diagnosed too late. There are two big steps the NHS can take to reduce the incidence of OASI:

- Adopt the consensus statement on assisted vaginal birth. This has been produced by a cross-disciplinary working party of obstetricians, midwives and patients and includes a recommendation to reduce the incidence of forceps birth. The risk of obstetric tearing is six times higher with forceps and their use can also lead to injury to the baby.
- Roll out the OASI care bundle nationally to reduce the incidence of severe obstetric tearing and to improve the diagnosis of tears immediately after birth. The OASI care bundle was developed by a team of midwives and obstetricians and a pilot project showed that it is effective.

I'd also like to see physiotherapy offered to women who have experienced tearing during birth so they are not left with long-term problems. The programme to introduce local pelvic health clinics, launched by the Sunak government, is a good step forward in achieving this aim.

7. IMPROVE POSTNATAL CARE

My own experience of postnatal care was dismal. I was left on the postnatal ward feeling exhausted and ill after a long labour that had finished with a post-partum haemorrhage and third-degree tear. Too weak to lift my own baby, I called for help, only to be told by a member of staff, 'Not my baby, not my problem.'

What I heard during the inquiry was that I wasn't alone. Lots of women shared stories of pressing buzzers that went unanswered or of being left alone in bloodstained sheets. Postnatal wards should be properly staffed, so that a woman who needs help, for example, to breastfeed her baby or to go to the toilet receives it immediately.

Some women have provided accounts of dirty postnatal wards, such as toilet cubicles with blood stains. Cleanliness should be a minimum requirement on a hospital ward, but wards should be comfortable and pleasant too. So many women find breastfeeding challenging, particularly after a traumatic birth. Too often, they are hectored about the importance of breastfeeding but are not given any help to do it. Midwives need to receive better training in breastfeeding support and hospitals need to understand that supporting a woman to breastfeed means spending time with her. Some women may choose to formula feed and should not be judged for this.

Women who have experienced baby loss or whose baby is in intensive care should not be placed on a postnatal ward with women who have their babies with them. And not all GPs offer a six-to-eight-week postnatal check. This needs to change – and the check needs to be offered for the mother as well as the baby and cover her mental as well as physical health.

8. IMPROVE MENTAL HEALTH SERVICES

One in twenty-five women, research shows, experience PTSD as a result of birth and many more find some aspects of birth traumatic.

Many find it hard to access mental health support. The maternal mental health services introduced in England are a good start, but they need to be expanded and fully resourced. Any woman who has PTSD after birth should have access to either trauma-focused CBT or EMDR therapy.

I firmly believe that health checks should be offered for partners as well as mothers. Henry, my husband, was traumatised by seeing me wheeled off to theatre haemorrhaging badly and not knowing whether I was going to come out alive. About one in 100 fathers or partners develop PTSD after birth, while about one in twelve men develop postnatal depression. As a society, we need to stop ignoring the mental health needs of dads and partners.

9. MAKE BETTER USE OF DATA

The NHS has a great advantage over health systems in other countries – as a single, large organisation, it holds the health records for every patient in the country. This gives it an opportunity to collect patient data at a national level and use it to identify the factors leading to poor outcomes, as well as the ones that lead to better outcomes. This knowledge can be used to improve maternity care for everyone.

At the same time, digital data can be used for information sharing. The new Connecting Care Records programme means that community midwives, hospital doctors and midwives and GPs will all have access to the same maternity record. Women often say that they spend too much time retelling their story to different people. If everyone has access to the same information, it will save time and, more importantly, reduce the stress caused to women by having to repeat their story over and over again.

POSTSCRIPT

10. INTRODUCE NEW MECHANISMS FOR DEALING WITH COMPLAINTS

I've heard from lots of women who said that their complaints to the hospital about poor care were not treated seriously. In some cases, hospitals denied or minimised what had happened to them. I'd like to see a mechanism by which complaints could be reviewed independently so that hospitals can't simply send out fobbing-off responses to complaints about poor care. In an ideal world, hospitals would treat complaints as an opportunity for learning and improvement.

MODERNISING PARLIAMENT

RECOMMENDATIONS FOR PARLIAMENT TO IMPROVE SUPPORT IN THE HOUSE OF COMMONS FOR MPS WITH YOUNG FAMILIES

Being pregnant, giving birth and becoming a mother while working as an MP were all much more difficult than they would have been had I worked in almost any other job. As MPs, we pass legislation that offers basic protections to mothers – but those same protections don't apply to MPs themselves. Here are my recommendations for making Parliament more accommodating for female MPs who want to start a family:

- Introduce maternity leave with written guidance for MPs. Government ministers are entitled to six months of paid maternity leave, but this does not apply to MPs. Yet in other parliaments worldwide, provision for maternity leave is the same as the national law.
- Make the proxy vote system more flexible. Currently, MPs can appoint a proxy MP to vote for them from one month before

their due date to six months after. It means that if an MP is away for longer than six months (perhaps because the MP or their new baby is ill), they are dependent on the slip system, in which the whips have discretion as to whether allow the MP to be absent. This enables whips to award or withhold slips as a form of party discipline.

- Allow all MPs to appoint a locum while they are on maternity leave. The locum would cover an MP's constituency duties while they are on leave. Without a formal arrangement, constituents are not represented properly during an MP's maternity leave.
- Allow MPs on maternity leave to attend select committee hearings virtually or to nominate another MP to attend meetings in their place. The replacement MP would then stand down at the end of their maternity leave.
- Change the way MPs vote. Currently, MPs vote by walking into the division lobbies, even if they are unwell or heavily pregnant. In the Scottish Parliament and Welsh Senedd, however, votes are registered electronically and rather than voting after each debate, voting is grouped into a single voting period at the end of the day, during core hours. This saves time as well as being less physically demanding.
- During the Covid pandemic MPs were able to vote remotely, and there is no reason why that practice could not be reintroduced in specific circumstances, benefiting MPs who are unwell or who have caring responsibilities (for example, taking a child to hospital).
- MPs who are on maternity leave or are seriously ill should be allowed to ask questions of a minister virtually, as happened during the pandemic.

- Give MPs' babies and children priority in the on-site nursery. The current nursery, which has forty places, is open to all pass-holders who work on the parliamentary estate. MPs should be prioritised for nursery places, given their unique role, late-night voting hours and the requirement to be near the voting lobby. (MPs are already given precedence in other parts of the estate – for example, the lifts are reserved for MPs to go ahead of staff during divisions.)
- Make the nursery more flexible by offering term-time care in order to better accommodate the recess, when MPs spend time in their constituencies rather than in Parliament. The nursery should include a drop-in crèche facility that could be used at times when other childcare isn't available, such as the school holidays or when Parliament is sitting beyond its scheduled hours.
- Parliamentary hours should be made more family friendly. Sometimes Parliament sits until late at night, which means that MPs may have to pay for or struggle to find additional childcare.

RESOURCES

You may find these resources helpful if you have been affected by traumatic birth or pregnancy or are interested in finding out more. Helpline numbers are given where available; otherwise the phone numbers listed are for general enquiries. If a contact email isn't given, that is usually because the organisation has a contact form on its website.

ANTENATAL RESULTS & CHOICES (ARC)
ARC provides emotional support and independent information relating to antenatal testing.
- Website: www.arc-uk.org
- Email: info@arc-uk.org
- Helpline: 020 7713 7486

ASSOCIATION FOR POST NATAL ILLNESS (APNI)
APNI offers support to women with postnatal depression.
- Website: www.apni.org
- Helpline: 0207 386 0868

BIRTH TRAUMA ASSOCIATION (BTA)

The Birth Trauma Association supports parents who have been affected by traumatic birth and campaigns for improvements in maternity care. Its support email is staffed by peer supporters who have themselves experienced birth trauma.
- Website: www.birthtraumaassociation.org
- Email: support@birthtraumaassociation.org.uk
- Helpline: 0203 621 6338

BLISS

Bliss offers support for parents and families of premature and sick babies. You can request a video call if you prefer.
- Website: www.bliss.org.uk
- Email: hello@bliss.org.uk
- Phone (general enquiries): 020 7378 1122

BREAKING THE TABOO

Podcast on women's health focused on birth trauma. Practical advice from experts and affected mothers/families.
- Website: www.theo-clarke.org.uk

FIVE X MORE

Five X More campaigns for better outcomes in maternity for Black women.
- Website: https://fivexmore.org

MAKE BIRTH BETTER

Supports parents and professionals impacted by birth trauma and offers training to professionals.

- Website: www.makebirthbetter.org
- Email: hello@makebirthbetter.org

MASIC FOUNDATION

MASIC supports women who have experienced anal sphincter injuries as a result of birth.

- Website: www.masic.org.uk
- Email: info@masic.org.uk
- Helpline: 0808 164 0833

MATERNAL MENTAL HEALTH ALLIANCE (MMHA)

MMHA is a network of organisations offering mental health support to mothers.

- Website: https://maternalmentalhealthalliance.org

MISCARRIAGE ASSOCIATION

The Miscarriage Association supports anyone affected by the loss of a baby in pregnancy.

- Website: www.miscarriageassociation.org.uk
- Email: info@miscarriageassociation.org.uk
- Helpline: 01924 200 799

NATIONAL BREASTFEEDING HELPLINE

The helpline offers information and support to anyone needing advice on breastfeeding.

- Website: www.nationalbreastfeedinghelpline.org.uk
- Helpline: 0300 100 0212

NATIONAL DOMESTIC ABUSE HELPLINE

The helpline is run by the charity Refuge. It is open twenty-four

hours a day, seven days a week, and offers free and confidential advice. A translation service is available if English is not your first language.
- Helpline: 0808 2000 247

NCT
The NCT runs antenatal classes and offers support for parents during pregnancy and postnatally.
- Website: www.nct.org.uk

PANDAS FOUNDATION
PANDAS supports parents with prenatal or postnatal depression, as well as other perinatal mental health challenges. Its helpline is open Monday to Friday between 10 a.m. and 5 p.m.
- Website: https://pandasfoundation.org.uk
- Email: supportme@pandasfoundation.org.uk
- Helpline: 0808 1961 776 or text via WhatsApp 07903 508 334

PEEPS
PEEPS supports parents, families and friends of people who have experienced hypoxic-ischaemic encephalopathy (brain injury as a result of oxygen deprivation). It has lots of useful downloadable resources.
- Website: www.peeps-hie.org
- Email: info@peeps-hie.org
- Helpline: 0800 987 5422

PREGNANCY ASSOCIATED OSTEOPOROSIS PATIENT GROUP
The Pregnancy Associated Osteoporosis Patient Group offers advice and support for women with pregnancy-associated osteoporosis.

- Facebook page: https://www.facebook.com/paogroupuk
- Email: paopatientgroup@gmail.com
- Phone: 0300 124 0441

PREGNANCY SICKNESS SUPPORT

Pregnancy Sickness Support offers support to women affected by hyperemesis gravidarum and campaigns to improve the care of those affected by the condition.

- Website: www.pregnancysicknesssupport.org.uk
- Email: support@pregnancysicknesssupport.org.uk
- Helpline: 0800 055 4361

SAMARITANS

The Samaritans helpline is open twenty-four hours a day, seven days a week. It is available to anyone experiencing emotional distress, including thoughts of suicide.

- Website: www.samaritans.org
- Email: jo@samaritans.org
- Helpline: 116 123

SANDS

Sands supports parents who have experienced baby loss. You can call the helpline if you need support after the death of a baby, whether it was recent or long ago.

- Website: www.sands.org.uk
- Email: helpline@sands.org.uk
- Helpline: 0808 164 3332

TOMMY'S

Tommy's researches the causes of miscarriage, stillbirth and premature

birth, as well as treatments to save babies' lives. They also provide trusted pregnancy and baby loss information and support from midwives.
- Website: www.tommys.org
- Email: midwife@tommys.org
- Helpline: 0800 0147 800

FURTHER READING

All-Party Parliamentary Group for Birth Trauma (2024) 'Listen to Mums: Ending the Postcode Lottery on Perinatal Care', UK Parliament.

Ayers, Susan and Ford, Elizabeth (2016) 'Post-traumatic stress during pregnancy and the postpartum period', in Wenzel, Amy (ed.) *Oxford Handbook of Perinatal Psychology*, Oxford University Press, pp. 182–200.

Dockrill, Laura (2021) *What Have I Done? Motherhood, Mental Illness and Me*, Vintage Publishing.

Jolin, Lucy (2019) *Coping With Birth Trauma and Postnatal Depression*, Sheldon Press.

Jones, Lucy (2024) *Matrescence: On the Metamorphosis of Pregnancy, Childbirth and Motherhood*, Penguin.

van der Kolk, Bessel (2015) *The Body Keeps the Score: Brain, Mind and Body in the Healing of Trauma*, Penguin.

Scotland, Mia (2015) *Why Postnatal Depression Matters*, Pinter & Martin.

Scotland, Mia (2020) *Birth Shock: How to Recover from Birth Trauma*, Pinter & Martin.

Svanberg, Emma (2019) *Why Birth Trauma Matters*, Pinter & Martin.

Thomas, Kim (2020) *Birth Trauma: A Guide for You, Your Friends and Family to Coping with Post-Traumatic Stress Disorder Following Birth*, Nell James Publishers.

Thomas, Kim and McCann, Shona (2022) *Postnatal PTSD: A Guide for Health Professionals*, Jessica Kingsley Publishers.

Thompson, Louise (2024) *Lucky: Learning to Live Again*, Ebury Spotlight.

ACKNOWLEDGEMENTS

I would like to thank the many people who have supported me both during the writing of this book and over the past few years as I campaigned to improve maternity care. Firstly, thanks to my husband Henry, who encouraged me right from the start to share my story of birth trauma and believed that I could make a difference by doing so. I was conscious that this was partly his story too and I'm so pleased that he was finally able to speak about his experiences as an affected father in this book, which was very powerful.

Dr Kim Thomas, CEO of the Birth Trauma Association, was instrumental to both this book and the Birth Trauma Inquiry in Parliament. She read and edited the many submissions from the public and provided me with an invaluable sounding board as my first reader. Thank you to so many families for trusting me with their stories.

Many politicians have supported my cross-party campaign, in particular Rosie Duffield and members of the All-Party Parliamentary Group on Birth Trauma.

Thank you to my mother for helping to look after my daughter, especially when I was unable to do so, and for being such a wonderful grandmother. Many friends have supported my campaign from early on, including Vanessa and Belle, and thanks in particular to Rachel and Molly, who bravely wrote their experiences down for me.

Thank you to the brilliant team at Biteback Publishing, starting with my editor Olivia Beattie. She helped me coax this book into life and showed me how to structure my memoir into a coherent narrative. Thanks also to my publisher James Stephens and Mark Wallace at Total Politics Group, who came to see me in Parliament one day for a coffee and said they believed that I could write a book. Thanks to Catriona Allon who did my edits, my publicist Suzanne Sangster who got this book out into the world and Martin Halfpenny for all the media advice he gave me for my birth trauma campaign. Diane Banks from Northbank also advised me on getting my book deal.

I acknowledge the work of my brilliant team in Parliament, especially James Cantrill. Max Austin and Elliot Malik have subsequently helped me with setting up the Global Birth Trauma Alliance. Thanks also to my amazing podcast team on *Breaking the Taboo*, including Bella Carter, Natasha Feroze, Adam Woodward, Alex Ward and Emily Ryder.

During the writing of this book, I also undertook The Novelry's ninety-day writing class and their specialist memoir course with Alice Kuipers, alongside mentoring sessions with Kate Riordan, which I found to be invaluable. Thanks also to my original writing group, which met many years ago, at the Arvon Foundation, including Dom, Jem, Laura, Maggie and Robin, who first encouraged me when I dared to think I might write a book one day. Thanks also to

ACKNOWLEDGEMENTS

my mother-in-law, author Caroline Montague, who has given me a lot of tips as a new writer.

I hope my daughter Arabella will be proud of me for writing this book. I am lucky to be her mum and I want her to know that she has brought me such joy.